LONDON

LONDON

A History of 300 Years in 25 Buildings

PAUL KNOX

YALE UNIVERSITY PRESS
New Haven and London

For information about this and other Yale University Press publications, please contact:
U.S. Office: sales.press@yale.edu yalebooks.com
Europe Office: sales@yaleup.co.uk yalebooks.co.uk

Set in Neue Swift by Tetragon, London
Printed in Slovenia by DZS-Grafik d.o.o.

Library of Congress Control Number: 2023952218

ISBN 978-0-300-26920-8

A catalogue record for this book is available from the British Library.

10 9 8 7 6 5 4 3 2 1

Contents

Illustrations

Preface

HAVING spent much of my career writing on world cities, urbanisation and urban social geography, I became increasingly aware, about ten years ago, that although I knew a lot about cities and urban development, I could not, as an 'urbanist', lay claim to be particularly knowledgeable about any one city. It was discomfiting. I set about rectifying this by focusing on my home town, Portsmouth, a place with a distinctive cityscape that is the product of an exceptional history. I found myself wishing I had known more about the city as I was growing up, and the book I eventually wrote, *Strong Island*, is in open-access format (https://vtechworks.lib.vt.edu/handle/10919/97919) to make it freely accessible, in particular, to secondary schools in the city.

Meanwhile, I had set about developing a deeper knowledge of London, cumulatively logging more than 800 kilometres (500 miles) walking its streets in the course of multiple visits. Two books ensued, one on the characteristics and distinctiveness of the districts of central London; the other on the 'anatomy' of outer London. Both were informed not only by reading and observing, but also by the privileges of access afforded by my involvement, as dean of a college of architecture and urban studies, with design professionals, builders, developers and community groups. These contacts gave me additional insight and somewhat different perspectives on the production and meaning of the built environment. Office visits, site visits and informal conversations gave depth and texture to issues that had hitherto been, for me, mainly empirical or theoretical in tenor. I came to see the totality of the built environment as economic and social history in material form, the legacy of successive phases of historical development and of the prevailing political economy of the time: something much broader, and richer, than the usual compass of solipsistic academic disciplines (the connoisseurship of architecture and architectural history especially come to mind).

This book is an attempt to bring such a perspective to a broad readership. I am indebted to Jo Godfrey at Yale University Press for helping to distil the idea into a history told through the lenses of a few selected buildings, though the responsibility for the selection is mine. It was a challenging but fascinating task, given the history of London's development and the rich legacy of its built environment. In the end, there was no room for the influential 'gentlemen's clubs' of St James's or for covered markets like Leadenhall and Old Spitalfields; for the furniture workshops of Shoreditch, the warehouses of Wapping Wall, or the industrial estates of Park Royal and the Lea Valley; for the City of London Guildhall or any of the thirty-two borough town halls; for any of the many fascinating examples of Victorian philanthropic housing, bath-houses, orphanages, settlement houses, asylums, almshouses and prisons; for Edwardian pubs and theatres; for twentieth-century cinemas, roadhouses and Underground stations; for twenty-first-century shopping malls or big-box superstores; or for many of London's more 'obvious' landmark buildings, such as the Old Royal Naval College in Greenwich, Buckingham Palace, the Palace of Westminster, Horse Guards, the National Gallery, the Royal Courts of Justice, Royal Albert Hall, the Bank of England, Broadcasting House, Wembley stadium, BT Tower, the O2 Arena, the Tate Modern… all of them living histories with their own biographies that are part of – and illustrative of – the broader history of the city itself. I hope that the selection I have made can begin to do justice to the endlessly fascinating city that is London.

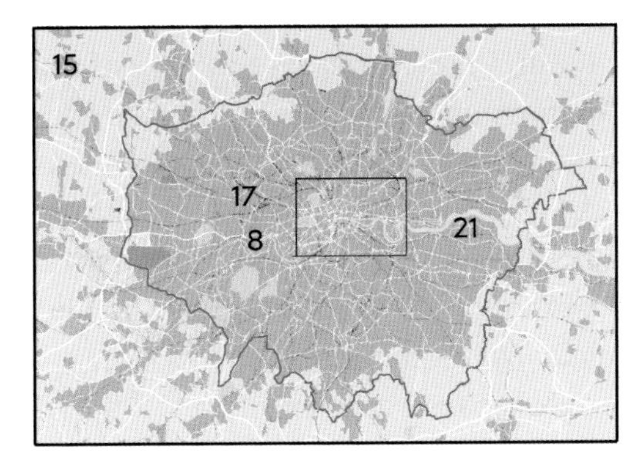

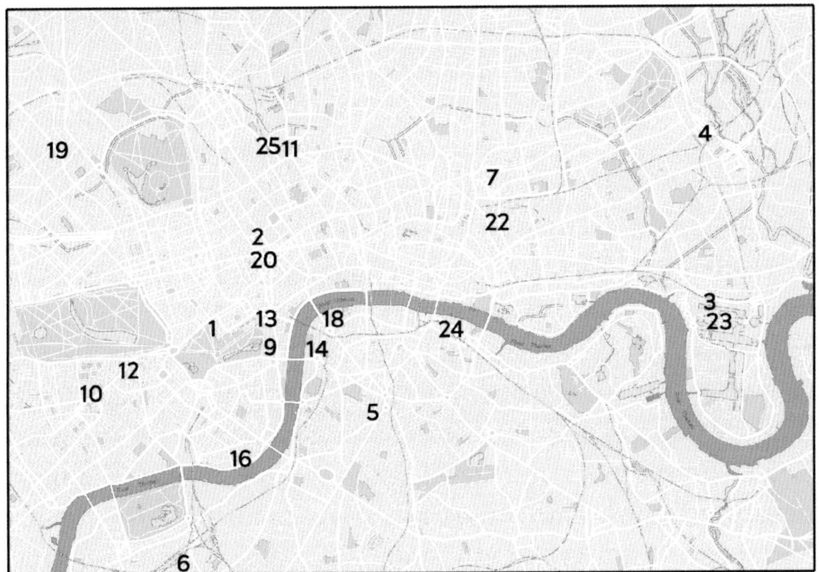

1 Spencer House, St James's
2 Bedford Square, Bloomsbury
3 No. 2 Warehouse, Import Dock, West India Quay
4 Fairfield Works, Bow
5 Lambeth Workhouse, Lambeth
6 Shaftesbury Park Estate, Battersea
7 Rochelle Street School, Bethnal Green
8 Christ Church, Turnham Green
9 Foreign and Commonwealth Office, Whitehall
10 Victoria and Albert Museum, South Kensington
11 St Pancras Station and Hotel, Camden
12 Harrods, Knightsbridge
13 Admiralty Arch, Whitehall
14 County Hall, Lambeth
15 Dunroamin, Amersham
16 Dolphin Square, Pimlico
17 Hoover Factory, Perivale
18 National Theatre, Waterloo
19 Abbey Road Studios, St John's Wood
20 Centre Point, St Giles
21 Penton House, Thamesmead
22 Jamme Masjid, Spitalfields
23 One Canada Square, Isle of Dogs
24 The Shard, London Bridge
25 Platform G, King's Cross

Introduction

Becoming London

> Behind everything in London is something else, and, behind that, is something else still; and so on through the centuries, so that London as we see her is only the latest manifestation of other Londons.
>
> H.V. Morton, *In Search of London* (1951), p. 207

A TEN-MINUTE walk along the half-mile length of Lupus Street in Pimlico takes you past an assorted legacy of seemingly ordinary buildings: a Victorian church and the Italianate terraces and squares that it was built to serve; a Victorian elementary school and philanthropic housing from the same era; interwar mansion apartment buildings; Modernist postwar council housing and shopping parades; and a brand-new sixth-form academy and public library. The eastern end of the street is dominated by the Church of St Saviour. In Decorated Gothic style, its elegant spire was the tallest in the entire city when it was built in 1882. The surrounding streets and squares were part of Thomas Cubitt's mid-century development of Pimlico, built on land leased from Robert, Earl Grosvenor, the 1st marquess of Westminster (some of whose ancestors had carried the Christian name of Lupus, hence Lupus Street). The stuccoed Italianate terraces and squares of Cubitt's Pimlico, with their balustraded balconies and iron railings, were characteristic of middle-class Victorian London, but only short stretches survive along Lupus Street itself. Just along from St Saviour's, across the street from a surviving block of Cubitt terracing, is the long, low frontage of Pimlico Academy. Opened in 2011 on the site of a former welfare-state-era school that had been much admired by Modernist architects, the new school and adjoining public library are in a restrained postmodern style, the street frontage echoing 1930s Bauhaus designs. Visible behind the school is the enormous mass of Dolphin Square, a 1930s luxury mansion block. Further along on the left, walking westwards, is another stretch of Cubitt terracing. Its counterpart on the opposite side of the street was destroyed by German air raids in the autumn of 1940, and the site is now occupied by a postwar apartment building. Across the street on the next block is Churchill Gardens Primary Academy, built in 1878 as Napier Road School for the London School Board in characteristic three-storey red-brick pared-down Domestic Revival style, with separate playgrounds and entrances for boys and girls. Further along is a series of seven- and ten-storey slab blocks that form the northern and western boundaries of the Churchill Gardens municipal housing estate. The western end of the street, where it turns toward the Thames, was hit twice by V1 flying bombs in 1944, but a small run of Cubitt terracing survives, along with a group of Peabody buildings constructed in 1876 in typical barrack-like Italianate style.

Together, this assortment of buildings can tell the history of the street; individually, each of them is the product of the broader history of the city itself. Although Lupus Street is a particularly vibrant example, in almost any of the city's streets London's history is writ large. Its built environment is history in material form, the legacy of successive phases of urbanisation. Every historical period has introduced new buildings – and new types of buildings – to London's streets. Individually, buildings embody the influence of social and economic needs, technological capabilities and aesthetic trends at the time of their construction. Some become the archetypical products of particular historical periods. Some become landmarks because of their association with particular people or important events – something that happens, in many cases, well after their construction. A few become iconic as a result of media coverage, professional recognition and resonance with the public. Meanwhile, as new occupants and new uses are found for existing buildings, all of them become living histories, their own biographies woven into the biography of the city itself. This book tells the story of London's development over the past 300 years through just 25 surviving buildings.

As living histories, buildings are simultaneously outcome and shaper of social, political, cultural and economic forces. London's buildings reflect the needs and intentions of particular patrons, architects and institutions, but they have also influenced the lives of successive generations of Londoners. Buildings provide functionality to economic enterprise, structure to political and cultural institutions, and durability to social networks. They are important elements of social worlds and play key roles in shaping people's experiences, identities and relationships. Ideology, religion, class, race and citizenship are all implicated in the built environment, as are changing attitudes toward the role and status of women, public versus private spheres of life, mechanisms of social control, and norms of taste and distinction. London's built environment is both legacy and conditioner of all these forces.

The approach adopted in this book stands in contrast to the conventional art-historical conception of architectural history: treating buildings as potential art objects, each imagined as a thing unto itself, too often resulting in a narrative framed around consecrated geniuses and great buildings.[1] To understand buildings as living histories means drawing together agents and structures, intentions and circumstances, builders and users, owners and tenants. It means recognising the 'betweenness' of buildings: between continuity and change, between their material form and their cultural and symbolic attributes.[2] It follows that the meaning and significance of individual buildings is provisional. As sociologist Thomas Gieryn observes, 'Buildings don't just sit there imposing themselves. They are forever objects of (re)interpretation, narration and representation.'[3] Buildings are constantly being adapted as settings for different users, as context for different observers, and as part of the fabric of the city – itself always restlessly 'becoming'.

Twenty-five buildings are too few, of course, to afford either a comprehensive or a thematic history of the metropolis. But in the biographies of just twenty-five buildings we shall meet the various actors – developers and financiers, architects, builders and their clients, politicians and planners, and, not least, the people of London themselves – who have shaped the city's evolving cityscape as it has recovered from the Great Fire of 1666 to become serially (and oftentimes simultaneously) a mercantile city, industrial workshop, imperial capital, sprawling conurbation, post-imperial city, progressive city, 'swinging city', multicultural metropolis, tourist destination and global financial centre: at once an engine of wealth and of inequality, imprinting both on its cityscapes.

The cast of characters behind the creation of London's evolving cityscapes after the Great Fire begins with landowners: from the landlords of the so-called Great Estates of the West End – the Bedfords, the Cadogans, the Crown, the Ecclesiastical Commissioners, the Fitzroys, the Grosvenors and so on – to modern conglomerate property development companies and estate agents. Many of London's large landowners have also acted as developers, while London's property market has always attracted speculative developers. Thomas Cubitt, who began building around 1810, was one of the first speculative developers to have his own construction company, complete with foremen, bricklayers and plasterers, operating out of workshops in Gray's Inn Road and Pimlico. Cubitt built much of north Bloomsbury and Belgravia, as well as Pimlico. Speculative developers large and small were also instrumental in creating London's interwar suburbs, while postwar redevelopment owed a lot to the interventions of developers like Joe Levy, Harold Samuel, Charles Clore, Felix Fenston, Jack Cotton and Harry Hyams.

The pantheon of architects we shall meet in subsequent chapters includes Robert Adam, William Kent, John Vardy, John Nash, Thomas Leverton, James Pennethorne, George Gilbert Scott, Richard Norman Shaw, Aston Webb, Berthold Lubetkin, Richard Seifert, Edwin Lutyens, Denys Lasdun, John Forshaw, Norman Foster and Richard Rogers. Less well known are the engineers of the city's infrastructure, though one name stands unmatched: Joseph Bazalgette, chief engineer to the Metropolitan Board of Works between 1856 and 1889. Bazalgette was responsible for the modernisation of the city's infrastructure, including the implementation of a sewerage system and the construction of new roads through demolished slums. His greatest achievement was arguably the embankment of the Thames, a brilliant piece of engineering that not only gave definition to the river's edge – and to the city itself – but also reclaimed land for new buildings, public gardens, a riverside boulevard and, beneath, massive sewer, gas and water pipes, electricity conduits, and a tunnel for the new Metropolitan District Railway.

While London's built environment has been supported by its infrastructure of utilities and transport networks, it has been conditioned by the politics and policies of its administrative framework. A major landowner and property developer in its own right, the City of London Corporation ('the City') is able to function as its own planning authority and has exercised a significant influence on the built environment in the 'square mile' of its jurisdiction. But the City of London Corporation has always pointedly refused to be part of metropolitan-wide administration. Beyond the Square Mile, politics and policies affecting the built environment have taken place within a fragmented administrative framework that has struggled for cohesion. The vestries of the ancient mosaic of parishes were, naturally, parochial in outlook. Local government reform came to the rest of the country in 1835, but London had to wait until the end of the century, while the City and the vestries quarrelled and prevaricated. For a long time, as geographer-planner Peter Hall pointed out, London took shape within a political economy steeped in Adam Smith's laissez-faire philosophy and Jeremy Bentham's utilitarianism.[4] Reformers and philanthropists such as Octavia Hill, J. Passmore Edwards, Angela Burdett-Coutts, Samuel and Henrietta Barnett, Sydney Waterlow, George Peabody and Edward Guinness were important mediators of the free-market forces shaping London's built environment, but it was not until the London County Council (LCC) was created (in 1889) and the vestries were replaced by municipal boroughs (in 1899) that London acquired a modern administrative framework. Within the LCC, Fabianism and the emerging Progressive Party of 'gas and water socialists' introduced a climate of radical reform that was eventually to blossom with the post-Second World War settlement of the welfare state. As the metropolis grew and its politics evolved, so its administrative framework changed, the Greater London Council (GLC) succeeding the LCC in 1965 until it was abolished in 1986. A limited amount of strategic governance was restored with the creation in 2000 of the Greater London Authority (GLA) with a directly elected mayor, thereby adding a new role in the cast of characters shaping and reshaping the metropolis.

The people of London have also played important roles in the biographies of individual buildings, as changing occupancy and adaptive re-use have added new chapters to the life-cycle of their homes, workplaces and institutions. People tend to impose themselves on their environment, modifying and adjusting it as best they can to suit their needs and express their values. Homes are remodelled, as generations of families go through their own life-cycles; as successive waves of socio-economic or ethnic groups move in or move on; or as buildings are converted to non-residential uses. Many of central London's mansions, town homes and suburban villas, for example, have been converted to offices or studio spaces, while some erstwhile country mansions in the outer suburbs have become commercial care homes or spas. Workplaces, meanwhile, are adapted or redeveloped, as declining industries are succeeded by new patterns of economic activity and as obsolescent buildings are converted to residential uses. Furniture workshops become media and IT studios; cinemas become churches, social clubs or bingo parlours; factories and warehouses become supermarkets or loft apartments. Similarly, institutional buildings may be converted to commercial uses: some government offices have been redeveloped as hotels or residences; asylums, prisons, workhouses and orphanages have become apartment buildings; obsolescent schools have become community centres; decommissioned churches have become cafés, thrift shops or apartments; and so on.

Much of this is driven by the changing overall social and economic geography of the metropolis. Successive waves of migrants and immigrants have arrived and gravitated to particular districts; changing demographics, evolving lifestyles and new patterns of household formation result in changing demand for everything from infant schools to care homes and from corner shops to superstores, whether in new or converted buildings. Structural economic change leaves the buildings of declining industries ripe for re-use or redevelopment, while investment in new industries and new technologies requires new spaces in new kinds of locations. In the process, entire districts change character. Notting Hill, for example, was developed in the 1850s as a middle-class suburb in an area formerly known for its brick-making, piggeries and slums. By the 1940s it had become established as the epitome of a down-at-heel area of cheap lodgings. In the 1950s and 1960s it became notorious for landlordism and race riots. In the 1970s low-income households were squeezed out of the district, as young professionals bought up properties, investing sweat equity and gentrifying the district. Many Victorian villas were brought back to prime condition, while second-hand stores, betting shops and laundromats were displaced by gastropubs, delicatessens and martial arts studios, prompting a new wave of 'super-gentrification' that has rendered the residential parts of the district into exclusive enclaves of ultra-wealthy households.[5] Like the metropolis itself, every district is constantly becoming something different.

The book is organised around a selection of buildings that reflect the imprint of broad historical periods, beginning with Georgian London. Yet of course Georgian London already incorporated a legacy of city building that had begun with the Roman settlement established around 50 CE on the north bank of the Thames. London's commercial core – the present-day City of London – grew up around the Roman settlement, while 3 kilometres (almost 2 miles) to the west a second nucleus developed: the centre of royal justice and administration around Westminster. The two were separated by farmland and marshland until the seventeenth century, and their very different character and functions have anchored the basic geography of the metropolis ever since. In the countryside surrounding these two cores were numerous small settlements: the seeds of what would become London's distinctive physiognomy as a 'city of villages', formalised in due course around the thirty-two boroughs and the City of London.

It was a physiognomy underpinned by physical geography.[6] The attractiveness of the landscape along the meandering Thames west of London attracted royalty and nobility, who established extensive reservations of parkland on the rich floodplain. Downstream to the east, where the riverbank was marshy, the river attracted activities of a very different complexion: maritime and processing industries and working-class housing. The Lea Valley, meeting the Thames from the north at the eastern margin of central London, formed another natural structuring element. The lacy waterways flowing through marshes and meadows marked the historic boundary between Middlesex and Essex, as well as a physical and psychological boundary between what became aspirational North London and plebeian Northeast London. London's transport network was also framed by physical geography. Roman roads had radiated from the capital to all points of the compass along better-drained ridges and gravel terraces, and stretches of several – notably Watling Street – were adapted by eighteenth-century turnpike roads. Later in the eighteenth century, canal-building took advantage of the Thames and Lea waterways, thus reinforcing the axial influence of the rivers on the structure of the metropolis.

Georgian London was situated within this physical framework, growing rapidly through the dynamism of an emerging new form of capitalism that thrived on capital extracted from three main sources: the rural enclosure movement, the Atlantic slave trade and the colonial enterprises of the East India Company. Great new warehouses were built to accommodate the products of Caribbean slave plantations and the imports of the East India Company, while the private wealth of the period came to be expressed in a built environment that carried the rationalism and refinement of London's new urban bourgeoisie and its belief in the moral significance of aesthetics. The 'beau monde' of the period depended on new settings in which to display their refinement: assembly rooms, spas and grand town homes that hosted balls, dinners and soirees; and new public buildings to accommodate concerts and art exhibits. The grand squares and terraced town homes developed by the Great Estates of the West End meanwhile established the template for much of the subsequent development of central London on a more modest scale.

Victorian London was extended geographically and reshaped by the imperatives of industrial capitalism, including the creation of many new kinds of buildings. Huge railway sheds and station hotels at Charing Cross, Waterloo, Victoria, Paddington, Marylebone, Euston, St Pancras, King's Cross and Liverpool Street brought goods and passengers to and from every part of the country. The growth of consumer culture saw the introduction of arcades, department stores, cafés, restaurants, tea rooms, dance halls, theatres, hotels and sports stadiums. London's domestic economy produced a legacy of factories and workshops and an impoverished population living in insanitary slums and reliant on almshouses, workhouses, dispensaries, orphanages and asylums. Meanwhile, the Victorian ideology of progress was manifest in libraries, art galleries, museums, mechanics' institutes, board schools and hospitals, while the new imperial mission was reflected in monumental architecture and in the institutional landscape of new and expanded government departments. They stood out in high relief against a general background of cramped stock-brick terraced housing. A new middle class, meanwhile, impelled the march of bricks and mortar towards the countryside, which in turn led to a new phase of church building that reflected sectarian competition for the religious adherence of the new suburbanites.

By the turn of the nineteenth century, the LCC was in place, introducing progressive housing policies, creating a unified transport system and improving London's infrastructure in line with its status as national capital. The LCC and the metropolitan boroughs bulldozed their way through slum after slum, flattening the houses of some 180,000 Londoners in the 1920s and then building new accommodation for them, prompting what was to become a long-running debate about the desirability of high-density, high-rise formats versus low-rise suburban estates for social housing. By then the social conventions and economic privations of Late Victorian and Edwardian society had been partially eclipsed by the hedonism and consumerism of the Roaring Twenties. While rural and industrial regions in the rest of the country experienced the worst of the Depression, London grew dramatically in population and areal extent and became a seedbed for social change. Increasing levels of owner-occupation and automobile ownership and the extension of the Underground network gave rise to a 'Metroland' of semi-detached houses, bungalows, roadhouse pubs, and the factories and offices of new industries and corporations. More central districts sprouted mansion blocks catering to an emerging class of young professionals.

After 1945, London's cityscapes were significantly recast through reconstruction and the emergence of the welfare state. More than 80,000 dwellings had been destroyed or damaged beyond repair during the Second World War, along with factories, warehouses and hundreds of historically significant buildings. Social housing was grafted onto the fabric of both the suburbs and inner-city districts on an unprecedented scale. New schools, health clinics and hospitals appeared throughout the suburbs, but the most widespread new features of the city's landscape were tower blocks and mid-rise buildings of social housing: the product of the golden age of Modernism in planning and architecture that had been foreshadowed by Patrick Abercrombie's *County of London Plan* (1943) and the radical Town and Country Planning Act (1947). The postwar economic boom saw the replacement of much of London's older stock of buildings, as well as the redevelopment of bomb sites, though the 1947 Town and Country Planning Act protected buildings of special architectural or historical interest that were officially 'listed' by the Ministry of Works (a function subsequently taken over by English Heritage, later renamed Historic England).

The 1960s was the era of 'Swinging London'; or, as historian John Davis puts it, 'Waterloo Sunrise',[7] with new waves of immigration helping to sustain the booming economy, while adding new layers of cultural identity to inner suburbs. In central London, speculative office development began to make up for the deficit caused by war and obsolescence. The pace of change, combined with increasing prosperity, prompted a strong conservation movement, underpinned by the Civic Amenities Act 1967. This introduced conservation areas, which in turn fostered the gentrification of some older neighbourhoods. Beginning in a few pockets in Camden and Kensington, gentrification spread north across Camden and Islington and west into North Kensington and Notting Hill. By the early 1970s, the focus was more on public opposition to the more ambitious plans of some developers and to the evangelistic Modernism of London's planners and architects. One key target of dissent was a proposed Ringway road system that would have torn through many districts and displaced around 100,000 people. Another was the GLC's proposal for the comprehensive redevelopment of Covent Garden with a new road system through the area, together with futuristic pedestrian walkways connecting office blocks, hotels, an international conference centre, schools and apartment blocks.[8] Meanwhile, the Ronan Point disaster of 1968 – the partial collapse of a new tower block of system-built social housing in Newham – contributed to a growing critique of high-rise council housing that eventually widened to a general loss of confidence in Modernist planning. The international economic system-shock of oil price rises stimulated by the Organization of the Petroleum Producing Countries (OPEC) in late 1973 put an end to the postwar building boom. An extended strike by coal-miners in 1974 led to the imposition of rolling power cuts and a three-day working week to conserve electricity. This was followed by a protracted period of high unemployment, combined with price inflation that was traumatic and socially divisive, culminating in the 'Winter of Discontent' of 1978–79.[9]

The fading promise of the postwar era slid into outright dissatisfaction, fuelling a 'counter-reformation' that was implemented by the Thatcher administration.[10] Thatcher's 'Big Bang' of financial reform coincided with the end of the Cold War, the consolidation of European political and economic integration, and the globalisation of manufacturing and finance, repositioning London as a global financial centre. The geography of the metropolis itself was subsequently reframed around the combination of a new transport infrastructure (the M25 orbital motorway, the Docklands Light Railway, Eurostar high-speed rail and, more recently, the addition of the Elizabeth Line to the Tube system) and large-scale regeneration schemes developed through public–private partnerships (Canary Wharf, Paddington Basin, Nine Elms, the South Bank, Olympic Park, King's Cross and London Bridge). The City of London, having relaxed its historic preservation policies, promptly found itself crammed with office towers. London meanwhile became an international destination city not only for investment capital, but also for tourists. Finance, high-tech and creative industries generated a great deal of wealth, accentuating the social polarisation inherent to the era with glossy new-build gentrification projects, riverside condominium complexes and deluxe residential apartment towers.

The biography of every building in London reveals something of this history. Selecting just twenty-five buildings that, collectively, illustrate 300 years of urban development is an interesting exercise. Choices have had to be made. Thus we have, for example, Bedford Square, but not Belgrave Square or Fitzroy Square; the Victoria and Albert Museum, but not the British Museum or the Natural History Museum; Christ Church, Turnham Green, but not All Souls, Marylebone, or any of the scores of London's other 'Commissioners' churches'; Dolphin Square, Pimlico, but not the Isokon flats, Taymount Grange or another of the many interwar mansion blocks; Penton House in Thamesmead, but not Churchill Gardens in Pimlico, Balfron Tower in Poplar or Alton West in Roehampton; and so on. Readers will surely think of their own candidates, perhaps including other kinds of buildings, such as the many fascinating examples of Victorian philanthropic housing, bath-houses, orphanages, settlement houses, asylums, almshouses and prisons; of Edwardian pubs and theatres; or of twentieth-century cinemas, roadhouses and

Underground stations. The point here is that all of them, like the assorted legacy of seemingly ordinary buildings along Lupus Street in Pimlico, represent living histories that can reveal a whole new side to the London that is too easily taken for granted. As we shall see in the twenty-five buildings selected here, the biographies of individual structures are distillations of many different aspects of London's rich and complex history.

A New Map of
LONDON
Most humbly Inscrib'd to the Rt. Wor:
shipfull Sr. Peter Delme Kt. & Aldern.
of London. 1720.
Haberdashers Hospital
Artillery Ground
Goodmans Fields
St. James's Park
The Marsh
The narrow Wall
the New way to Kensington
THE RIVER THAMES
A Scale of Half a Mile

I

GEORGIAN LONDON

At the beginning of the Georgian era, in 1714, London's population was around 600,000. The city had recovered from the Great Fire of 1666 that had raged for days, destroying more than 13,000 houses and many of the City's civic and ecclesiastical buildings, and displacing almost 90 per cent of the population. The rural fringes to the north and east of the City were transformed, as both the poor and the moderately prosperous moved in. Displaced aristocratic families moved in the other direction, to Piccadilly and St James's. Wenceslaus Hollar's map, drawn soon after the Fire, shows the extent of the devastation. Ogilby and Morgan's map, drawn just eleven years later, shows how quickly the city was rebuilt. With more than 8,000 new houses and numerous new public buildings, London had re-established itself around the old street pattern. Some saw it as an opportunity missed: a rare chance to plan the capital and lay it out in the Grand Manner, commensurate with the great continental cities of the time. Charles II, a monarch with a strong regal impulse, certainly wanted the burnt-out streets to be replaced with grand boulevards, imposing buildings and statuary. Christopher Wren devised such a plan, as did courtier John Evelyn, cartographer Richard Newcourt and physicist Robert Hooke. All four plans featured broad, straight streets with vistas of landmarks in public squares. Nothing came of them. Building in the Grand Manner was associated with the exercise of autocratic power and the 'popery' of France – anathema to English cultural sensibilities,

1 'London in 1721'.

as well as to the utilitarianism of City merchants. There were more practical reasons, too: a shortage of labour, lost records of property ownership, and worries that an extended process of reconstruction would cause the City to lose its commercial advantage over continental rivals.

Charles II died in 1685, and three years later parliament ousted his Catholic successor, James II, in a 'Glorious Revolution' that put an end to any notion of royal pretensions in city building. Until, at least, the last years of the Georgian era, when the prince regent had John Nash carve out an awkward processional route between Regent's Park and Pall Mall. Meanwhile, the Glorious Revolution had much broader significance for Georgian Britain. The Protestant monarchy of William and Mary meant a major shift in foreign alliances and prompted a number of major wars, culminating in the Seven Years' War of 1756–63. The exigencies of war, combined with Britain's expanding colonial portfolio, induced significant financial and legal reforms and encouraged the use of land as collateral for domestic industrial and commercial investments.[1] London received a disproportionate share of the investment, with much of it directed to the city's role as a centre of international trade. Thanks to the rising Atlantic trade on the one hand and the activities of the East India Company on the other, Britain's imports rose more than three-fold during the eighteenth century, while exports rose almost seven-fold. A large proportion of that passed through the Port of London, dealt with by London-based merchants. London's wealth was also swollen by the incomes of absentee landlords of the sugar and tobacco plantations of the Caribbean and of the merchants who organised the transatlantic slave trade on which they relied (at least until the slave trade was outlawed by Britain in 1807).

With a weakened monarchy, Georgian financial and administrative reforms tended to benefit the landed gentry, who dominated both Houses of Parliament. Between 1660 and 1830,

2 'London after the Great Fire of 1666' by Wenceslaus Hollar, 1667.

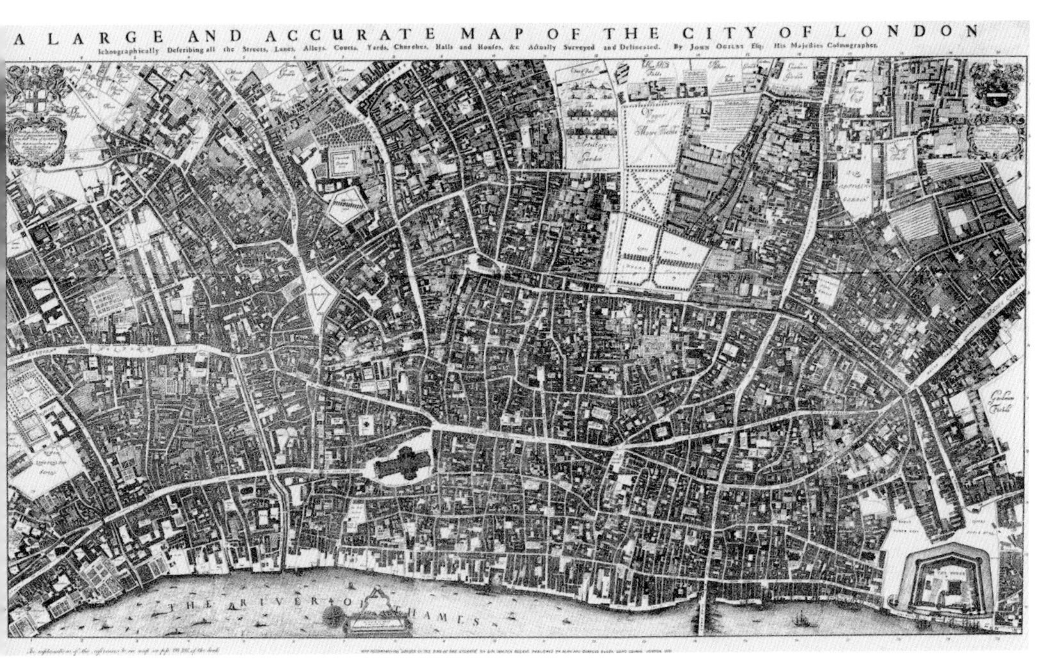

3 'A Large and Accurate Map of the City of London' by John Ogilby, 1677.

parliament passed roughly 3,500 acts modifying ancient common rights to property. These acts enabled wealthy families to enclose common lands and to sell, mortgage, lease, exchange and improve land previously bound by ancient rights, inheritance rules and other legal entails. It was effectively 'accumulation by dispossession' and the chief beneficiaries – aristocratic landowners – could use the land as collateral for investment. Meanwhile, the enclosure of the countryside removed the prior rights of local people to land they had used for generations, depriving them of a living and creating a reserve army of cheap labour, a large fraction of which made its way to London in search of work, thereby intensifying the social inequality that came to be a hallmark of the metropolis.

The newly enriched landowning gentry became the core of the country's governing elite and the apex of London society. Parliament met between January and May, bringing the political classes and cream of society to the capital for 'the Season'. The wealthiest families built palatial town homes like Spencer House (Chapter 1) as their base for the Season, and became the sponsors of a new regime of taste and aesthetics that was central to the political, philosophical and scientific discourse that characterised the 'Age of Reason' in Georgian Britain. The Glorious Revolution had sparked a huge cultural shift. There was a new interest in the history and iconography of ancient republican Greece and Rome and, in particular, the sixteenth-century adaptations and refinements of classical architecture by Andrea Palladio (in the Veneto) and Inigo Jones (in London). Recoiling from the increasingly elaborate Baroque styles of the seventeenth century, the patrician classes hurried to embark on a Grand Tour of Europe to take in the villas of the Veneto and the ruins of Greece and Rome. The super-wealthy Lord Burlington was a major sponsor of Palladian architecture in London. He and his 'gang' of architects – William Kent, John Vardy and Isaac Ware –

> ruled that the only proper adornments for buildings, both inside and out, were grammatical elements comprised of the five classical orders [Doric, Ionic, Corinthian, Tuscan and Composite] and the somewhat limited number of expansions and variations exemplified in the works of Palladio and Indigo Jones.[2]

Burlington sponsored Giacomo Leoni's English translation of Palladio's *Four Books of Architecture* in 1715. A second important publication that year was Colen Campbell's portfolio of drawings, *Vitruvius Britannicus*. James Gibbs' *Book of Architecture* (1728) was also influential.

In addition to their fancy homes, London's elite also sought more public settings in which to show off their wealth, taste and manners.[3] At the same time the city's aspirational bourgeoisie required access to elite society in order to acquire and cultivate their own taste and sociability. The problem was mutually resolved by the appearance of clubs, assembly rooms, spas, public walks and pleasure gardens. Regular assemblies featuring balls, banquets and lectures became the staple of the city's social round, often in purpose-built premises with a ballroom, a card room and a tea room. The Pantheon, a spectacular domed hall on Oxford Street (on the site of what at the time of writing is a Marks and Spencer store), was the premier event space for assemblies, masquerades and subscription concerts. London's population also had access to several spas. One of the earliest was Epsom, some 24 kilometres (15 miles) from the centre of the city. Other spas were developed (to varying degrees of success) around mineral springs in Acton, Clerkenwell, Dulwich, Hampstead, Islington, Kilburn, Richmond, Streatham and Sydenham. The best spas typically centred on a 'great room' for taking the waters. Outdoor socialising was accommodated in pleasure gardens and walks. 'Promenades fulfilled many of the functions of assembly rooms, but out of doors. They were places in which polite society exchanged views, developed social or sexual relationships, and established its identity.'[4] Much of Georgian Chelsea functioned as a riverside pleasure resort, where people could come for the day or perhaps take lodgings for the summer. Lambeth's exurban character, meanwhile, lent itself to its development as a series of pleasure gardens. The most famous was the very fashionable Vauxhall Pleasure Gardens, where visiting nobility and upper-middle classes from north of the river could enjoy food, drink, music and plays.

Yet while London's growing educated middle classes were keen to congregate in these new social arenas, they were equally anxious to avoid the seedy, coarse and debauched side of London and its less well-off citizens, famously depicted in William Hogarth's engravings of London's casual brutality, squalor and epidemic gin drinking. Thus the Age of Reason became an age of social stratification and spatial segregation, not only separating the rational from the mystical, but also the cultivated from the coarse, the healthy from the sick, the virtuous from the corrupt, the deserving from the undeserving.[5]

The city within the old Roman walls lost population as more of the central district came to be occupied by specialised commercial buildings. At the same time, London was beginning to spread out, well on its way to becoming a polycentric city of villages. Some of Britain's wealthiest families hedged their bets between London and their provincial estates by building an additional grand house in the countryside around London: Chiswick House, Chiswick; Frognal House, near Sidcup; Kenwood House, Hampstead; Marble Hill House, Richmond; Wimbledon Park House, Surrey; and Roehampton House, near Richmond Park, for example. Ridge-top villages nearest to central London were the sites of the very earliest exurban development, attracting prosperous 'carriage folk' well before the railway age. High ground with pleasant views – such as were afforded at Camberwell, Clapham, Hackney, Norwood and Peckham – attracted clusters of villas and town houses. Meanwhile, new turnpikes, such as Cambridge

Heath Road, Mile End Road, Kensington Road, Edgware Road, Clapham Road, Brixton Road, Uxbridge Road, Hampstead Road and the Surrey New Roads, attracted ribbon development: mostly terraced housing and workshops in the east and south, detached and semi-detached villas in the west and northwest.

Speculative builders were the mainspring of London's expansion, filling in the inner suburbs. Their efforts were framed by the post-Fire Rebuilding Act of 1667, which laid the basis for a regularised street hierarchy and produced a degree of architectural conformity that was without parallel in Europe. The act required houses to be built in one of four types or 'rates', each with its own specifications 'for better regulation, uniformity, and gracefulness'. It formed the organisational basis for the irrepressible expansion of eighteenth-century London, ensuring that streetscapes throughout the metropolis became visual compositions of simple repetitive harmony. In the same spirit of improvement, parts of the road system in central London were realigned, some new roads cut through, and several street markets were removed from major thoroughfares. The increasingly widespread adoption of brick as a building material meanwhile endowed London with a distinctive appearance. Nevertheless, a common impression of eighteenth-century London was of 'narrow streets, congestion, lack of vistas, unplanned development, and lack of refinement'.[6]

London's first post-Fire building boom followed the Treaty of Utrecht 1713 and saw the development of parts of the West End around Hanover, Grosvenor, Cavendish and St James's squares. With the country at war between the 1740s and the 1760s, relatively little new building took place, but London was already becoming distinctly layered:

> Thus in 1760 a large part of London was occupied by buildings of the first generation on the site, another large area was occupied by buildings of the second or third generation, while in the City,

> Southwark, and parts of Westminster the fabric embodied elements from a period extending over at least six hundred years.[7]

When the Treaty of Paris ended the Seven Years' War in 1763, landowners and speculative builders once again looked to create new estates. This saw the development, for example, of the Portland, Portman and bishop of London's estates in the West End, the Bedford Estate (Chapter 2) and Southampton Estate in Bloomsbury and Fitzrovia, the Skinners' Company Estate, Brewers' Company Estate and New River Estate in Clerkenwell, and the Thornhill Estate in Islington, among others. South of the river, Robert Mylne developed a succession of housing schemes across Southwark, after St George's Fields had been drained. After the opening of the Regent's Canal in 1820, wharf-side yards, factories and workshops were drawn to its basins at Paddington, St Pancras, City Road and Limehouse, and nearby landowners quickly moved to develop housing for the local workforce. A Paddington Arm of the Grand Union Canal linked the new East India, West India and London Docks and warehouses (Chapter 3) to the Midlands, placing London in a pivotal position between the country's nascent industrial base and its transoceanic trade. By the close of the Georgian era, the population exceeded 1 million. Seven new bridges spanned the Thames, knitting the city together in a 'new, balanced completeness'.[8] London was becoming a metropolis.

1 Spencer House, St James's

SEEN from Green Park, Spencer House has the look of a museum or art gallery. In neoclassical style, its huge triangular pediment crowns a Doric colonnade that frames seven bays of tall windows. Yet the building is fenced off from the park and the imposing façade is missing the skirt of entrance steps that would be expected of a public building. In fact, Spencer House can only be approached by way of the backstreets of St James's. The close-up view from St James's Place, where the narrow street broadens to a small residual square, dispels any notion that the building is anything other than a private establishment. There is a single doorway, imposing enough, but uninviting. The eastern end of Spencer House abuts directly onto a brick town house, while the southern flank of the building, accessible only by a private yard designed for servants and tradespeople, is mostly brick.

When it was built in the 1750s, Spencer House stood at the extreme western fringe of the city, facing the royal park. It was one of the grandest aristocratic town houses ever built in the city, and its construction marked 'a watershed' in the development of taste.[1] Aside from Apsley House, it is the only great eighteenth-century private London mansion to survive intact, though the interior has been serially remodelled,

4 Spencer House from Green Park.

5 Spencer House, 1800.

renovated and restored. It was commissioned by John Spencer, the 1st Earl Spencer, who wanted a town house that might establish his position in London society. He had wealth and title, but in the capital he was just another rich boy. The grandson of the 3rd earl of Sunderland and the great-grandson of Sarah, duchess of Marlborough, he had inherited both of their fortunes while still a minor. This included tens of thousands of acres of prime agricultural land spread across central England and the Home Counties, an impressive art collection and several homes, including country mansions at Althorp in Northamptonshire and Wimbledon Park in Surrey. The two houses he inherited in London were deemed inadequate. Having married the day after he turned twenty-one, he set about getting himself elected to parliament, finding a site on which to build a London town house and fulfilling his ambition to become a member of the exclusive

Society of Dilettanti ('a club, for which the nominal qualification is having been in Italy, and the real one being drunk').[2] He had accomplished two of the three within a year – he would not be eligible for membership of the Society of Dilettanti until he had made a Grand Tour of Europe.

Spencer was by no means exceptional among the landed elite in his anxiety to establish a fine London residence. Vast sums were dropped on residences that were to be occupied for only part of the year. A good house 'had an incalculable value in constructing and maintaining an identity in the West End – a "proper figure", attracting social and financial credit'. A grand house 'could be used in the manner of a trump card, to better others, or a wild card, to compensate for lack in other areas'.[3] For Spencer, his London mansion was to be his trump card. Whether or not they were parliamentarians, the country's new elite needed to be in London for the Season and to have a residence

6 The main entrance to Spencer House, on the north façade.

capable of ensuring a base from which to secure or reaffirm membership of the 'beau monde'.[4] The Season was a time for transacting business, securing credit, consulting lawyers, buying or selling property, shopping, fixing engagements and marriages and, not least, socialising and entertaining: seeing and being seen. Many opted for leasing one of the big town homes in the new terraces and squares of the West End. The Jermyn Estate in St James's and the Grosvenor Estate in Mayfair exercised a special magnetism in the 1720s and 1730s,[5] but a couple of dozen of the wealthiest aristocrats felt the need to stand out from this crowd with a pompously ostentatious mansion of their own. Spencer was one of these.

The site that Spencer found was in St James's, almost next door to St James's Palace and its Court, and a short walk through St James's Park to the Houses of Parliament. By the time Spencer signed a lease on the site, the district was already an aristocratic enclave. The earl of Bridgewater's huge Bridgewater House was next door; Buckingham House, the duke of Buckingham's town residence, was just across the corner of Green Park (and would soon be purchased by George III and renamed Queen's House); Sarah Churchill, duchess of Marlborough, had recently built Marlborough House next to St James's Palace; and St James's Square was home to the duke of Kent, the duke of Norfolk, the duke of Portland and the earl of Strafford. Almack's fashionable Assembly Rooms were nearby on King Street, while the Society of Dilettanti met at the Star and Garter on Pall Mall. It was the heartland of the Season and the perfect setting for a new young man about town.

Spencer House was the crucial first step in realising the earl's ambitions: an impressive establishment in which to conduct political and financial business and which, through its size and opulence, would reflect his wealth, status and taste, advancing his position in society and winning the respect of his contemporaries. John Vardy was the architect fortunate enough to receive the money-is-no-object commission. Vardy had been designing a house in Palladian style for the previous owner of the site, Baron Montfort, whose suicide put the land on the market. Spencer took Vardy on, while at the same time taking advice on design from his mentor, Colonel George Gray, the secretary of the Society of Dilettanti. Gray also brought an opportunistic element to the project. The Society of Dilettanti had been planning an academy of arts on the north side of Cavendish Square. It was to have had a classical façade based on the Temple of Rome and Augustus at Pola in Istria (now Pula, in Croatia). Masons had already begun working a large quantity of Portland stone that the society had stockpiled, only for the project to unravel just as Spencer was engaging Vardy. Gray saw an opportunity, and the result was the striking west façade of Spencer House in the form of a neoclassical temple front dressed entirely of Portland stone, a material previously associated in London only with public or institutional buildings.[6] Vardy's contribution was to present it as a Palladian composition featuring a Doric colonnade of seven bays, each containing a pedimented window. The five middle bays were crowned with a great pediment topped by statues of three Roman deities: Ceres, the goddess of plenty; Flora, the goddess of flowers and gardens, a symbol of eternal youth; and Bacchus, the god of wine and revelry and patron deity of the Society of Dilettanti. The north façade featured a Palladian-style pavilion, balustrade, Doric pilasters and Venetian windows.

Overall, it was a turning point in confirming classical principles of proportion, composition, scale and harmony as the new touchstones of taste and prestige. Spencer House embodied a close association between notions of what was deemed good aesthetically and what was assumed to be good in terms of the organisation of society. 'In regard to the power structure of society, the classical ideal provided a cultural rationale for the favored position of the privileged and prosperous classes, and, hence, for the rigid stratification of society.'[7]

But it was the interior layout, decoration and furnishing of the building that was central to its function as a social setting and totem of refinement. At Colonel Gray's insistence, Vardy was required to collaborate with James 'Athenian' Stuart in designing the interiors. The Greek influences introduced by Stuart were especially favoured by Gray and the Society of Dilettanti. Together, Vardy and Stuart were expected to provide a layout suitable for display and entertainment, with a circuit of reception rooms on the ground and first floors arranged around a grand central staircase and balcony. The idea was to prompt guests to stroll around a sequence of impressive interiors, each decorated differently, and leave after their circuit was complete without doubling back. The ground floor consisted of a large entrance hall, anteroom, morning room, main dining room and Lord Spencer's drawing room – known as the Palm Room because of its gilded plaster columns in the style of palm trees – which he later used as a library. On the first floor – the *piano nobile* – was the Great Room (used for balls, dining or receptions), a music room, Lady Spencer's drawing room and the Painted Room, the climax of the 'circuit' with its bow window overlooking Green Park. The second floor contained the Spencers' private apartments: unseen by guests, and therefore relatively modest in size and decoration. The third floor was reserved for servants' quarters, connected to the rest of the house by a network of passageways, staircases and specialised basement rooms that ensured the circulation and functionality vital to the smooth running of the household.

As with the exterior statuary, Vardy and Stuart drew directly on actual examples from Greece and Rome, not only as guarantees of neoclassical authenticity, but also to introduce symbolism, metaphor and allegory: 'coded meanings, often related to the function of the house and individual rooms or to past events from the Spencers' lives'.[8] It was both a tacit acknowledgement and a challenge to the presumed connoisseurship of

7 The Palm Room, Spencer House.

the Spencers' guests (and, later, to generations of architectural historians). Vardy's design for the entrance hall, for example, referenced the antechambers to classical temples, where animal sacrifices would have been made. Specifically, he drew on the Tomb of Cecilia Metella (first century BCE) and the Temple of Vespasian (first century CE), featuring a frieze of rams' and oxen's skulls and ancient knives and hatchets. In the dining room he incorporated a frieze of swags and putti derived from the Temple of Fortuna Virilis in Rome; and so on.[9]

The overall effect was flashy and grandiose, unashamedly ostentatious. The staterooms were crammed with neoclassical decorative motifs and objects. Priceless vases and ewers stood on side tables carved with masks of Bacchus and supported by winged panthers. Walls were decorated with gilded mirrors and with moulding and frieze-work featuring egg-and-dart patterns, trumpets, palm branches, axes and helmets, oak-leaf and acanthus garlands, fish-scale scrollwork and medallions of the Three Graces. Ceilings and alcoves were coffered and gilded, doorways were pedimented, and columns topped with Corinthian capitals.[10] It was all deliberately and grotesquely expensive, and just what the young earl wanted in order to establish his place in London society.

When the house finally opened in the spring of 1766 it attracted a great deal of attention. Colen Campbell included plans of Spencer House in an updated edition of his *Vitruvius Britannicus*, a survey of the most admired buildings in England. Arthur Young, a writer and connoisseur, remarked after a visit: 'I do not apprehend there is a house in Europe of its size better worth the view of the curious in architecture and the fitting up and finishing of great houses than Lord Spencer's in St James's Place.'[11] Sir William Chambers, a leading architect of the period, described the house as 'magnificent'. Robert Adam, another leading architect (and rival of James 'Athenian' Stuart), was rather less enthusiastic, describing the interior as 'pityfullissimo'. Thomas Malton, a prominent painter of architectural views, found fault with the exterior, describing it as 'a striking example of the impropriety of employing the Doric order in private houses'.[12] Joseph Friedman, whose compendious history of the building served as the basis for its restoration in the 1990s, noted that

> Some complained that the pediment was 'too large and heavy', others that it was too 'lofty' ... that the addition of an entrance door would have improved the front's appearance. Others complained that the columns were too massive and the order too severe; that the basement was 'too large' and the *piano nobile* 'too small'.[13]

Nevertheless, London's newest landmark generated enormous excitement among the city's elite and was generally well received by the public at large.

Public and professional opinions aside, the broader significance of Spencer House was its role in the ecology of the beau monde of Georgian London. Aristocratic town homes, along with gentlemen's clubs, assembly rooms, spas, public walks and pleasure gardens, were the arenas in which a new ruling elite was forged. In the process, the rest of London's population was influenced in some important ways. The wealthy new elite, with its exclusive group identity and tight social network, gave rise to a resilient power structure that for generations played a huge role in shaping London's physical development, its social structure and its cultural milieu.

The mansions and town homes of Mayfair and St James's provided the setting for many of the most important events in the social calendar. With both Houses of Parliament dominated by landed gentry, these events were at the centre of politics, as well as landmarks in the social calendar. Social entertainment in the beau monde was as much a part of the political process as parliamentary debate. Under the guise of balls, dinners and suppers, introductions were made and strategic political alliances formed and cemented. The presence of the landed aristocratic elite

> became seen as essential to good government. The visibility of powerful lords in London would, it was hoped, act to counter any tyrannical ambitions harboured by the crown ... [E]xtensive stays in the metropolis and the very concept of 'the season' were reframed as important components of noble obligation and modern government.[14]

Spencer House occupied a pre-eminent position in all this. The staterooms of the house became a theatre for the pageant of society and an arena for the tireless manoeuvring that could make or break political careers. Throughout the Season, the Spencers hosted lunch parties, receptions, banquets, concerts and masquerades on a grand scale. Their guests naturally included wealthy members of the nobility and politicians, but also eminent writers, philosophers and artists. This continued under the 2nd earl, supercharged by the circle headed by his sister, Georgiana, who was widely regarded as one of the most alluring and talented women of her generation. She had married the fabulously wealthy duke of Devonshire, a senior statesman possessed of vast estates, palatial houses and priceless art treasures. Some of the most influential figures of her time were part of her circle, including Marie Antoinette, the prince of Wales (later George IV), Lady Melbourne (the prince's lover) and the 2nd Earl Grey (who later became prime minister). Georgiana was the great-great-great-great aunt of Diana, princess of Wales and, like Diana, was a socialite and fashion icon with a gregarious personality, an unhappy marriage, a tenacious loyalty to her children and a social calendar that was written up in detail by the popular press.

The popular press was an important new element in Georgian Britain and its reporting (and satirising) of the fashions and behaviour of the elite was influential in fostering modern consumption culture and the assimilation of taste among an increasingly wealthy urban bourgeoisie. Although titled and seriously wealthy individuals may not have wanted to mix socially with the aspirational classes who could afford to attend the same assemblies, spas, exhibitions and pleasure grounds, both groups wanted, simply, to see and be seen. As nineteenth-century sociologists Thorstein Veblen and Georg Simmel observed, this sparked a dynamic of emulation (Veblen) and differentiation (Simmel), where the aspiring group emulates the fashions and manners of the socially superior group, which in turn adopts new strategies of distinction and differentiation in order to maintain its social distance. But the late Georgian elite could hardly have pushed their levels of consumption or their extremes of fashion much further in differentiating themselves. Instead, their response to the emulation of their social inferiors was to marry into the bourgeoisie in order to acquire new wealth, differentiating themselves with money and the power that came with it.[15]

Generations of the Spencer family continued to live in Spencer House until 1895. By then, the beau monde of the Georgian era was a distant memory, overtaken by the new social structures and consumption patterns introduced by the Industrial Revolution. Meanwhile, the wealth of the country's landed aristocrats had been significantly impacted by an agricultural depression that began in the 1870s. Then parliamentary reform diluted their political power: the Reform Act of 1884 extended the franchise to 60 per cent of the male population. Four years later the creation of local elected authorities (in the form of county councils) undercut the traditional rural power base of the landed aristocracy. Eventually, when the Parliament Act of 1911 established the formal dominance of the House of Commons over the House of Lords, the political power of the nobility – and their influence within London society – was appreciably diminished. Another blow was the introduction of inheritance taxes in 1894, as the government introduced estate duty, a tax on the capital value of land, in a bid to raise money to pay off a £4 million government deficit.

Several great London aristocratic residences were among the first casualties. Harcourt House, on Cavendish Square, was demolished in 1906. It was followed by Harewood House (Hanover Square) in 1908, Camelford House (Park Lane) in 1913, Devonshire House (Piccadilly) in 1925, Grosvenor House (Upper Grosvenor Street) in 1927, Chesterfield House (Curzon Street) in 1937 and Norfolk House (St James's Square) in 1938. Many others, including Spencer House, were let to tenants. The 5th Earl Spencer found himself in straitened circumstances as a result of dwindling income from his country estates and some panicky, ill-advised investments. Faced with escalating maintenance costs and the breakdown of the Season, he sold off the family's rare book collection and some other artefacts, and leased the house to

Barnett Isaacs, one of the richest and most flamboyant men in Victorian England. A succession of other tenants included Mrs Ogden Goelet, wife of a prominent New York property developer, followed by an Austrian nobleman, the Baron de Forest. In 1910, the Spencer family returned to the house, but it was let again in 1920–23 to Prince and Princess Christopher of the Hellenes. Between 1926 and 1943 it was occupied by the Ladies' Army and Navy Club, before being requisitioned as wartime office space for the nation's nursing services. The most valuable contents of the house, along with chair rails, chimney pieces and doors, had been taken to the Spencers' country home at Althorp. By the time the war ended, the house was in a state of dereliction. A nearby bomb had brought down the ceiling of the Painted Room, the façades were blackened by smoke, windows blown out and boarded up and the garden overgrown. By 1948, the family had succeeded in leasing Spencer House to the auctioneers Christie's, whose salerooms had been flattened in the Blitz. When Christie's eventually moved out in 1956, a new lease was signed with the British Oxygen Company, which moved out in 1962 to be replaced by the Intelligence Unit of *The Economist* magazine.

By this time there was an emerging appreciation for the character of older buildings, boosted by urban conservation and historic preservation movements coordinated by the Civic Trust, which had been founded in 1957 by middle-class interests, in reaction to postwar clearance and redevelopment schemes. After *The Economist* moved out in 1984, Lord Rothschild secured a ninety-six-year lease from the current freeholder, the 9th Earl Spencer, brother of the late Lady Diana Spencer. Rothschild's investment trust company, RIT Capital Partners, undertook a ten-year programme of restoration. By 1989, the staterooms and garden had been returned to their original appearance, filled with copies of original furniture and pieces on loan from the royal collection, the National Trust and the V&A. The upper floors now serve as offices, while the staterooms are rented out for civil weddings and exclusive social events. When Russia's President Putin rented Spencer House for a diplomatic banquet in honour of the queen during his state visit to the UK in 2003, it marked the building's return to a central role in the ecology of London's high society. As a living legacy of the Georgian beau monde, it has been an attractive setting for gala dinners and receptions held by international fashion brands, and for the weddings, garden parties, recitals and dinners held by the wealthiest residents, overseas property owners and celebrity visitors to Global London.

2 Bedford Square, Bloomsbury

APPROACHED from any direction, Bedford Square is film-set perfect, a symmetrical square of handsome Georgian town houses surrounding a leafy central garden. Each side of the square forms a terrace of houses in yellow brick, with the two houses in the centre of each terrace stuccoed with pilasters and pediments, giving them the appearance, at first glance, of a single mansion. The houses have three storeys plus basements and attics, with front doors topped by rounded fanlights and semicircular arches in the style of Adam. Most of the houses have retained the original wrought-iron balconies to the first-floor windows, with iron railings along the 'moat' of the lightwell that serves the basement. Every house in the square is on the National Heritage List at Grade I ('of exceptional interest, sometimes considered to be internationally important'), while the gardens in the centre of the square are listed at Grade II* ('particularly important, more than special interest') and the garden railings and lamp standards are listed at Grade II ('nationally important and of special interest').

Andrew Byrne, in his architectural study of Bedford Square, describes it as unique.[1] But as Simon Jenkins points out, Bedford Square is also 'London architecture at its most characteristic'.[2] John Summerson, the

8 Bedford Square town house.

doyen of Georgian architectural history, remarks that the square was built on the leasehold system 'which brought half London into being',[3] while Donald Olsen, in his comprehensive volume on planning and development in eighteenth- and nineteenth-century London, observes that 'Bedford Square set the pattern for later squares in London, which from that time were virtually all built to a single uniform and symmetrical design'.[4] In other words, the significance of Bedford Square rests on its influence as a mature template for London's late Georgian, Regency and early Victorian townscapes. It stands as an exemplar of the elements that characterise London's distinctive terraces and squares, such as narrow three-storey frontages in London stock brick, laid Flemish-bond style (with alternate headers and stretchers in each course); three tall sash windows on each floor, reducing in height from the first floor upwards; stone dressings, basement wells and cast-iron railings.

London's squares and their adjacent networks of rectilinear terraces brought a degree of order to an otherwise sprawling metropolis. They owe their existence to the windfall privatisation of London's medieval fringe belt of hospitals, abbeys, priories, convents and ecclesiastical palaces in the wake of the Reformation. The beneficiaries were a select group of families of Tudor and Stuart courtiers whose heirs would become 'Landlords to London'.[5] A few families – including the Russells, the Grosvenors and the Cadogans – gained control of London's prime development land: the Great Estates to the west of the City. The generous size of their holdings gave the owners of these estates the opportunity to exercise an exceptional degree of architectural and urban design control when they eventually developed their estates, one after another, in response to the building booms of the seventeenth and eighteenth centuries. Francis Russell, the 4th earl of Bedford, had led the way in the 1630s with the development of land that was formerly the kitchen garden of Westminster Abbey, the Convent (later 'Covent') Garden. The manor of Bloomsbury, seized at the Dissolution, was assigned to the 1st earl of Southampton, Thomas Wriothesley, whose namesake, the 4th earl, pioneered the idea of a 'little towne' built around a square – Bloomsbury Square – with a market and cheaper houses in side streets in 1665. The earl of Leicester followed with Leicester Square in 1671; the duke of Monmouth began the development of Soho Square in 1678; Henry Jermyn, earl of St Albans, broke ground on St James's Square in 1684; Grosvenor Square followed in 1695; and Berkeley Square in 1698.

These early developments were the antecedents of Bedford Square, which was laid out during the big building boom that followed the end of the Seven Years' War in 1763. By this time, the economics of estate development were well understood. By setting tall houses next to each other in long runs, builders were able to maximise the density of large homes. The cost of the land set aside for the gardens and open space of the squares was more than compensated for by the increased rents that could be charged for the status, amenity and fresh air enjoyed by residents of the homes facing the garden. For the aristocratic landlords of the Great Estates, the leasehold system was especially important in their calculations. Their estates were 'settled' in law, which meant that they were not entitled to sell any of the land outright, thus preserving the family inheritance. The land could, however, be leased for a fixed term. So, instead of selling their freehold interest to developers, aristocratic landowners leased it to speculative builders. Under the terms of the lease, the builders would erect buildings to a specified standard and keep them in repair for a certain length of time – typically ninety-nine years, the 'London lease'. On the expiry of the lease, the land and the buildings on it would revert to the freeholder.

> For landlords the advantages were clear. Granting leases was likely to be the only way in which they could increase both the revenue and the capital value of their landholding … Because at

> the end of the lease the land and buildings on it reverted to the landlord, there was the possibility of a substantial long-term gain if development was carried out properly.[6]

Naturally, leases tended to be very detailed, often stipulating the minimum sum to be spent on building. In addition, building façades might be the subject of clauses requiring them to be properly aligned with adjoining houses and of similar height. Building materials might be specified, or architectural drawings attached to the lease. Other clauses might stipulate the thickness of outer walls, the use of materials in the interior, or the dimensions of joists, wall plates and rafters.[7] The overall outcome was the uniformity and symmetry that became a hallmark of London's Georgian estates.

Just as Bedford Square was being planned, this tendency toward uniformity was reinforced by a government policy that effectively mandated the appearance of London's new streetscapes. In the spirit of improvement that characterised the age, the London Building Act of 1774 was drafted to regulate the quality and construction of new buildings and make them as fire-proof as possible. The sizes of rooms and their layouts were standardised, and four types or 'rates' of buildings were specified in terms of size and structural quality. First Rate houses had more than 84 square metres (900 sq. ft) of floor space and were to face principal streets. Second Rate houses had between 46 and 84 square metres (500–900 sq. ft) of floor space and faced principal streets, lanes of note and the Thames. Third Rate houses had 33 to 46 square metres (350–500 sq. ft) of floor space and faced mid-ranking streets. Fourth Rate houses occupied less than 33 square metres (350 sq. ft). In addition, the act restricted exterior timber ornamentation, specifically requiring window sash boxes to be recessed into the brickwork. Earlier acts had already required external window sills, with the windows themselves set back slightly from the façade.

The houses built in Bedford Square, of course, were First Rate. The estate had long since passed into the hands of the Russell family, dukes of Bedford, through marriage. The 4th duke of Bedford began seriously to consider resuming development of the Bloomsbury part of the estate soon after the Treaty of Paris concluded the Seven Years' War. The construction of New Road (now Marylebone Road/Euston Road) along the northern fringe of his estate had effectively staked out a new northern perimeter for London, making the fields and orchards in the northern reaches of the estate ripe for development. New Road had been built in the 1750s as a link between Paddington and the City, to provide a route for sheep and cattle to be driven to Smithfield Market and to facilitate troop movements across town; but by the 1760s it was already attracting a ribbon of residential development. The duke aspired to develop his land in a more orderly way, such that it might match the reputation of his great-grandfather, who had developed Covent Garden almost a century and a half before. A frequent visitor to take the waters at Bath, he hoped to create a 'Bedford Circus' in London along the lines of King's Circus in Bath, a grand ring of three-storey town houses that had been completed in 1766. But the 4th duke died even before plans could be drawn up. His successor was a five-year-old grandson, and so the Bedford estates were held in trust by the boy's grandmother, the dowager duchess of Bedford. Together with the late duke's chief agent, Robert Palmer, she set about putting her stamp on her late husband's plans.

The economics of estate development called for a rectilinear arrangement of terraces and squares, rather than a circus; but this did not mean that the centrepiece could not be grand. Palmer's principal responsibility was to devise a ground plan and draw up leases. Thomas Leverton, an established architect, was one of the first to take up a building lease, and he is credited with influencing the design not only of his own house (number thirteen) but also the rest of the square. The regular plot sizes of the ground plan

ensured a regular rhythm to the streetscape. The conditions laid out in the building leases were stringent: 'facings, balustrades and windowsills had to be of Portland stone, roofs of slate, gutters and rainwater pipes of lead, floors of best Memel or Riga wood, the pavements wide and of York stone'.[8] The floors were to be laid with 'good yellow seasoned deals free from sap', and the houses as a whole were to be built 'with hard place brick, ... the walls ... to be flushed solid with good mortar'. Equally stringent restrictive covenants were included to ensure the respectability of the development. No trades were permitted, and nor was any change of use from residential allowed. Lessees were precluded from doing anything in or upon the premises which 'may be or

9 'First Rate' houses on Bedford Square.

grow to the annoyance, grievance, damage or disturbance' of the freeholders.[9]

Building agreements were signed in 1776, with the majority of the plots taken by Robert Grews, a carpenter, and William Scott, a brick-maker. They built the whole of the south side of the square themselves, along with many of the houses on the other sides and on nearby streets. Each side of the square was treated as a single unit. The building elevations are dominated by tall windows on the first floor, underscored by continuous banding at floor level. The doorways are the most decorative part of the elevations, with semicircular arches and fanlights with decorative glazing bars and Coade stone surrounds. The latter are among the earliest surviving examples of their type in London. Coade stone was a new product, made in Lambeth by Eleanor Coade's Artificial Stone Manufactory using a secret formula involving raw clay, ground-up fired clay and various minerals, all pressed into plaster moulds and then fired again at a very high temperature. Frost-resistant and much cheaper than quarried stone, it became one of the distinctive building materials of the Georgian era, used in London by virtually all the leading architects of the time.[10] Whole streets were adorned not only with mass-produced Coade stone door surrounds, but with all kinds of architectural detailing: pilasters, columns and capitals, dentils, cornices and allegorical statuary.

Entrance steps to the town houses span basement wells surrounded by cast-iron railings with urn or flambé torch finials. Inside, the ground floor consisted of a room to the front and a room to the rear, with a staircase to one side. The first-floor plan typically consisted of a large room at the front spanning the width of the house, with a second room behind. Basements extended under the pavement beneath the square itself and ran through to a rear lane that served mews buildings. Mews are a unique and distinctive element of London's cityscape, a practical solution to the problem facing the developers of the Great Estates: how to accommodate the horses, carriages and associated servant class without detracting from the distinction of the neighbourhood. The solution, first introduced in the 1630s as part of Inigo Jones' Covent Garden scheme, was to place a lane between the terraced streets, with mews buildings on both sides of the lane, behind their respective town houses.

The square's central garden oval was grassed over, laid out with gravel walks, and fenced off with cast-iron railings. Before long, it was planted with shrubbery and trees. The idea of the relaxing sensibilities of nature was very fashionable, influenced by Edmund Burke's *Philosophical Enquiry into the Origin of Our Ideas of the Sublime and Beautiful* (1757) and its emphasis on the picturesque.[11] Only leaseholders had access to the garden, which was

10 The central pair of town homes on the north side of Bedford Square.

maintained by a committee of residents. The square itself served as the focal point for a whole new network of streets and mews laid out by the estate. Gower Street to the east, Store Street to the north and Bedford Avenue to the south all took shape at the same time as the square, with Scott and Grews responsible for many of the houses. The building of Bedford Square and the adjacent streets 'inaugurated the systematic transformation of the pastures of northern Bloomsbury into a restricted upper-middle-class suburb'.[12] The development of the estate continued through the completion of Gordon Square in 1860. By that time there were more than thirty squares in the West End. The Great Estates had formed an archipelago of inwardly oriented residential enclaves, each with discreetly located streets of shops and little side streets and mews for the staff and tradespeople necessary to keep the big households going. They were London's newest districts: insulated, class-segregated communities that were to prove impermeable, for a long time, to the normal urban processes of penetration and succession by progressively less wealthy generations of households, as housing becomes worn, obsolescent and relatively less expensive. The landlords of the Great Estates had collectively established a distinctive template for urban design in London. By requiring sound building construction, disciplined exercise of architectural aesthetics, stylistic continuity and an ordered arrangement of building fronts around central gardens, they achieved a special sense of place in each estate.

Bedford Square's exclusivity was sustained by gates with small lodges that were erected around the margins of the Bloomsbury Estate by Thomas Cubitt in the 1820s: an early example of an exclusionary gated community. The gates permitted the passage of gentlemen's carriages and persons on horseback, but prohibited the passage of 'omnibuses, empty hackney carriages, empty cabs, carts, drays, wagons, trucks, cattle and horses at exercise, or funerals' and were closed to all traffic from eleven in the evening until seven in the morning.[13] Servants were expected to patronise the shops south of Great Russell Street, while shopkeepers were not even allowed to send their boys to make a delivery. A shopkeeper 'would only be admitted if he came himself, lest the tone of the neighbourhood should in any way be lowered'.[14]

The houses around the square were marketed to the haute bourgeoisie, rather than the aristocratic elite. They were soon occupied by upper-middle-class tenants who wanted the distinction of 'an address' but could not afford the likes of Mayfair, St James's or the better parts of Marylebone around Portland Place. The square and the streets around it gradually became a lawyers' district, due to the proximity of the Inns of Court, a kilometre (half a mile) to the southeast. Among the more notable judges and lawyers to reside in the square itself were Sir Nicholas Tindal, lord chief justice of the common pleas; the justices Sir James Burrough, Sir John Bayley, Sir Joseph Littledale and Sir John Patteson; and senior lawyers Sir John Richardson, Sir Soulden Lawrence and Sir Robert Graham.[15] Lord Eldon, who served as lord chancellor almost continuously from 1801 to 1827, lived at number six, the stuccoed residence in the middle of the east side of the square, between 1804 and 1815. He was deeply unpopular because of his strident opposition to any kind of progressive change (including the abolition of slavery and restrictions on child labour) and because he was instrumental in framing the notorious Corn Laws, which led to a steep rise in the price of bread. In March 1815, as the Corn Law Bill was under discussion in parliament, an enraged mob gathered outside his house, where they 'instantly tore up the railings before his door, and these were used as weapons to force an entrance through the doors and windows'.[16]

Gradually, the square's changing cast of residents came to reflect the evolving socio-economic character of the upper-middle class and its emerging professional subgroups. By 1850 there were almost as many medical men in the square as there were in Harley Street. Among them were Thomas Wakley, the founder editor of *The Lancet*; Thomas Hodgkin, best known for his account of a form of lymphoma and blood disease that bears his name; and Dr Neil Arnott, physician extraordinary to the queen and consultant to the Poor Law Commission. The architectural profession was represented by Lewis Cubitt, the architect of King's Cross Station (and brother of London's master builder, Thomas Cubitt), and, later, William Butterfield, architect of Keble College, Oxford, and scores of churches in Gothic Revival style. Henry Cavendish was one of the first prominent scientists to lease a house in the square. A reclusive eccentric, he established a museum, a laboratory and a library of some 12,000 volumes in his house. He was reputedly so reclusive that he ordered his dinner by leaving a note on the hall table for his servants. His female staff were under threat of instant dismissal if ever he were to catch sight of them. Just off the edge of the square, on what is now Bayley Street, lived Marc Isambard Brunel, engineer of the Thames Tunnel and developer of machine tools for the mass production of the pulley blocks that Samuel Bentham, the Royal Navy's inspector general, had invented: a landmark in the history of technology, the first application of machine tools used for mass production. Another emerging profession, education, was represented at number forty-seven, on the south side of the square, where Elizabeth Reid, an ardent anti-slavery reformer, used the rooms as Ladies College, which evolved into Bedford College and eventually, in new premises, part of the University of London.

By the turn of the century, Bedford Square had become part of the haunt of the so-called Bloomsbury Group, a mixture of writers, artists and thinkers formed around the novelists Virginia Woolf and E.M. Forster, the biographer Lytton Strachey, the economist John Maynard Keynes, the art critics Roger Fry and Clive Bell, the civil servant Saxon Sydney-Turner, and Walter Lamb, long-serving secretary of the Royal Academy. Lady Ottoline Morrell, who lived at number forty-four, regularly hosted Thursday and Friday evening 'at homes' for members of the Bloomsbury Group, as well as for literary figures Henry James, Aldous Huxley, T.S. Eliot and D.H. Lawrence. The Bloomsbury Group's iconoclasm, their progressive attitudes towards pacifism and feminism, and their predilection for transgressing sexual boundaries earned them a great deal of notoriety. They have been credited by some with fostering a modern sensibility that was symptomatic of – or even catalytic to – the transition from high Victorianism to Modernism. They might equally be portrayed, though, as self-appointed arbiters of taste, intellectual snobs whose private incomes and social status insulated them from the reality of life in London.

By the late nineteenth century, Bedford Square's days as an enclave of upper-middle-class privilege were already under threat from the broader sweep of change across the metropolis. The creation of the LCC in 1889 introduced a swathe of municipal reforms, including the removal of three of the five entrance gates to the Bloomsbury Estate in 1890. In 1893, the LCC removed Bloomsbury's two surviving gates, as well as most remaining gates elsewhere in London. Bedford Square was suddenly a convenient and accessible location between the three great railway termini of Euston, St Pancras and King's Cross to the north, and the offices of both Whitehall and the City to the south. The Great Estates had been spared the disruption of railway building by an act of parliament that restricted rail termini north of the Thames to locations north of New Road. Now, though, the social and economic geography of north-central London was decisively recast. Non-residential tenants began to move into Bedford Square, beginning with the Physical Therapeutic Institute in 1901.[17] Several others, including offices of the Royal Academy of Music and the Royal Agricultural Society of England, had moved in by the start of the First World War, and by the start of the Second World War there were just six private houses left.[18] During the Second World War the square was the focus of the so-called 'Battle of the Railings': ostensibly a campaign to supply scrap metal for the war effort, but in many ways a proxy battle over the elite symbolism of private gardens. By late 1941, the railings around all of the Bloomsbury squares had been requisitioned for scrap, excepting those at Bedford Square. The reprieve was one of the first conservation victories of the Georgian Group, which had only been founded in 1937.

The physical fabric of the square has been fully protected since the listing of its buildings, street furniture and garden by English Heritage in the 1950s and its designation as part of Bloomsbury Conservation Area in 1968. Nevertheless, the role of the square within London continues to evolve. By the end of the

Second World War, it had been given over almost completely to offices of one sort or another. Having been something of an enclave for lawyers and, later, medical men, the square became a magnet for publishers' offices. Among them have been Michael Joseph, William Heinemann, Hodder and Stoughton, Jonathan Cape, Edward Arnold, Bloomsbury Publishing and – last but not least – Yale University Press. More recently, the square's proximity to the British Museum, the British Library and University College London – reinforced, perhaps, by the cachet of having publishing houses as neighbours – has brought educational institutions to the square. They include offices and facilities associated with New York University, the University of North Carolina, Royal Holloway College, the London School of Tropical Medicine, Sotheby's Institute of Art, the Bloomsbury Institute, the Paul Mellon Centre for Studies in British Art, the New College of the Humanities, Amity University, the Architectural Association School of Architecture and École Jeannine Manuel. The rest of the buildings are leased by a mixture of real estate and legal services, accountants, tax and investment consultants, charities and trusts, literary and theatrical agents, and just a handful of private residences. Nevertheless, Bedford Square still retains the appearance of a residential square, largely because of its listed buildings and conservation area status. The square has also benefited from English Heritage's Campaign for London Squares, backed by the Heritage Lottery Fund, which removed an accumulation of unnecessary and unsightly clutter, refurbished street lighting and paving, and laid broad bound-gravel aprons around the oval garden.

Nikolaus Pevsner, whose multi-volume connoisseurial surveys of the buildings of England have become a definitive reference for architectural historians, pronounced Bedford Square 'without any doubt the most handsome of London squares', though he noted, rather archly, that the detailing of the buildings themselves 'argues against the involvement of a designer familiar with classical principles'.[19] Such shortcomings aside, the square must be understood as a pivotal element in London's history: a mature model of the city's speculative seventeenth-century squares that was translated to nineteenth-century inner suburbs, including Islington (e.g. Arundel Square, Barnsbury Square, Gibson Square and Lonsdale Square); the East End (e.g. Arbour Square, Tredegar Square and York Square); and South London (e.g. Albert Square, Cleaver Square, Walcot Square and West Square). Most consist of three-storey runs of terraced houses in London stock brick, with sash windows, basement wells, cast-iron railings and Coade stone dressings, giving inner London a distinctive, repeated grain and appearance.

VIA
sky
OPEN
Kozel
Kozel

3 No. 2 Warehouse, Import Dock, West India Quay

ONE of the few buildings to survive the comprehensive redevelopment of London's docklands, No. 2 Warehouse on the West India Quay is tucked away at the extreme northwestern corner of the Isle of Dogs. Dwarfed among the gleaming new high-rise developments of Canary Wharf and spruced up to accommodate new tenants, it can come across as rather Disneyfied: a token effort at conservation, preserved along with a few renovated dockside cranes, ships' anchors and buoys to lend a whiff of place-based identity to the anonymous forest of new luxury apartment and office towers and hotels. There can be no doubt, though, as to its original function, with its barred windows and vertical bays – called loopholes – where goods would have been hoisted up and swung into storage through the doors.

The functional and symbolic importance of the warehouses cannot be overstated. In sheer physical terms, the warehouses of the West India Docks were a remarkable achievement: a range of nine that eventually stretched uninterrupted along the quayside for more than a kilometre (half a mile): 'one of the great monuments of European commercial power'.[1]

11 No. 2 Warehouse, West India Quay.

Collectively, the West India Docks were also the mainspring of a whole new district, Poplar, which grew up to accommodate the stevedores, lightermen and casual labourers who worked in the docks. The greatest significance of the West India Docks, though, is their role in the Atlantic slave economy. London was the home port for many of the ships that set off for West Africa with manufactured goods, weapons, cloth and tobacco to exchange for enslaved Africans, who were then transported to the plantations of the Caribbean and the North American Atlantic seaboard and exchanged for sugar, rum, tobacco and cotton.[2] London's wealth and Britain's Industrial Revolution were fuelled in part by profits from Caribbean plantations and the enslaved Africans who toiled there.[3] By the late eighteenth century, the West India trade accounted for nearly a third of London's imports, nearly a fifth of its exports and a quarter of Britain's total income. The West India Docks were built expressly to handle this trade. As such, the warehouses stand as testament to a crucial chapter in the history of Britain, as well as the African diaspora.

The construction of the West India Docks resolved an acute problem of congestion at the port of London. Access to the resources, raw materials and markets of an expanding empire, together with the development of domestic manufacturing techniques, had consolidated Britain's position as a trading nation. In particular, the conclusion of the Seven Years' War in 1763 had secured the trade of both the West Indies and the Atlantic seaboard of North America for Britain. London accounted for a large share of it all, including huge East Indiamen (the merchant sailing vessels of the British and Dutch East India companies) bringing tea, silk and cotton textiles, indigo, opium and porcelain from India and China, smaller ships bringing wine from Portugal, timber from the Baltic, building stone from Dorset, coal from Newcastle and so on – as well as the ships bringing sugar and rum from the West Indies. All of them were required to unload in a short stretch of the Thames between London Bridge and Wapping – either at the 'Legal Quays', a monopoly of the City of London Corporation, or at the bishop of Winchester's wharves in Southwark. It enriched City grandees and the bishop of Winchester, but the archaic system was cripplingly inadequate. London's ever-increasing volume of trade meant that the river was permanently clogged with ships. On arrival, they moored wherever they could find room, blocking the shipping channel for other vessels while they waited for lighters and barges to transfer cargo to the limited wharf-side areas.

Inadequate storage facilities meant that unsecured cargoes were stacked on quays, waiting to be processed by customs and leading in turn to further delays in unloading cargoes. Goods left out on open quays – especially high-value consumables like sugar, rum and coffee – meanwhile presented an irresistible temptation to criminals, whose ranks included 'river pirates, night plunderers, light horsemen, heavy horsemen, game watermen, game lightermen, mudlarks, scuffle-hunters, copemen and a number of inferior revenue officers who joined in the game'.[4] Each followed their own methods, some working at night and armed, some prowling in the mud at low tide, waiting for goods to be cast overboard by accomplices, others starting fights during unloading and seizing goods during the general commotion. Local newspapers regularly reported the theft of hundreds of bottles of liquor:

> They also took ... candlesticks, tobacco, packets of wool, bottles of chlorodyne and of Dr Powell's balsam of aniseed, bales of cow-hair ... boxes of Jordan almonds, bags of oats, wheels of cheese, pineapples and other fruits ... And these were only the cases mentioned by part of the press.[5]

Some relief to the congestion had been provided by the establishment in 1786 of customs and excise 'sufferance wharves' (on the Surrey bank and downstream from the Tower) for lower-value goods. And merchants' concern over pilfering and theft had led to the creation, in 1798, of a Marine Police Establishment, the forerunner of the Metropolitan Police. But neither the sufferance wharves nor the small new river police force was sufficient to resolve the issues of congestion, delay and thievery. The 'West India interest' – merchants, shipowners, plantation owners, absentee landlords and slave factors (who bought up cargoes of slaves and then resold them to the plantations)[6] – took up the idea of creating a new 'wet dock' set off from the river with its own secure warehouses. William Vaughan, a London insurer and heir to West Indian plantations, published a treatise, *On Wet Docks, Quays and Warehouses for the Port of London*. Another leading proponent of the idea was Robert Milligan, a Jamaica planter who was a partner in a firm of slave factors and owner of two sugar plantations worked by more than five hundred enslaved Africans.

The group's first proposal, for new quays and warehouses in Wapping, was vigorously opposed by the City of London Corporation, by wharf owners along the Legal Quays, and by the Thames lightermen and coopers who worked there. After various counter-proposals had been advanced, a report by a Select Committee of the House of Commons resulted in support for two schemes, one for London Docks at Wapping and another for West India Docks on the Isle of Dogs. Both were endorsed by parliament, with the West India Docks the first to be approved. The Act for Rendering More Commodious and for Better Regulating the Port of London received Royal Assent in July 1799. The required land was to be purchased by the City of London Corporation and then sold on to the West India Dock Company through trustees. The act also required all rum, coffee and sugar imported to London to be unloaded in the West India Dock for twenty-one years following its construction. This clause removed much of the speculative risk, and there was little difficulty in raising the initial capital of £500,000. Most investors were drawn from the commercial and financial community of the City, along with absentee slave-owners, slave factors and overseas merchants involved in the 'West India interest'.

The site selected for the new docks was 3 kilometres (2 miles) downstream from the Legal Quays, where the river makes its distinctive U-bend around what was the marshland of the Isle of Dogs. The land here was used only for pasturing cattle; much of it was covered with reeds and regularly inundated by high tides. There were a few ship-breakers' yards, rope-makers and timber merchants along the riverside, but only a handful of permanent inhabitants: one of them drove the cattle off the marshes, another worked a ferry across to Greenwich.[7] But the land was cheap, there was space to build very large docks and extensive warehouses, and the river was relatively deep and free of congestion. The innovative plan was to dig out two docks across the neck of the Isle of Dogs, with independent access from each dock to the Thames by way of locks and basins at either end. This would allow a vessel arriving from the West Indies to unload in the northern dock – the Import Dock – then sail round to the southern dock – the Export Dock – and load up with cargo. The docks were vast in scale: the Import Dock held a body of water 12 hectares (30 acres) in extent. Dug out to a depth of 7 metres (23ft) deep, it could accommodate scores of vessels at any one time. The Export Dock was almost as big. Clay from the excavations was used to make 24 million bricks for the walls lining the docks, while the rest of the spoil was used to build up the ground level of the quays.

A competition for the design of the warehouses attracted some of the leading architects of the day, including John Nash, John Soane, George Dance the Younger, James Wyatt and Thomas Leverton (of Bedford Square). But the priority of the directors of the West India Dock Company was economy. The sheer scale of the project would be spectacular enough. The contract was given

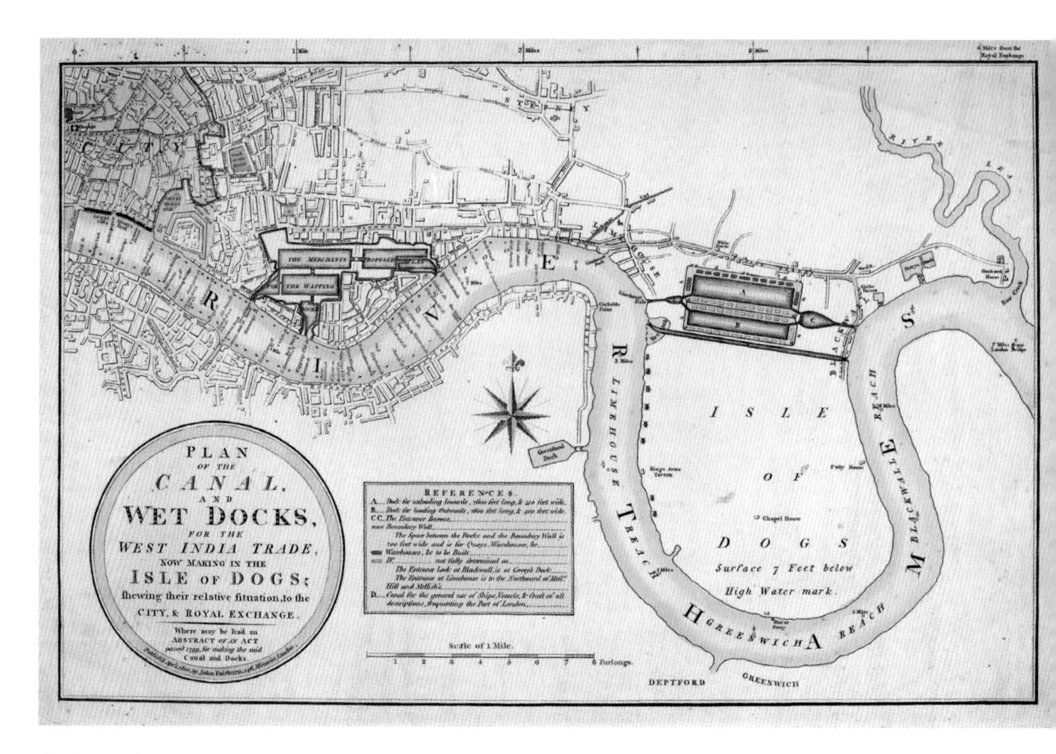

12 Plan of the canal wet docks for the West India trade, 1800.

13 Bird's-eye view of West India Docks and warehouses, 1802.

to George Gwilt, a surveyor who agreed to reside at the docks and devote his full attention to dock affairs with his eldest son, also George, as clerk of works. The first six West India warehouses – numbers 2, 3, 4, 6, 7 and 8 – were completed in only two years, between 1800 and 1802. Bricklaying proceeded at a rate of about a million bricks each week, this at a time when both labour and materials were scarce, due to geopolitical turmoil. Gwilt's design for the warehouses was not particularly advanced, however. At a time when the cotton mills of Belper in the Lower Derwent Valley were incorporating structural cast iron and brick or tile flooring as part of their innovative multi-storey, fire-resistant designs, the only use of cast iron in the West India warehouses was in the barred window frames. It proved to be a false economy, as within twenty years of their opening, sagging wooden floors of the warehouses had to be propped up with structural cast-iron columns designed by engineer John Rennie.

Nevertheless, the warehouses were virtually a fortress, built securely enough to become Britain's first bonded warehouses, where payment of duties on the stored goods could be deferred until the cargo was sold on. This had enormous implications for the re-export trade and the development of London as an entrepôt. The whole complex was surrounded by a brick wall 9 metres (30ft) high. Beyond the wall on the far side of the surrounding cart road was an iron railing and a ditch 24 feet wide by 7 feet deep, crossed only by swing bridges. Beyond that, empty fields. Only dock company or customs employees were allowed unaccompanied access to the premises; even ships' crews were excluded. The dock company established its own security force to protect the stored goods. No. 2 Warehouse alone could house approximately 8,000 hogsheads of sugar on the main floors, 2,000 hogsheads of coffee in the attic and 2,000 casks of rum in the cellars. The price of efficiency, economy and security was banality. 'In the Gwilts' hands, austere neo-Classicism, fashionable as well as suited to conveying strength and impregnability, lapsed into bulky monotony.'[8] Joseph Conrad, in his novella *The Children of the Sea*, wrote that 'Brick walls rose high above the water – soulless walls, staring through hundreds of windows as troubled and dull as the eyes of over-fed brutes.'[9] The one extravagant flourish on the part of the company was to commission a statue of Robert Milligan by the noted sculptor Richard Westmacott. It was erected at the main access to the Import Dock in 1813, with a plaque inscribed with praise for his role in establishing the docks.

When No. 2 Warehouse opened in 1802, the first ship to discharge its cargo was the *Echo*, out of Jamaica. Business boomed in the early years, thanks largely to the company's twenty-one-year monopoly clause. The Import Dock could discharge eighteen ships at a time, with a turnaround time of just a few days, rather than the month or more it had taken under the old system. The total number of ships discharged rose from 354 in 1804 to an early peak of 641 in 1810.[10] British slave trading was abolished in

14 Numbers 1 & 2 Warehouses, Import Dock, West India Quay.

1807, but British colonial slavery was not abolished until 1833, and the plantation economies of the United States, Cuba and Brazil, where slavery was not abolished until 1865, 1886 and 1888 respectively, continued to send cargoes of sugar, coffee, rum and mahogany, along with camphor, tea, pepper, pimento, rice, tin, copper, ginger and molasses. As the British Empire gained in size and strength through the nineteenth century, so London's port functions increased. New docks were dug on the Isle of Dogs and along the banks of the Thames, creating a 'dockland' that would become the nexus of empire. The London Dock at Wapping had begun construction even before the West India Docks had opened. The Surrey Docks at Rotherhithe followed soon afterwards, along with the East India Docks at Blackwall. St Katharine Dock, upstream next to the Tower, opened in 1828; Royal Victoria Dock in 1855; Millwall Dock in 1868; and the Royal Albert Dock in 1880. Altogether the docklands occupied more than 160 hectares (400 acres) of land and 445 hectares (1,100 acres) of water.[11] All of the docks, following the example of the West India Docks, had vast bonded warehouses, often five or six storeys high.

The docklands provided about 50,000 jobs. Stevedores, skilled in the art of loading and unloading cargo, were the labour aristocracy of the area, along with lightermen and the operators of winches and cranes; but most were casual labourers who never knew whether they would be hired on a given day. The ebb and flow of goods at the docks determined the fortunes of hundreds of thousands of working-class people, and 'there was in this sense no more significant site in the landscape of empire'.[12] Late Victorian tourist guidebooks routinely recommended a trip into the docklands in order to appreciate the awesome scope and range of London's influence. Early editions of *Baedeker* promoted the docks as an unmissable spectacle, 'the centre from which the commerce of England radiates all over the globe'.[13] The dock workers themselves were witness on a daily basis to the glories and spoils of empire. On the one hand it generated a distinctively patriotic streak in the culture of working-class East End communities, while on the other the same communities were renowned for industrial and political militancy.[14] The West India Docks were the site of a pivotal moment in British labour history in 1889, when a dispute over bonus payments during the unloading of the cargo steamer *Lady Armstrong* prompted a walk-out. The dockers demanded a raise of a penny an hour (bringing the rate to sixpence an hour; equivalent to £8.22 an hour in 2023),[15] 'which seemed exorbitant only to the dock owners'.[16] Within a week, the whole labour force of London docks and their ancillary functions – by now 130,000 men – was on strike, and within another three weeks the dispute was resolved in favour of the dockers. It is widely considered a milestone in the development of the British labour movement, signalling the growth of 'new unions' of casual, unskilled workers (in contrast to the craft unions already in existence).

Meanwhile, the initial commercial advantage enjoyed by the West India Docks did not last long. Although the Import Dock remained one of the most spacious of all, the newer docks, beginning with the Royal Victoria Dock, were cut with wider entrances and deeper berths, and were able to take advantage of new technologies – the arrival of merchant steamships in the 1830s, the railway in 1851, and the introduction of hydraulic locks, capstans and cranes in the 1850s. With the loss of trade to competing docks, the Import Dock's surplus warehousing capacity was resolved by way of a merger in 1838 with the East India Dock Company, which had insufficient warehousing. Further competition from newer docks meant declining profits, leaving the new company unwilling to invest in major improvements to either dock. Instead, the company finally invested, in 1886, in additional new docks of its own, 32 kilometres (20 miles) downstream at Tilbury. By the 1900s, the company had merged with the Victoria, Albert, St Katharine and London Docks to form a single vast entity, while the Port of London Authority

(PLA) was created in 1908 to oversee commercial enterprise on the river.

During the early twentieth century, London gradually lost ground to other ports that were modernising and enlarging their facilities to serve specialised markets. The West India Docks carried on until the Second World War, when air raids on day one of the Blitz – 7 September 1940 – obliterated 80 per cent of the storage space. Only warehouses 1 and 2 on the Import Dock (now called the North Dock) were left operational. After the war, London's docklands as a whole recovered enough to account for around a third of Britain's seaborne trade. But circumstances were challenging. Apart from competition from other British and continental ports, the world – and Britain's position in it – was changing. Post-colonial adjustments and changes to international trade blocs did not help, but the development of shipping container technology recast the entire network of ocean-going shipping. The West India Docks, like the rest of the docklands, were suddenly and terminally obsolescent. Recognising this, the PLA created the necessary infrastructure for handling containerisation at Tilbury. When the North Quay berths closed in 1971, warehouses 1 and 2 were already closed and shuttered. By 1980, trade in the docklands as a whole had declined to almost nothing. Docks and warehouses were abandoned, and the government took control of the land. The result was the reincarnation of the Docklands, capitalised, centred around West India Docks – themselves renamed and rebranded as Canary Wharf – as a financial services district (see Chapter 23).

No. 2 Warehouse, like scores of others along the Thames – in Southwark and Rotherhithe, along Wapping High Street, on the Isle of Dogs and in Blackwall, all with fine river views – proved structurally sound and sufficiently grittily 'authentic' for conversion to loft apartments and studio spaces to accommodate the Docklands' incoming gentrifiers. It was duly converted in 1998–2000 to provide a mixture of apartments, restaurants and shops by the developers Manhattan Loft. No. 1 Warehouse, next door, was converted to become the Museum of London Docklands. In a misguided and tone-deaf attempt at signalling the history of the docks, the statue of Robert Milligan, which had been put in storage during the Second World War, was brought out and installed on the quayside, with its bas-relief on the plinth depicting Britannia receiving Commerce: a rather wan-looking Britannia is improbably seated on a lion and hailed by the female figure of Commerce, with cherubs and a large horn of plenty at her feet. The plaque on the plinth references Milligan's 'genius, perseverance and guardian care' in establishing the docks (but omits his prominent roles in the Atlantic slave economy). The statue was removed in 2020 in the midst of Black Lives Matter protests, and is scheduled to become part of the museum's permanent collection, once local communities have been consulted about how it should be presented.

of
LONDON,
FROM
An Actual Survey made in the Years 1824, 1825 & 1826.
C. and J. GREENWOOD.
London
Explanation
Public Buildings
Park & Pleasure Grounds
Woods & Plantations
Fields
To
His Most Gracious Majesty
KING GEORGE THE FOURTH
THIS MAP
Explanation
Boundary of the City of London
Boundary of the City & Liberty of Westminster
Boundary of the Borough of Southwark
LIMEHOUSE REACH
GREENWICH

II

VICTORIAN LONDON I: WORKSHOP METROPOLIS

When Queen Victoria began her reign in 1837, London was already the largest city in the world, with a population of more than 1.5 million. By the time she died, in 1901, that population had grown almost three-fold, to 4.5 million – or 6.5 million including the emerging suburbs of Greater London. The continuously built-up area had reached Hammersmith and Notting Hill in the west, Holloway and Crouch End in the north, Tower Hamlets and Stratford in the east, and Streatham and Penge in the south. Patchy ribbon development connected exurbs and villages like Surbiton, Kingston, Twickenham, Sutton, Croydon, Wimbledon, Tooting, Hounslow, Willesden, Hendon, Edmonton and Tottenham. All of them were about to become integrated into the fabric of the metropolis. London was feeling the full effects of what the economist Karl Polanyi called the 'Great Transformation' as industrial capitalism took hold, bringing rapid urbanisation, economic growth and radical changes to economic, social, cultural and political life.[1] It also brought new kinds of buildings, new urban landscapes and new landmarks.

As the accelerating Industrial Revolution generated thousands of new factories, workshops and warehouses, London became distinctive as a European capital with a significant industrial base, as well as a thriving port. By 1900, about one in every three workers in London was involved in manufacturing of

15 'London in 1827'.

some sort.[2] As the largest and wealthiest consumer market in the country, London tended to specialise in both luxury goods and everyday items. The reason London has never appeared as an industrial metropolis in the popular imagination is largely because of the diversity of these activities and the fact that they were localised in different districts within the expanding and diversifying fabric of the city: cabinetmaking in Shoreditch and Bethnal Green; watchmaking in Clerkenwell; gunsmiths in the Minories near Aldgate; the garment industry, sugar refining and brewing in Whitechapel; the leather industry in Southwark and Bermondsey; shoemakers in Bethnal Green; instrument making and the manufacture of electrical apparatuses in Soho, Millbank, Vauxhall and Clerkenwell; and upholsterers, bookbinders, furriers, umbrella makers, cigar makers, brush makers, French polishers and matchbox makers throughout the East End. London also had a fair share of big factories and work yards: heavy engineering in Lambeth and Pimlico; bleaching mills, oil mills and iron foundries along the Wandle at Wandsworth; chemicals and coal by-products in Silvertown; match production in a great new works at Bow (Chapter 4); potteries in Lambeth, Fulham and Mortlake; railway engineering in Stratford; and rope-making and shipbuilding along the Thames below Tower Bridge.

The transition to the industrial era required an entirely new infrastructure and a more orderly and healthy society that could be sustained only through stronger and better-organised governance, greater social control and a more literate population. It was a transition that involved a complex of interdependent and sometimes conflicting social and political processes as it unfolded across urban space, but the outcome was that London's landscapes came to be punctuated by an array of public institutions (the courts, prisons) and municipal facilities (schools, libraries, public baths, asylums, dispensaries, hospitals, etc.). To progressive Victorians, board schools like Rochelle Street

School (Chapter 7) were 'beacons of the future';[3] and libraries were 'citadels of culture, emporiums of civilisation'.[4] It was all supported by an entirely new infrastructure of gasometers, water towers, sewage pumping stations, power plants, railway stations, tram networks and sanitary cemeteries: iconic embodiments of Victorian technological achievement, 'compulsively admired and marvelled at'.[5] At the same time, the deployment of gas, electricity and plate glass, together with the efforts of local authorities to widen streets and regulate the built environment, helped to create 'a lighter, airier, more salubrious city within which civil conduct could be both secured and publicly displayed'.[6]

New churches and chapels were also important landmarks in the spreading metropolis. The new class fractions generated by the Industrial Revolution were broadly matched to multiple denominations of Christianity – though with the one glaring exception of the fundamentally irreligious working class.[7] The growth of nonconformism produced a rash of Methodist and Congregationalist churches, Baptist chapels, Quaker meeting houses and Salvation Army citadels. Between 1810 and 1840, nonconformists built more than 33,000 places of worship while Anglicans built only just over a thousand new churches.[8] The nonconformists' target markets were the growing ranks of the lower-middle classes, for whom they offered not only spiritual support, but also the agency of social mobility, socialisation and education. 'Chapels became centres of working class resistance, where workers developed their own culture of self education, running their own administrative affairs, and honing skills in oratory.'[9] Church- and chapel-building became an aspect of sectarian competition, new and restored churches representing not only a commitment to particular devotional practices, but also a claim to territory.[10] Commissioners' churches such as Christ Church, Turnham Green (Chapter 8) staked out the claims of the established Anglican Church, subsidised by parliament through Church Building Acts of 1818 and 1824.

Meanwhile, in order to maximise the productivity of labour with minimal expenditure, it was necessary to compress vast numbers of the working classes in close proximity to the means of production. The price of urban land and the economics of construction resulted in the crowding of impoverished populations into cellars, tenements and jerry-built terraces. It meant that communicable diseases were rife. Warrens of slums with narrow, poorly lit, unpaved streets and alleys with no proper drains or satisfactory water supply were soon identified as breeding grounds for life-threatening diseases and occasional epidemics of smallpox, cholera and typhoid. As the eminent historian Asa Briggs noted, the 'Sanitary Idea' emerged as one of the leading themes of the age.[11] Charles Dickens terrified his readers with descriptions of London's slums; Gustave Doré illustrated them; and Charles Booth carefully mapped their extent. In response there emerged a second, parallel, ideology: of paternalism and reform. It developed its own expression in the built environment in the form of almshouses, workhouses, dispensaries, orphanages, asylums, hospitals, model housing and model communities: buildings charged with powerful moral meanings for Victorians because they were rooted in issues of justice and virtue. It was, though, a morality framed by a judgmental attitude towards the poor and the idea that they could be neatly divided into three categories: the industrious poor; the incapacitated poor, such as the disabled, orphaned, chronically sick and elderly; and the morally degraded poor who were too lazy to work, instead wallowing in vice, crime and immorality. As Henry Mayhew put it in *London Labour and the London Poor* (1851): 'those that will work, those that cannot work, and those that will not work'.

The appalling conditions in the slums and in Victorian workhouses such as Lambeth Workhouse (Chapter 5) inspired a significant amount of voluntary action and philanthropy. Women's voluntary groups helped to establish childcare and child labour issues as matters of public concern and public policy, sowing seeds that would later germinate as part of the welfare state, and in the process carving out new professions for women in public health and social work.[12] Industrialists and financiers such as George Peabody, Sydney Waterlow and the Guinness family were all willing and able to build decent housing (for Mayhew's 'those that will work') that yielded profits that were, for the period, strikingly modest: typically around 5 per cent. J. Passmore Edwards helped to fund hospitals, drinking fountains, libraries, schools, convalescent homes and art galleries, while the likes of Octavia Hill, Angela Burdett-Coutts and Samuel and Henrietta Barnett combined personal philanthropy with advocacy of reform. The reform movement was underpinned by activist associations such as the Health of Towns Association, the Society for the Improvement of the Conditions of the Labouring Classes and the Association for Promoting Cleanliness amongst the Poor. 'Model' bath-houses were established in London from 1845 by the Association for the Establishment of Baths and Washhouses for the Labouring Poor, while the Metropolitan Association for Improving the Dwellings of the Industrious Classes, the East End Dwellings Company, the Four Per Cent Industrial Dwellings Company and the Artizans', Labourers' and General Dwellings Company, among others, offered middle-class investors a mechanism through which to invest in model housing developments such as Shaftesbury Park (Chapter 6) for 'decent' working-class families,[13] rather than simply donating money for model housing.

But voluntarism, philanthropy and activist associations were no match for the pace of urbanisation and the inexorable logic of laissez-faire economics. The conditions endured by the industrious poor in philanthropic housing were bleak. The Kaplans, who rented a tenement flat in the Four Per Cent Industrial Dwellings Company's Rothschild Buildings in the East End, 'had virtually nothing except each other': 'We had orange boxes for to eat on ... we had three chairs.' As much as they tried to keep the place clean, and despite standing bed legs in tins of paraffin, spending food-money on insecticides like Keating's Powder and fumigating with sulphur candles, they suffered, along with their neighbours, from infestations of bed bugs. 'We used to be up all night. You couldn't *sleep*.' Finding enough money for food was a constant concern:

> Breakfast? Hard bit of bread and have to take that off to school. We never had breakfast those days ... Nothing when we came home. Cold banana. Cold banana. My sister always says to me 'If I ever see a banana again I'll scream!'

Annie Kaplan recalled that

> My mother never played with us ... My mother didn't have the time. She was a very good mother but she never had time for all that. We never had a party, no birthday, no toys, nothing. No, my mother didn't even know when was our birthdays.[14]

Gradually, the combination of intensifying slums and the realisation that markets require a degree of collective action to function adequately led to a more generalised response: local government intervention in the marketplace in order to impose standards and to ensure the provision of key services and basic amenities. Along with the 'hidden hand' of market dynamics, the visible hand of the state was needed. Led by Sidney Webb's Progressive Party, London's 'gas and water socialists' stood for progressive taxation, housing reform and the provision of municipal infrastructure. But it was the threat to public health – cholera epidemics, in particular – that led to a more widespread public willingness to raise taxes and impose regulations to address a range of public health needs, including the regulation of land use, the provision of water and gas supplies, the creation of municipal cemeteries and the introduction of new building codes. Yet the provision of decent, affordable housing was stymied by the dismal arithmetic of wages and rent, clearance costs and building costs. The impasse was broken towards the end of the nineteenth century by the combination of two key reforms. In 1889, the London County Council (LCC) was created as a metropolitan-wide authority, injecting party politics into every aspect of the built environment.[15] And in 1890, the Housing of the Working Classes Act empowered the new LCC to demolish the worst slums and build new tenements and blocks of flats. The LCC began by targeting the Old Nichol rookery in Bethnal Green and replacing it with London's first council housing project, the Boundary Street Estate.

4 Fairfield Works, Bow

THE best view of the Fairfield Works (now part of the 'Bow Quarter') is from a train passing along the main line between Liverpool Street and Stratford: the only clear view, in fact, of the massive south façade of the main building. Pevsner, for the most part reliably restrained in recording the buildings of England, describes it simply as 'awesome'.[1] Its 'great brooding mass' of red brick stretches alongside the railway for 137 metres (450ft), with forty-eight five-storey bays of double windows separated by projecting piers and buttressing. The overall effect is indeed awesome. The east elevation of the main building, on Wick Lane, is similarly massive but shorter in length, with only five double and nine single bays, punctuated by goods entrances and terminating in a gated entrance to a cobblestone driveway, the former workers' entrance to the works. On the far side of the complex, along Fairfield Road, a gatehouse and a series of cottages are integrated into a fancy boundary wall, all in red brick. The whole ensemble, which pre-dates the main works building by some thirty years, is an exercise in neo-Gothic ornamentation. The original owners clearly wanted to make a statement. The boundary wall features deep pointed-arch recesses and the buildings include elaborate chimney stacks, crow-stepped gables, a gambrel-roofed (witch's hat) pavilion, projecting

16 Fairfield Works, built 1909–11. Now Bow Quarter's Manhattan Building.

porches and terracotta panels with bas-relief scenes and motifs. The main gate here opens to a courtyard fronting a yellow-brick building with an elaborate passageway framed by a white stone surround and polished granite columns. Above the passageway is a clock set in a Venetian-style panel with its own elaborate stone scrollwork and heraldic shields. Looming behind is an Italianate water tower.

The Fairfield Works was established by the firm of Bryant and May, one of several in the East End whose principal business was manufacturing matches. Matches were big business throughout the nineteenth century and well into the twentieth. They were needed by everyone: for lighting fires, candles, cigars, cigarettes, oil lamps, gas lamps and gas cookers. Millions were consumed every day. Bryant and May matchboxes, with their yellow and black labels, were ubiquitous. Special-edition boxes, such as the 'England's Glory' label, with union flags and a picture of a battleship, became iconic. Matchboxes were an important part of an East End 'cottage' industry, where women and children eked a supplementary living on piece-work. The Fairfield Works, where the matches themselves were manufactured, was, in contrast, representative of the emergence of large-scale industrial production in London. At the same time, the factory's operational issues were symptomatic of changing class and gender relations. Before too long, the Fairfield Works would become a pivotal scene of class conflict, a landmark in British labour history and the site of an important chapter in environmental health and safety. Eventually, the notoriety of the works would come to be obscured, as the derelict works was converted to one of London's first redevelopments as a gated residential community.

William Bryant and Francis May had established a general trading company in 1843. Within a few years the firm had contracted with a Swedish match-maker, Lundström's, to import matches to meet the ever-increasing British demand. Business was so good that, within a decade, they decided to acquire the

17 Bryant and May's Fairfield Works in Bow, c. 1865.

British rights to the Lundström safety match and enter the manufacturing business. They purchased a 3 acre (1.2 hectare) site in Bow, and with advice from Lundström's engineers they built their own factory, along with a warehouse, offices and directors' cottages. The premises on Fairfield Road had two important locational advantages. Just to the east was the River Lea, with a convenient wharf for the delivery of raw materials. To the west and the south were the growing streets of working-class housing in Bow and Poplar, respectively, representing a huge pool of cheap female labour. Fairfield Road itself was relatively new, having been established after Bow Fair (which gave the road its name) was abolished for being too rowdy.

Both Bryant and May were Quakers, with a strict but paternalistic approach to business, much like the Cadbury brothers in Birmingham and Joseph Rowntree in York. They wanted to create a model operation, not only in terms of profitability, but also in terms of modern technology and the treatment of workers. That is how, in fact, the Fairfield Works was seen by contemporary observers – though this, of course, was in the context of the brutal, exploitative and dangerous conditions in most of London's mid-century workplaces. By 1881, the site covered around 2.5 hectares (6 acres) and had a workforce of over 5,000, mostly women, with an output of roughly 300 million matches per day. The company was booming financially, paying dividends of 20 per cent or more from the late 1870s into the mid-1880s. Working conditions may have been significantly better than in most factories, but they were by no means easy. There were twelve-hour shifts in the summer and ten-hour shifts in the winter, with an hour for lunch. Working with the white phosphorus used in making Bryant and May's 'strike-anywhere' matches was hazardous: it could cause 'phossy jaw', an illness involving terrible pain, swelling of the gums, the loss of teeth, decay and disintegration of the jaw bone, disfiguration of the face and, for some, death. Fines were imposed for the slightest breach of factory regulations, such as omitting to clear away litter from under a workbench. Late arrival meant being shut out for half a day; and pay was so poor that being fined could mean working all day for nothing.

The appearance of a new social subgroup – waged working-class women – represented a new and significant threat to the established order and a potential threat to relations between the sexes. The Victorian middle classes tended to think of women as belonging to one of three categories: mother/wife, celibate spinster or tart (amateur or professional). The idea of respectably employed women of any class was unnerving; and especially so if it involved the working poor.

> Welcome or not, the new figure of the 'factory girl' strode onto the public stage, and began to occupy a particular place in nineteenth-century fiction and media. She was always a 'girl', never given the dignity of maturity no matter her actual age, and her portrayal

> by mostly male and middle-class journalists and commentators would reveal many of the fears and preoccupations of the unquiet Victorian subconscious.[2]

The matchwomen of the Fairfield Works were close-knit and independent-minded, with a strong sense of solidarity. They were also a brash and boisterous lot, with a disarming confidence and a refusal to 'know their place' that was characteristic of a tight community dominated by Irish immigrants and their descendants. Charles Booth, who had seen so much of London in compiling his seventeen volumes of *The Life and Labour of the People in London* (1889), noted that the matchwomen were 'a rough set of girls'.[3] Their intimidating and scandalously unfeminine comportment played on bourgeois fears that women with jobs would end up just like men – rejecting domesticity in favour of the attractions of pubs and music halls! Worse, it played on contemporary fears of an alienated 'mob' emerging from working-class neighbourhoods: 'haunts of vice' that harboured moral degeneration, which in turn was seen as a fundamental cause of both poverty and disease. Another nineteenth-century statistician, G.B. Longstaff, asserted

> That the town life is not as healthy as the country is a proposition that cannot be contradicted ... The narrow chest, the pale face, the weak eyes, the bad teeth, of the town-bred child are but too often apparent. It is easy to take an exaggerated view either way, but the broad facts are evident enough; long life in towns is accompanied by ... degeneration.[4]

It was a view that was widespread among London's comfortably off middle and upper-middle classes and, especially, churchmen who felt threatened and disappointed by the stubborn irreligion of the working classes. The Reverend Andrew Mearns' sensational thirty-page pamphlet, *The Bitter Cry of Outcast London*,

18 East façade, Fairfield Works.

19 Fairfield Works gatehouse complex, Fairfield Road.

published in 1883, was an instant bestseller. 'We must face the facts,' he wrote, 'and these compel the conviction that THIS TERRIBLE FLOOD OF SIN AND MISERY IS GAINING UPON US.' Tellingly, Mearns' first paragraphs noted the non-attendance of the working classes at church: 'It is perhaps scarcely necessary to say of the hundreds of thousands who compose the class referred to, that very few attend any place of worship.'[5]

Others sought to soften the edges of laissez-faire capitalism and 'rescue' the poor from low wages and poor housing. Annie Besant, an activist and writer committed to women's rights, birth control, secularism, workers' rights and Fabian socialism, took up the cause of the matchwomen. Having met some of them, she wrote up a sensationalised account of conditions in the Fairfield Works in her political weekly, *The Link*. Published in June 1888 under the title 'White Slavery in London', it played, in an unselfconsciously patronising way, on the sentimentalised trope of Hans Christian Andersen's waiflike 'Little Match Girl'. The matchwomen were portrayed as touchingly childlike, having to endure ruthlessly exploitative conditions imposed by rich and powerful factory owners. The fact that the women came out on strike just a month later gave rise to a conventional historical narrative in which Besant and her progressive colleagues have been credited with organising and orchestrating the strike. A Blue Plaque on the wall of the gatekeeper's cottage on Fairfield Road says so: 'The Match Girls Strike of 1888 was led here by Annie Besant.'

But in fact, as labour historian Louise Raw has shown, the strike was planned and initiated by a cell of politically astute activists within the factory; Besant and others only became aware of the strike after the fact.[6] Indeed, the women of the Fairfield Works had been on strike several times before: in 1881, 1885 and 1886. At issue on each occasion was not only low pay, but also resentment at irksome fines for petty misdemeanours. Stories of the insensitive hubris of the company directors, propagated by

Annie Besant, did not help. In 1871, the women had marched on parliament, supporting the directors' protest against a proposed tax on matches. The following year, the directors erected a testimonial fountain outside Bow railway station in commemoration of the defeat of the proposed tax, but the rumour was that they funded it by docking the matchwomen's wages. A decade later, the directors were rumoured to be at it again, docking workers' wages to pay for a statue of Prime Minister William Gladstone to mark his half-century in British politics. All this while drawing handsome dividends for themselves.

The 1888 strike was triggered by the dismissal on 5 July of the organisers of a campaign to refuse to sign a statement of satisfaction with working conditions – a move that the management hoped would provide a counter to Besant's essay. A strike committee helped ensure that by the following day the entire factory was on strike. This is where Annie Besant did play a significant role, organising a strike fund and engaging the support of prominent reformers. The matchwomen had rallied around Besant as their public voice. In an anonymous letter to Besant dated 4 July 1888, the women wrote:

> Dear Lady they have been trying to get the poor girls to say that it is all lies that has been printed and trying to make us sign papers that it is all lies; dear Lady nobody knows what it is we have put up with and we will not sign them. We thank you very much for the kindness you have shown to us. My dear Lady we hope you will not get into any trouble on our behalf as what you have spoken is quite true.

On 16 July, the *London Evening Standard* reported that the London Trades Council 'had taken up the cause of the match girls' and 'strongly urged the girls to stay out'. By the next day, even as the newspaper was reporting that the Trades Council had met Wilberforce Bryant and several directors, who insisted that 'the firm could entertain no proposition for compromise, and nothing but an unconditional surrender',[7] Bryant and May had capitulated, reinstating the victimised 'ringleaders' and scrapping the system of fines and deductions. As the London Trades Council accepted after an inquiry, wages at the factory were comparatively high and there was no evidence for Besant's claim that Frederick Bryant had compelled every worker to contribute towards the cost of the statue of Gladstone. Nevertheless, the strike was a landmark in the history of the British labour movement, consolidated as part of a 'New Unionism' the following year by striking dock workers, many of whom were matchwomen's husbands, sons, brothers, uncles and friends from Bow and Poplar. By 1894, there were twenty-six unions in London with more than 2,000 members.[8] The events were also a precursor to the 'welfare capitalism' that emerged in the first half of the twentieth century, as large firms began to assume some responsibility for the well-being of their employees, offering insurance, retirement plans and health benefits. Bryant and May did not go that far at first, but they took the first steps by introducing a full-time company doctor and dentist, providing a staff canteen for the women to eat their lunch away from the factory floor and granting time off for women who wanted to go hop-picking in the summer.

The strike over, Bryant and May continued to prosper. To meet demand, the company needed to introduce new machinery, which in turn required a new factory. Built in 1909–11, it was the massive concrete-framed red-brick structure that runs parallel to the railway on the southern side of the works. Drawing on new American ideas of 'scientific management', the factory was organised for the entire production process to flow through the building. Timber was taken into the sawmill on the ground floor and reduced to match splints on the upper floors, before the dipping in fourth-floor match rooms. Boxing and packing finished up in the east wing, adjacent to Wick Lane and the nearby wharf on the River Lea. It was considered a model factory. The directors, anxious to put the notoriety of the strike behind them, entertained visitors to tours. A visit by representatives of London newspapers in 1912 was reported in the *East London Observer*:

> The new factory at Bow is surely one of the finest structures in the world ... Special care has been taken to provide the best ventilation, heated dining rooms, cloakrooms, lavatories, and other arrangements for the comfort of the workpeople ... Principles of hygiene have been considered with as much care as the methods of turning out matches expeditiously. One is struck throughout with the light and air and spotless cleanliness of the place, and the general impression of spaciousness ... Like the rest of the building, the kitchen and scullery are as clean and sweet as could possibly be desired ... A further proof of the firm's regard for the welfare of the workpeople is shown in the arrangements for looking after any ailment from which they may be suffering. A matron and a fully equipped dispensary are at their service, and a doctor is retained. A visitor to the works cannot but be struck by the humane side of this great organisation ... The employees have little to do except to wait upon the great machines and occasionally fill boxes with safety matches.[9]

The following year the firm hosted an inspection by a visiting party of dignitaries that included the mayor and ex-mayor of Poplar, several councillors, guardians and sick asylum managers, the town clerk, the medical officer of health and the borough surveyor. The reporter respectfully noted that

> The directors have been at great pains and expense to make their employees comfortable and the conditions under which they work healthy. The visitors Friday were fully impressed by this aspect of the works, and realised that the matches are NON POISONOUS AND HARMLESS.[10]

The capitalised comment was no coincidence. In 1892, the *Star* newspaper had disclosed in detail a case of phossy jaw in an employee at Bryant and May. The smell from the woman's cancerous bone had been so great that her husband and children had been unable to attend to her. The Home Office, responsible for inspecting factories, eventually investigated. An internal memorandum outlined the facts: altogether there had been forty-seven cases of phossy jaw at Bryant and May between 1878 and 1898; nine had been fatal. The government was reluctant to embarrass a major company publicly, while company managers stalwartly stonewalled the issue. Marmaduke Hare, rector of Bow and chairman of Poplar Board of Guardians, wrote to the *London Evening Standard* in July 1898 in support of the company: 'I may safely assert that there is no class in England more independent, more high spirited, more vigorous in mind and body than the match-girl ... Of course, the use of phosphorus has its dangers ...'[11] But the issue was insistently pursued by progressive campaigners like the duchess of Sutherland, the countess of Portsmouth, Lord Hugh Cecil and Canon Wilberforce. By the early 1900s, Bryant and May had stopped using white phosphorus for the production of its match heads, and in 1908 its use was completely banned by the government. It was another important landmark, this time as a precedent in environmental health and safety.[12]

For the next fifty years or so, the Fairfield Works attracted little attention. Demand for safety matches gradually fell off and the company moved some of its production to Liverpool, amid a series of corporate mergers and acquisitions. The Fairfield Works closed in 1979 with the loss of 250 jobs and stood derelict for a decade, until it was acquired by the developer Kentish Homes. Inspired by the popularity of loft conversions in Brooklyn and Manhattan, and emboldened by an ongoing property boom and the emergence in London of a 'yuppie' consumer culture, the developer commissioned Orms Architects to convert the works to a gated residential enclave. It was among London's first large-scale regeneration projects. Orms envisaged the converted works looming over Bow's mixture of aging council housing and drab Victorian terraces like a great 'citadel'. Early brochures were crafted to appeal to the aspirational lifestyle of young first- or second-time East End buyers and 'Dockland Yuppies' (rather than wealthy City types). As Patrick Wright observed, 'The pictures left no doubt that as well as being young and prosperous, the ideal residents of the Bow Quarter would also be athletic sensualists.'[13]

Having developed a bold overall plan, based on the American trend for 'loft living' in converted warehouses and garment factories,[14] Orms resigned from the project, citing budget restrictions. In 1993, Kentish Homes went into receivership, having been caught financially overextended as the property boom fell into a slump – the same slump that stopped the Canary Wharf project (Chapter 23) dead in its tracks. But it is the nature of property cycles to swing back from slumps, and the Fairfield Works conversion (like the Canary Wharf project) was far enough along to recover its momentum. Under new investors, the works cottages and gatehouse were converted to residences and the factory floors repurposed as apartments. Brand-new apartment buildings and a row of town houses were added on the northern part of the site. Facilities included a limited amount of underground parking, a leisure centre, a café/bar and a minimarket. Protected by security gates, the works was rebranded as the Bow Quarter – with advertisements shamelessly over-reaching, with comparisons to Greenwich Village in New York and the Latin Quarter in Paris. Labouring the point (and seemingly not bothered, as Wright put it, that 'there were still those who tormented themselves with the image of oblivious yuppies enjoying a massage and slurping champagne where slave-driven women once ached with phossy jaw'),[15] individual buildings were given American-sounding names to evoke the idea of loft living. The original office building became the Arlington building; the 1911 factory buildings became Lexington and Manhattan; the new apartment buildings were Park East, Park Central and Park West; and the minimarket was Fifth Avenue. For a long time, the Bow Quarter stood as an inward-looking enclave, with low levels of interaction with the surrounding neighbourhood: less of a citadel, more of a blockhouse (an image that was underscored when the water tower was used by the Ministry of Defence throughout the 2012 Olympics to locate surface-to-air missile defences). But the regeneration of Stratford after the 2012 Olympic Games and the development of London Stadium and the surrounding park – just across the River Lea – has appreciably repositioned the Bow Quarter and its neighbourhood within London's gentrifying landscape. Gradually, the surrounding streets have been upgraded, with new-build apartment blocks and town homes replacing Victorian terraces and brownfield sites.

5 Lambeth Workhouse, Lambeth

THE surviving buildings of Lambeth Workhouse – the administrative complex, water tower, lodges and former receiving wards to either side of the entrance to the site – are tucked away amid a jumble of late twentieth- and early twenty-first-century development just off the A3, hemmed in by new private apartment buildings and surrounded by the chaotic mixture of low-, medium- and high-rise housing that has overwritten most of this pocket of Victorian Lambeth. The exceptions are the adjacent Lambeth magistrates' court building (contemporary with the workhouse and now a Buddhist Centre), a late Victorian fire station (now a private residence) a few yards further along Renfrew Road, and an annex of the workhouse infirmary (now a community centre). The workhouse complex is dominated by an administrative block (now a cinema museum) and its impressive water tower (now a private residence). Both the administrative building and the water tower are listed Grade II structures and hint at the imposing presence that the entire complex must have represented in its day. The three-storey administrative block is in ornate Venetian Gothic style in yellow stock brick, with polychrome red-brick-and-stone dressings and detailing in blue brick and terracotta. It is flanked by two-storey wings that housed the master's residence and offices, respectively; each wing had its own extension – one was used as a messroom for

20 Administrative block detail, Lambeth Workhouse.

male staff and the other for female staff. The water tower, 30 metres (100ft) high, is also in Venetian Gothic style, in the same yellow stock brick, with buttresses at each of the four corners and bands of red brick at decreasing intervals of height.

London's Victorian workhouses were the product of a radical reform of poor laws that had been in operation since 1601. Under the Elizabethan poor law system, local parishes had been responsible for providing accommodation in workhouses for the indigent whose advanced years or 'impotence' (physical disability or blindness) meant that they could not support themselves through work; and for granting 'outdoor' relief to other 'impotents' in their community in the form of cash supplements, as well as in-kind grants of food, fuel and clothing. A revision to the system in 1795 introduced means-tested indoor relief to the able-bodied poor. The new and more costly system – known as the Speenhamland System – was still organised at the parish level and funded through local rates; but industrialisation and urbanisation soon made the parish-based system unworkable. The problem was particularly acute in London and other big cities, as destitute labourers from rural counties arrived in search of work, placing a heavy financial burden on local parishes. Attitudes to poverty had also changed amid the upheavals of industrialisation and urbanisation. The laissez-faire doctrine of Adam Smith and the utilitarianism of Jeremy Bentham combined to sustain a widespread belief that idleness was the root cause of poverty. The poor laws, they believed, interfered with the 'natural' laws of supply and demand, bred dependency and promoted pauperism.

A Royal Commission, charged in 1832 with reviewing the situation, recommended that able-bodied people and their families should no longer receive relief. The resulting Poor Law Amendment Act of 1834 established a central Poor Law Commission, with local 'poor law unions' formed by combining parishes and administered by elected officials called 'guardians'. 'Outdoor' relief was to be kept to a minimum. Instead, the poor were to be housed in workhouses, where they would be clothed and fed. Children who entered the workhouse would receive some schooling. In return, all would have to live and work under conditions that would deter any but the truly desperate from applying for relief. In workhouses, the poor were to be classified and separated, subjected to menial task work, required to observe silence at meals and to endure strict discipline and overbearing monotony. In this way, it was expected that people would seek relief only as a last resort, thereby reducing the overall cost of welfare and frightening the idle poor into independence.

In London, many parishes had already tightened relief policies and expanded indoor capacity because of the pressure on the old system. Lambeth, for example, had introduced the laborious and demeaning task of stone-breaking as a deterrent to workhouse residence.[1] At that time the workhouse was located at the west end of what is now Black Prince Road, a few streets north of Vauxhall Pleasure Gardens. It was built in 1726 in 'Brick-House' style for 270 inmates.[2] By 1840, nearly a thousand people were crammed into the building. Residents were obliged to hand-grind corn on heavy millstones to produce low-grade flour for workhouse bread. Margaret Crowther cites a note delivered to the poor law commissioners at Somerset House:

> Gentlemen, Do for God's sake take into consideration the sufferings of the poor of Lambeth Work-house ill used and half starved – the Master a perfect brute swearing at sick and aged driving them to Work when scarce able to stand. Some of you I know to be men of feeling – my information I know is correct. Yours Respectfully, A Parishioner.
>
> P.S. The food scarce fit for Hogs.[3]

Paupers who transgressed were classified as 'disorderly' on the first offence and 'refractory' if the offence was repeated within a week. Punishments could be severe, and the workhouse master was empowered to impose solitary confinement or a reduction in diet.[4] Lambeth Workhouse had a special refractory ward, even more sparsely furnished than the rest of the workhouse, with barred windows, and doors that could be securely locked if necessary.

In 1866, Lambeth's workhouse master, George Day, was forced to resign after paupers' complaints about illegal punishments were upheld by the poor law commissioners. This came amid increasing concern among the medical profession at the everyday environment in workhouses. Florence Nightingale, at the height of her influence, wrote witheringly about the incompetence of workhouse masters and mistresses, but was most concerned with the way that the 1834 act had thrown together the sick and infirm with other categories of the poor. In 1865, the medical journal *The Lancet* instigated its own Sanitary Commission to investigate conditions in London workhouses, following months of negative press coverage of the deaths of two paupers, Timothy Daly and Richard Gibson, whose bodies bore unmistakable signs of severe neglect.[5] Sanitary commissioners routinely reported cramped wards, with inmates occupying thin mattresses on iron slats, with no soap, shared combs and towels; 'lunatic' wards with no medical oversight; and fever cases dispersed through wards, infecting other inmates. In Lambeth, the only paid nursing staff were the male superintendent of the infirmary, a female superintendent sick-nurse, who also acted as midwife, and male and female superintendents of the lunatics.

The Lancet's clinical descriptions were important in mobilising professional opinion and influencing the Poor Law Board; but it was a series of sensational articles in the *Pall Mall Gazette* that was most influential among the broader public. Frederick Greenwood, the magazine's editor, sent his brother James to

Lambeth Workhouse disguised as one of the 'casual' poor, down and out on his luck and seeking shelter for a few nights. His reporting caught the imagination of readers, who could see how they themselves might feel during their first night in a casual ward: forced to take a communal bath in water that 'looked like mutton broth', lying on a straw pallet stained with a stranger's blood, listening to coughing fits; next morning tasting gruel; then endlessly turning a crank to grind corn. Not least among the details that gripped readers were Greenwood's euphemised descriptions of sexual depravity among homeless men and boys sleeping together naked. Published under the pseudonym of the 'Amateur Casual', the articles were not only a first instance of undercover reporting, but also one of the greatest media sensations of the century, the first news story to go viral. The initial instalment was picked up by *The Times* and carried by more than 200 newspapers across Britain and Ireland.[6]

A cholera epidemic in 1866–67 intensified middle-class concern over workhouse conditions and helped pave the way for the Metropolitan Poor Law Amendment Act, the first explicit acknowledgement that it was the state's duty to provide hospital care for the poor. The act combined unions and parishes into districts that were required to separate infirmaries from workhouses, administratively if not always physically; they were aided in this by the establishment of a Metropolitan Poor Fund for institutional medical relief. It prompted a spate of new workhouse and infirmary buildings across London. In Lambeth, the foundation stone for a new building in Renfrew Road was laid in 1871 by the chairman of the Board of Guardians, John Doulton, one of the largest employers in Lambeth and manufacturer of art pottery, bone china, architectural terracotta and high-quality drainage pipes. The building had been designed by R. Parris and T.W. Aldwinckle following a limited architectural competition. The ornate Venetian Gothic style and polychrome brickwork of the administrative block was a significant flourish. Kathryn

Morrison, author of the definitive study of workhouse architecture, describes it as 'an eclectic, almost palatial, style', in contrast to the 'utterly plain' appearance of most of the New Poor Law buildings erected in London after 1867.[7] The most significant aspect of Parris and Aldwinckle's design, though, was that the layout followed the 'pavilion' principle, based on the most innovative hospital designs of the time. Pavilion layouts had independent wings, either completely isolated or linked to each other through open galleries, with open corridors, large windows to facilitate the flow of air and light, and toilets positioned near to exits to allow the expulsion of foul air. Originating in France, the design was strongly advocated by Florence Nightingale. The most influential example was the new St Thomas's Hospital in Lambeth, across from the Houses of Parliament, which opened just as the foundation stone for the new Lambeth Workhouse was being laid.

Lambeth Workhouse was the first in London to adopt the pavilion plan, and one of the earliest nationally to do so. The layout allowed for the surveillance, segregation and specialisation that was held to be central to the moral order of the workhouse. As a newspaper report of the building's opening in 1874 noted:

> A system of rigid classification has been carried out in this design, and this separation of the several classes has been carried down to all minor offices. Each class has its own and distinct dayrooms, dormitories, staircases, lavatories, waterclosets, airing-grounds, and workrooms; the only common-place of meeting being the chapel and dining-room, where conversational intercourse is forbidden. The several classes in each sex are for aged, able-bodied of good character, and two subdivisions of able-bodied of bad character, together with accommodation for a limited number of boys and girls.[8]

21 Administrative block and master's offices, Lambeth Workhouse.

Families were separated, with male inmates accommodated to the north and females to the south, able-bodied in the inner pavilions and the aged in the outer ones. There was also a small amount of short-term accommodation for children, who could expect to be shipped off to Lambeth's industrial school after a few days. (The Industrial Schools Act of 1857 gave magistrates the power to remove poor, neglected or disorderly children to a residential school with a standard curriculum of basic trade work, housework and religious instruction.) In line with the Metropolitan Poor Law Amendment Act, a new infirmary was added in 1877 next to the Renfrew Road workhouse, along with a new 'casual' ward. In 1887–88 a 'test' workhouse (admittance only on acceptance of willingness to endure the test of deliberately harsh conditions) was opened on the old Black Prince Road site, leaving only the aged and infirm on Renfrew Road.

22 Converted water tower, Lambeth Workhouse.

Meanwhile, workhouse conditions were still inhospitable. Days began with a rising bell at 5 a.m. from March to September (7 a.m. for the rest of the year), followed by prayers before breakfast. The standardised, unappetising diet took no account of individual differences in weight and appetite, leaving some residents permanently hungry. Day work would typically involve stone-breaking or crushing bones for fertiliser. Among the unfortunate individuals to have experienced conditions in the Lambeth Workhouse were two of Jack the Ripper's victims. Mary Ann ('Polly') Nichols had been in and out of Lambeth Workhouse since 1882, before her death in 1888. When found, she was wearing two petticoats from Lambeth Workhouse. The Ripper's second victim, Annie Chapman, was also found wearing clothing bearing the mark of Lambeth Workhouse. Like most of the Ripper's victims, Annie was not a regular prostitute; rather, she was a street vendor – a flower seller, in fact – who occasionally resorted to prostitution simply to avoid starvation. This was the predicament she faced on the day she was murdered. According to a friend of Annie's interviewed by the *Daily Telegraph*:

> She said she felt no better, and she should go into the casual ward [of the workhouse] for a day or two. I ... asked if she had had anything to eat. She replied 'No, I have not had a cup of tea today.' I gave her twopence to get some, and told her not to get any rum, of which she was fond.[9]

Also in and out of Lambeth Workhouse, albeit fleetingly, were the young Charlie Chaplin, his mother Hannah and half-brother Sydney. Their story is representative of a type of inmate very different from Polly Nichols and Annie Chapman – underscoring the Victorian obsession with classification and segregation. The Chaplins had lived very comfortably in West Square, just a couple of blocks north of the workhouse. Charlie's mother and father were both successful vaudeville entertainers. But his parents separated, his father's maintenance payments ceased as alcoholism accompanied his slide from popularity as an entertainer, and his mother's voice began to falter. She also suffered a series of mental breakdowns. Left in poverty, the family had no option but the workhouse. Charlie and his brother were soon taken off to Lambeth's industrial school, while his mother was kept in various institutions until they could earn enough to look after her.[10]

By the turn of the century, the deterrent effect of the workhouse had significantly reduced the number of able-bodied adults seeking accommodation. At the same time, societal attitudes toward poverty and welfare had begun to change. Charles Booth's survey of the poor in London and Seebohm Rowntree's survey of York both concluded that poverty was the result of behavioural patterns induced by low wages.[11] Workhouse conditions steadily improved:

> The workhouse in 1900 was criticised less for its cruelty than for its dreariness, its regimented squalor, its failure to deal appropriately with different types of inmate. Meat dinners, blankets, heating, pianos, books, pictures and even doctors, nurses, spectacles and false teeth, all proliferated in workhouses during this period.[12]

Increasingly, as the causes of poverty were better understood, local communities organised around friendly societies, co-operatives, blanket societies and coal societies, and the enlightened self-interest of wealthy industrialists provided influential examples of model housing and model communities. Once precedents for social insurance had been established through the Workmen's Compensation Act and the Unemployed Workmen Act, the poor laws were seen as problematic and anomalous. At the same time, working-class political demands for change were also making themselves felt through burgeoning working-class organisations, including trade unions and socialist groups such as the Fabian Society. There was sufficient concern and controversy over the poor laws and their implementation to prompt a Royal Commission. Its findings, presented in 1909–10, ran to twenty-seven volumes, broadly acknowledging that the current structures were no longer fit for purpose. But the existing system was stoutly defended by its large and influential body of administrators and guardians, and reform was finally stymied by the difficulties of calibrating local taxation across wealthy and poorer localities.

In 1922, Lambeth Workhouse and infirmary were amalgamated and renamed Lambeth Hospital. Responsibility for the poor laws was transferred to local authorities in 1929, and the administration of Lambeth Workhouse (now a 'Public Assistance Institution') was taken over by the LCC until the final abolition of the Poor Law in 1948. One by one, the wards and outbuildings of the workhouse and infirmary fell into disuse and disrepair, to be replaced by a mixture of maisonettes, town homes, NHS clinics and small businesses. Apart from the administrative complex, lodges, receiving wards and water tower, the only surviving element is the former casual ward at the southwestern end of the infirmary on Wincott Street: now a community centre. The master's house was converted in 1998 to house the Cinema Museum, a non-profit organisation that grew out of the Ronald Grant Archive of material relating to the history and development of cinema. The abandoned and badly deteriorated Grade II listed water tower was featured as a look-what-money-can-do project in 2015 for the Channel 4 television show *Grand Designs*. At the top, the cast-iron water tank was converted into a reception room, linked by way of a brick elevator tower to a two-storey glass-fronted living-room cube at the foot of the tower: an example of the excess and spectacle that had become a hallmark of the *Zeitgeist* of neoliberal London.

SIMPLY
ALARMING
SECURITY
59

6 Shaftesbury Park Estate, Battersea

WHILE London's workhouses were the refuge of the abject poor – Mayhew's 'those that cannot work, and those that will not work' – working-class households were left, by and large, to make the best of it in slum conditions. Trapped in aging tenements, the ever-growing population of both the 'respectable' and the 'rough' working classes seemed to be condemned to cramped and insanitary accommodation. The housing question was the most acute and most intractable economic and social problem of the period. Wages in unskilled and low-skilled occupations were simply insufficient to pay for decent housing, while developers could not make a satisfactory profit from sound, sanitary housing at rents affordable by the great bulk of the working classes. A succession of government reports, combined with a steady flow of sensational newspaper and magazine articles and pamphlets, provided plenty of evidence of the social costs associated with squalor (intemperance, immorality and criminality; appalling levels of infant mortality; endemic tuberculosis and dysentery). Meanwhile, the looming threat of the slums was underscored by occasional outbreaks of mob violence, a succession of epidemics of cholera and

23 Shaftesbury Park, terraced housing.

smallpox, and regular outbreaks of typhus, measles, chickenpox, influenza, whooping cough, mumps, diphtheria and scarlet fever.

The impasse was undone by two important innovations. First, the financialisation of philanthropy and the emergence of social enterprise institutions, as paternalistic industrialists and model dwellings companies sought to demonstrate that there was no necessary contradiction between private profit and decent, affordable working-class housing.[1] Second, the introduction of suburban rail services (and later of subsidised fares) that made cheaper land on London's rural fringes available for the development of 'Cockneyfied' suburbs.[2]

Shaftesbury Park Estate was the product of both innovations: a 'workmen's city' developed by a model dwellings company on market-garden land a short walk from Clapham Junction railway station. It was 'the most assiduously publicised and widely discussed housing experiment of its day',[3] largely because it allowed working-class families to live affordably in terraces of soundly built 'cottages' rather than in austere model tenements or jerry-built slums. Graham Balfour, who contributed a chapter on Battersea to Charles Booth's *Life and Labour of the People in London* (1889), considered Shaftesbury Park Estate to have become 'the most perfect specimen of a working-class residential district'. It was reported on throughout the English-speaking world and around Europe, attracting attention from social reformers, builders and national and local governments. It has survived more or less intact, a grid of long, parallel streets with shorter cross streets, all with building frontages with a consistent use of materials and Gothic detailing, so that the streetscapes have a distinctive identity.

Shaftesbury Park Estate was developed by the Artizans', Labourers' and General Dwellings Company (ALGDC), a limited liability company that offered middle-class investors a mechanism through which to invest, rather than donate. Investing in such companies became known as '5 per cent philanthropy',

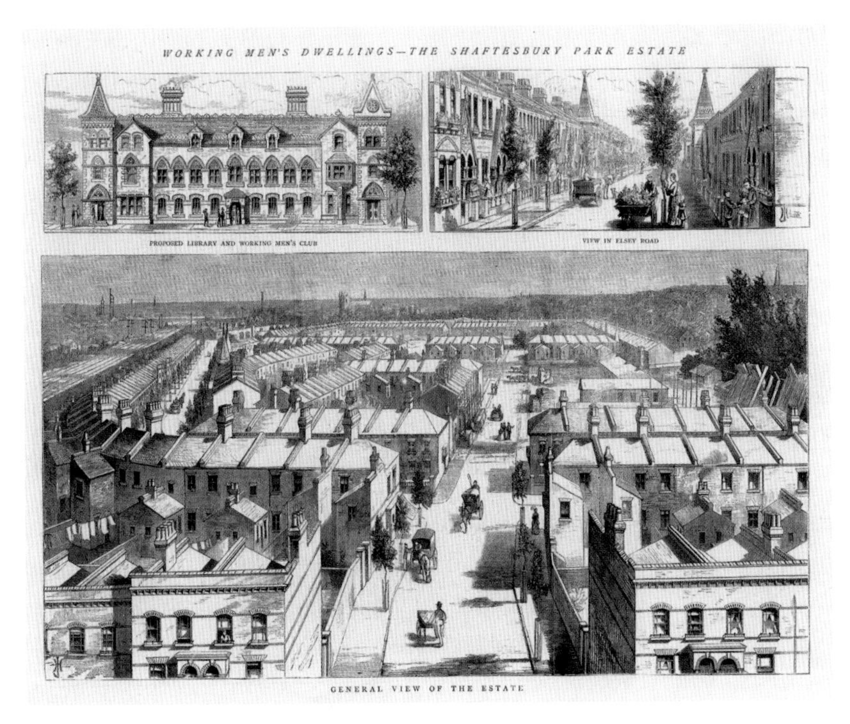

24 Shaftesbury Park Estate, c. 1874.

since this was the most common financial return promised to investors. Limited liability model dwellings companies could, as the *Morning Post* put it in 1848, 'show to those who possess capital, that they may invest it with great advantage and profit to themselves in consulting the convenience and comforts of their poorer brethren'.[4] London's first model dwelling company was the Metropolitan Association for Improving the Dwellings of the Industrious Classes (MAIDIC), formed in 1841. George Peabody, an American banker and diplomat, established his own philanthropic trust for model housing in 1862, and the following year Sydney Waterlow formed the Improved Industrial Dwellings Company, promising investors a 5 per cent return annually. Like the MAIDIC, both focused on building five- and seven-storey tenements in London's inner neighbourhoods. The ALGDC was formed in 1867, and by the mid-1880s twenty-eight model housing societies of one sort or another were paying between 4 and 5 per cent dividends, showing that decent dwellings for low-income households – if not the very poor – could be tolerably remunerative. It has been estimated that in London almost 30,000 families were housed by these model housing societies.[5] Their success was due in part to the 1875 Artisans' and Labourers' Dwellings Improvement Act, which empowered the Metropolitan Board of Works to purchase and clear unhealthy slum areas and then sell the sites to developers for working-class housing. The conventional view among historians has long been that the efforts of model dwellings companies were simply swamped by the pace of urbanisation, and then overtaken by an emergent welfare state. In strict numerical terms, model housing projects were indeed relatively insignificant. But in terms of their role in establishing principles and precedents for the development of 'respectable' working-class communities in decent, affordable housing they were hugely influential.

Shaftesbury Park Estate, in particular, was important as the first large-scale, low-density development. It was not only a precursor of the wholesale suburbanisation of the working classes, but with its planned central square, primary school and corner shops was also a forerunner of model suburbs like Hampstead Garden Suburb. It has been credited with being an important influence on the thinking behind the LCC's Edwardian 'out county' council estates, and an antecedent of interwar speculative garden villages. Unlike most model dwellings companies, with their paternalistic upper-middle-class sponsors, Shaftesbury Park Estate was rooted in working-class sensibilities. It was conceived by William Austin, a jobbing contractor and former labourer, who organised the support of a small group of clerks and workingmen to found the ALGDC. Austin's innovative concept was to build low-rise housing on cheap land on the suburban fringes, preferably near existing railway lines to allow workers to commute into inner-city workplaces. As the prospectus put it:

> this company was established for the erection of improved dwellings near to the great centres of industry, but free from the annoyances arising from the proximity of manufactures ... The Shaftesbury-park Estate is readily accessible from Kensington, Victoria, Waterloo, Ludgate-hill, and London-bridge, at low fares.[6]

Austin found a site that ran alongside the London, Chatham and Dover Railway line, on farmland owned by Earl Spencer (of Spencer House, Chapter 1) that had been leased for market gardening. Spencer sold the land in 1868 to a developer, James Lord, who in turn sold it to the ALGDC in 1872.[7]

What Austin and his fellow directors wanted to achieve, above all, was 'well-arranged, honestly-built houses' that would provide a healthy environment for residents. They had limited interest in architecture and design – 'All we have attempted to do is to endeavour to relieve, by ornament, what might otherwise be rather dull and monotonous'[8] – but were strongly committed to providing the functional infrastructure necessary for a thriving community. This included plans for a meeting hall, school, co-operative store, library, gymnasium, coal depot, baths and washhouses and a small station on the adjacent London, Chatham and Dover Railway line; but neither churches nor pubs were to be allowed. Three acres (1.2 hectares) were set aside for recreation and pleasure grounds, including a swimming pool. At the centre of the development was Brassey Square, a small park with a central bandstand, a symbolic heart of the community, as well as an amenity. Robert Austin, formerly a carpenter with the company (and no relation to William), designed an estate of 1,200 two-storey cottages, laid out along tree-lined streets, with gates at the estate entrances in Grayshott, Tyneham and Sabine roads. The plan was to build the cottages on the industrial partnership system (otherwise referred to as the 'co-operative principle' or 'associated labour'), by which the workmen would receive a share of the profits. The boldness and innovative nature of the plan captured the imagination of the 7th earl of Shaftesbury, who agreed to act as president of the company and to have the new estate named in his honour. He formally opened the first phase of the estate – about 350 houses – in November 1873, referring to Shaftesbury Park Estate as a 'Workmen's City', 'founded, raised, regulated, and paid for by the working people of England'.[9] The claim was a bit of a stretch, but the political potential of the notion did not go unnoticed. The following year, the new prime minister, Benjamin Disraeli, stepped in to formally open the southwest entrance of the estate. The *Evening Standard*'s report quoted Disraeli as saying:

> I have never in my life been more astonished than by what I have unexpectedly witnessed to day – to see this city, as it were, rising in the desert (applause) ... I have always felt that the best security for civilisation is the dwelling (hear, hear) ... It is the real nursery of all domestic virtues, and without a becoming home the exercise of these virtues is impossible (applause).[10]

The houses on the estate – 'sturdy little dwellings' with 'diminutive front gardens' – came in four sizes. The first or 'clerk' class had a bay-windowed front parlour, a back parlour, kitchen, larder and scullery, with three bedrooms and space for a bathroom on the first floor. Class 2 houses were similar, but most lacked the bay window and none had upstairs bathroom space; Class 3 houses had no back parlour; and Class 4 houses had only two bedrooms.[11] They were all built in London stock brick with Gothic detailing: blind pointed arches picked out in contrasting red and black brick, decorative lintels in Coade stone, terracotta plaques with the date and company monogram, paired front doors with projecting canopies, and window sills with cast-iron window-box retainers. The terraces were tied together with a low brick wall and entrance piers capped in Coade stone, the corner houses embellished with towers and turrets to add a distinctive touch.

Where possible, the houses were sold on ninety-nine-year leases: not so much to seed the creation of a new class of owner-occupiers as to raise money for the next stage of company investment. Prices ranged from £170 to £310 – equivalent to £25,000 to £45,750 in 2023, when houses on Ashbury Road, Eversleigh Road and Tyneham Road were selling for between £850,000 and £1.2 million (a dramatic illustration of London's overheated housing market, even allowing for the installation of indoor toilets and central heating, and serious interior makeovers with fancy kitchens). Most houses on the estate ended up being rented, however. Both owners and tenants were expected to behave in keeping with the estate's aspirations for working-class respectability.

25 'Sturdy little dwellings', Shaftesbury Park.

Having lodgers was forbidden, while alcohol, officially, could not even be consumed in private. The pubs and fish-and-chip shops on Lavender Hill were the beneficiaries. By the mid-1870s, Shaftesbury Park Estate was already a social fortress of the respectable working class. The estate had 'a Co-operative Store, a Labour Loan Society, its own *Social Review*, a rifle corps, numerous sporting teams, a music and drama society, a Workingmen's Club, branches of friendly societies, and an Annual Flower Show'.[12] The ALGDC

> seemed to have cut the knot that tied housing reform to 'philanthropy plus five per cent'. Through 'industrial partnership' and a unique financial model it could build better houses for less than the speculative builder, pay its workmen more than standard wages, sell or let its houses below the market level, and yet produce a return on capital not of five, but six per cent.[13]

But in 1877, the appositely named William Swindlehurst, a director who had become the company's manager and secretary, was arrested for fraud, along with two others. All three were tried at the Old Bailey, found guilty and imprisoned. It led to a change of approach, as the company sought to overcome the consequent financial constraints. The principle of industrial partnership was abandoned and – rather than relying on working-class subscribers – wealthy investors were pursued. A new board reduced the dividend to 2 per cent and raised rents twice in a single year. The plans for building the train station were shelved, as were all notions of a permanent meeting hall and gates at the estate entrances. Brassey Square was built over, together with the site that had been reserved for the train station.

Nevertheless, the changing geography of the metropolis was in the estate's favour. As London's transport network improved, it allowed the metropolis to spread out. Realising that commuting was beyond the pocket of the working classes, parliament had introduced the Railway Regulation Act of 1844, which required all passenger railway companies to provide at least one cheap service each way every day over the whole length of their lines, at a speed of not less than 12 miles (19km) per hour, including stops at all stations, at the maximum fare of a penny a mile. In return, the railways were exempted from paying tax on revenue from these passengers. But the continued growth of the metropolis, coupled with the loss of housing resulting from uncoordinated road and railway-building, intensified the problem of housing London's working classes, and in 1883 another Cheap Trains Act was passed, 'further encouraging the migration of the working classes into the suburbs'.[14] The use of workmen's tickets rose from just over 7 million in 1888, to just over 67 million in 1902.[15] Parliament's support for low fares for working-class commuters was driven by a desire to reduce population density in inner-city slums, with an eye, meanwhile, to freeing them up for commercial redevelopment. Win–win. It has also been suggested that it was tacitly understood as a way of giving a geographical focus to working-class suburban districts and so 'save' other localities for the middle classes.[16] The emergence of extensive tracts of affordable suburban housing significantly altered the social geography of the metropolis and introduced social segregation to the suburbs – hitherto the more-or-less exclusive domain of more affluent households. It drew the condescension of intellectuals such as William Morris, who observed that 'I was born at Walthamstow in Essex in March 1834, a suburban village on the edge of Epping Forest, and once a pleasant place enough, but now terribly cocknified and choked up by the jerry builder.'[17]

By the 1880s, Battersea was within a twopenny-return workman's fare to central London, and well connected with Vauxhall and Lambeth by a tramway that ran along Lavender Hill. Shaftesbury Park Estate was seen as a bastion of respectability. Charles Booth's *Life and Labour of the People in London* documented the composition of the estate: 47.5 per cent of the households were classified as Booth's Class E, the 'real backbone' of the London working class, while another 45 per cent belonged to Class F, 'Higher class labour and the best paid of the artisans'. Graham Balfour's chapter noted that 'Here it is that the intelligent portion of the Socialism of the district is chiefly to be found, and the colony represents perhaps the high-water mark of the life of the intelligent London artisan.' The 1891 census listed a population of labourers, factory workers, warehousemen, porters, domestic servants, tailors and dressmakers, shop assistants, carpenters, policemen, printers, railwaymen, clerks and schoolteachers. The estate was symbolic of the growing respectability of the upper levels of the Victorian working classes and 'betokened the rise of a private domestic culture and the individual pursuit of self-improvement and self-esteem'. Shaftesbury Park Estate 'provided a respectable launching place for those able to achieve some upward social mobility', while 'the polished front door knob and whitestoned front step proclaimed moral and physical order within'.[18]

House historian Melanie Backe-Hansen has provided an insight into the biography of one particular Class 3 house on the estate: 29 Morrison Street.[19] Its first occupant, in 1876, was a Mr J.R. Cook, who rented the house for a few months from the ALGDC. It was then sold for £210 to Alfred Idle, an assistant librarian, who moved in with his wife Elizabeth and nine children. They stayed for eleven years before moving out and renting the house to Bruce Kedge, a 'porter–messenger', his wife Mary and their seven children. The Kedge family continued as the occupants until the 1930s: in 1915, after both Bruce and Mary had passed away, their second-eldest daughter, Mabel, moved back in with her husband Edward Gaitt, a bus driver, and their eight children. They stayed at number 29 until March 1937. The new occupants were George Gannon, a general labourer working for Southern Rail, and his wife Hilda. By 1945, they had been replaced by another couple, George and Daisy Farrall. When the house was sold again in 1958, 'Drainage plans reveal that it was at this time, over 80 years after the house was first built, that a bathroom was fitted inside the house.'[20]

Morrison Street received a direct hit by a V1 rocket on the morning of 17 July 1944, which completely destroyed seven of the houses just along from number 29, together with several houses on the eastern side of Brassey Square. Otherwise, the estate has remained largely intact. It was designated a conservation area in 1976, coinciding with the enthusiasm among gentrifying households for Victorian buildings. Many of the freehold properties were purchased by young professionals, replacing working-class households that had dominated the estate for the previous century. Much of the rest of the estate, however, is social housing, the Peabody Trust having acquired the stock from the ALGDC's successors in a series of transactions between the 1960s and the 1980s. Although most of Peabody's stock is leased at social rent levels, some houses are rented at market rates, and some have been sold, adding to the gentrification of the area. But when Peabody sells houses, it imposes restrictive covenants that control alterations to the houses. On the one hand, this has ensured the continuity of the distinctive physical character of the estate; on the other, it has kept property values high, protecting the value of the trust's investment (but also contributing to house-price inflation and London's continuing affordability problem).

ROCHELLE
STREET
SCHOOL
1899

7 Rochelle Street School, Bethnal Green

A PROMINENT panel on the old caretaker's house on the southwest corner of Arnold Circus in Bethnal Green proclaims 'Rochelle Street School 1899'. Beneath is a tall boundary wall with a narrow entrance framed in stucco with 'Boys' embossed across the top. Behind, facing Rochelle Street itself, is a massive school building in yellow stock brick with red-brick pilasters and dressings, a ribbed chimney stack and rows of oversize arched windows: a classic Victorian board school in pared-down Queen Anne style. Around the corner, protected by a low brick wall topped by iron railings, is another school building in similar style, its long façade dominated by ten bays of tall, white-painted multi-pane windows. This was the original part of the school, built in 1879 on what at the time was called Nichol Street, in the heart of what was widely regarded as the most unhealthy, impoverished and dangerous of London's Victorian slums, the Old Nichol.

The school building on Nichol Street was for infants. It was a frontier outpost of a reform movement that sought, on the one hand, to ameliorate social conditions, instil wholesome values and enforce obedience to authority; and, on the other, to meet the need for

26 Rochelle Street Infant School.

basic numeracy and literacy in the industrial workforce. It was a manifestation not only of the beginning of an unprecedented expansion of the public sphere, but also of the moment when the balance tipped from Church to state in the organisation of social well-being. The school soon expanded to include a primary school building to serve its new catchment area: the residents of London's first public housing scheme, most of whom were part of the latest wave of Jewish immigrants to the city. Having played some part in assimilating them into the mainstream of East End life, Rochelle Street School settled into its role as a cornerstone of a close-knit East End community, before closure and adaptive re-use absorbed the school buildings into the ecology of Global London's creative industries.

As London grew in extent after the Fire, the western end of Bethnal Green, around Shoreditch, developed as one of London's first manufacturing districts, specialising in chair-making and silk-weaving. Most of the land in the east of the district remained as market gardens until the late seventeenth century, when investors began to pick up on the inexorable growth of the metropolis. One of them was John Nichol, a lawyer, who invested in several acres of land just beyond a priory that occupied the eastern side of Shoreditch High Street. He leased his land to various builders and gave them permission to dig for bricks, setting in motion the construction of what would become known as 'The Nichol' and, eventually, 'The Old Nichol'. All the early streets on the estate were named after him: Nichol Street (later Old Nichol Street) had been built by 1683; New Nichol Street and Nichol Row were under way by 1708; and Half Nichol Street was added in 1732.[1] The streets were narrow and many of the houses were built with 'billy-sweet', a mortar that included street dirt and that never really dried out. Ground-floor rooms were below street level, the floors laid directly on the earth.[2] The rest of the estate was steadily developed in piecemeal fashion to accommodate workers in the thriving silk-weaving trade that spread eastwards from Spitalfields. To cope with the booming industry, weavers' houses were even built in the gardens of the priory.

But soon after the rest of the Nichol Estate had been laid out, the East End's weaving industry collapsed under pressure from cheaper continental imports. The houses were subdivided, with rooms and yard spaces converted to workshops and 'manufactories', as people sought new lines of work. By 1860, the district had become home to a broad mixture of shoemakers, carpenters, workers in cane and veneer; upholsterers and French-polishers; seamstresses and makers of waistcoats, shirts, headgear, collars, stays and millinery supplies, such as buttons, feathers and artificial flowers; and households scraping a living 'clobbering' (renovating) second-hand clothes or making matchboxes and clothes pegs. The district also had more than its share of shoplifters, pickpockets, dog stealers and prostitutes. One street contained more than sixty people who had been in prison for one offence or another.[3] There was a big turnover, reflecting the precarious circumstances of many households. A school inspector in the 1880s calculated that, of 1,204 families on his books, 530 had moved within the year.[4]

In the late nineteenth century, the overcrowding and social problems of the district were intensified by another wave of immigration. The East End was already home to a mix of refugees from other countries: French Huguenots, German Palatines, Sephardic Jews from Portugal, Spain and the Netherlands, and Ashkenazi Jews from the Low Countries and Central Europe. They were joined in the 1880s by between 40,000 and 50,000 Jews who had fled the pogroms in Russia. Many of the poorest among them found their way to what was now the Old Nichol. It was already, at best, an impoverished district, and before long houses were overcrowded to such an extent that the whole area became a super-slum, acutely vulnerable to disease. The crowding of the impoverished population into cellars, tenements and jerry-built houses meant that communicable diseases were rife. Tuberculosis and dysentery were endemic; infant mortality was high; and there were regular outbreaks of smallpox, typhus, measles, chickenpox, influenza, whooping cough, mumps, diphtheria and scarlet fever. Residents of the Old Nichol were what the Victorian reformer Mary Carpenter had in mind when she wrote of the 'perishing class'.

By the 1880s and 1890s, the whole of Bethnal Green had assumed symbolic importance as the land of the outcast, stigmatised as harbouring, in the eyes of the Victorians, the morally degraded poor who were too lazy to work, wallowing instead in vice, crime, immorality and irreligion. The district had long been notorious as one of London's worst. In 1848, Hector Gavin, a medical officer of health whose responsibilities included the Old Nichol, wrote that it surpassed the rest of the East End 'in filth, disease, mortality, and wretchedness ... it abounds with the most foul courts, and is characterised by the presence of the greatest nuisances, and perennial foulness'. An article in the *Illustrated London News* on 24 October 1863 described the district as

> one painful and monotonous round of vice, filth and poverty, huddled in dark cellars, ruined garrets, bare and blackened rooms, reeking with disease and death, and without the means, even if there were the inclination, for the most ordinary observations of decency and cleanliness.

Charles Booth's painstakingly detailed maps showed the inhabitants of Old Nichol Street, Rose Street, Nichol's Row, Mount Street and part of Turville Street as 'Vicious, Semi-criminal', the lowest of his seven categories. Most of the rest of the Nichol fell into the next-worst category, 'Very Poor, Chronic Want'. Karl Marx simply described it as a 'notorious district' because of the prevalence of child labour. Later, writer and journalist

Arthur Morrison, having visited the Old Nichol, wrote a barely fictionalised novel, *The Child of the Jago*, a vivid account of a child's struggle against poverty that became a bestseller.

It was into this setting that Nichol Street Infant School was placed. The school was an expression of the reform movement that had been developing ever since the 1842 *Report on the Sanitary Conditions of the Labouring Classes of Great Britain* and the salutary revolutionary events on the Continent in 1848. London's slums were effectively *terra incognita* to the better-off, but they were nevertheless understood as a threat to the very material and spiritual foundations upon which the established order depended. Shocking details in the 1842 report encouraged progressive-minded liberals to form themselves into voluntary associations. Throughout the nineteenth century there were bursts of hand-wringing and pamphleteering by liberal reformers and do-gooders. By the 1860s, the liberal response was led by wealthy philanthropists such as George Peabody and Sydney Waterlow, who were willing and able to build worker housing that yielded modest profits. But philanthropic housing was self-interested benevolence,

> helping to maintain the existing order of industrial capitalism by ensuring the physical and social reproduction of labour, inculcating a curious mixture of deference and self-help, promoting respectability, and – by providing centrally-located housing at relatively low rents – allowing the perpetuation of a low-wage economy in which workers lived close to potential workplaces and could be hired or laid off at short notice.[5]

Such philanthropy did not, in any event, reach the poorest of the poor in districts like the Old Nichol, who could not afford the rents.

Meanwhile, amid the complex of social and political processes unfolding across the country, there was an increasing awareness of the plight of the poor, the threat they might pose both to the physical, social and moral well-being of the rest of the city, and to the ideology of progress that had become central to the Victorians' metanarrative of empire and industry. Employers were unhappy that their employees were sickly (and therefore less productive), fearful of labour unrest turning into mob violence, and increasingly in need of a more literate and numerate workforce. The respectable middle classes were worried about the breakdown of moral order and the contaminating effects of crime and drunkenness. Everyone was fearful of being constantly exposed to life-threatening diseases. One way or another, informed opinion had reached a critical point. The slums were a fearsome danger to everyone; philanthropy was insufficient; and free markets, left to themselves, were not going to achieve any kind of solution. It would take public intervention to begin the task of redemption.

The creation of a system of public education was at the forefront of the task. Before 1870, formal education was provided mainly by voluntary religious organisations. Funded by private subscription, they taught reading, writing and arithmetic; girls were also taught needlework and domestic skills. One such organisation was the nonconformist Society for Promoting the Lancasterian System for the Education of the Poor (later renamed the British and Foreign School Society for the Education of the Labouring and Manufacturing Classes of Society of Every Religious Persuasion), the sponsor of 'British Schools'. Another was the Church of England's National Society for Promoting Religious Education, the sponsor of 'National Schools'. Both had their origins in the first decades of the nineteenth century and both used the 'monitorial' system of instruction, whereby older or better scholars taught the younger or weaker pupils in a single school room, often in purpose-built facilities. Their pupils were mainly from respectable working-class families, leaving the 'perishing class' of children of the 'undeserving' poor to their own devices. For working-class parents who could afford it, the gap was filled by tiny 'dame' schools. For a small fee, teachers who were barely literate themselves – and often simultaneously engaged in domestic chores – taught reading and sewing in tiny rooms without ventilation, furniture, equipment or books. Completely beyond the realm or control of the authorities, they were nevertheless an important component of working-class culture.[6]

For some, 'ragged schools' supported by local philanthropists and churches provided an alternative, offering basic literacy and a little vocational training for the children of the very poorest families, along with, perhaps, a soup kitchen and some adult classes. The first ragged schools in London were founded by the London City Mission Society, an evangelical organisation dedicated to bringing the benefits of the gospel to the urban poor. The Scriptures provided the main text, supplemented by other books of an inspirational nature, including Samuel Smiles' best-seller, *Self-Help*. The Mission Society's annual report for 1840 listed five ragged schools in London, including one in Shoreditch and another in Bethnal Green. They were grim, bleak places, widely believed to be centres for the spread of infectious diseases.[7] Charles Dickens' visit to the society's Field Lane school near Farringdon in the mid-1840s inspired him to write *A Christmas Carol*. By 1870, the London Ragged School Union consisted of 250 schools.[8] Three of them served the Old Nichol: Virginia Row Ragged School, opened in 1856 with one paid teacher; Bethnal Green Gospel Mission Ragged School, on Old Castle Street, opened in 1867; and Nichol Street Ragged School, dating from 1849, the largest, had twelve volunteers and one paid teacher.[9]

Even so, tens of thousands of children were still without any formal education at all. The solution eventually came in the form of the Elementary Education Act of 1870, a product of the consensus regarding the need to ensure that all working-class children attended a school for some part of their lives, if only to moralise the working class:

> The 1870 Education Act reflected the balance of power between two coalitions then campaigning for educational reform: the National Education League, supported by the newly enfranchised working classes under the 1867 Reform Act, by dissenters, the TUC [Trades Union Congress], and forty Liberal MPs; and the National Education Union comprising the Anglican Church and the Tory party.[10]

The act's provision for locally elected public school boards, empowered to levy a rate to establish schools in underserved neighbourhoods like the Old Nichol, was pathbreaking. The legislation required that sufficient schools be provided to educate all local children between the ages of five and twelve (extended to thirteen in 1871) and allowed school boards to make their own by-laws relating to school attendance and to appoint attendance officers to pursue those evading the regulations. With the act, the grip of the Church and religious organisations on people's lives and in public affairs was significantly loosened. At the same time, it marked a turning point in what would, in future, be expected of the state in terms of responsibility for the welfare of its citizens.

The London School Board appointed E.R. Robson as its architect in July 1871 and formally prioritised the establishment of schools in the least favoured parts of the city. The Old Nichol was an obvious target, and the board promptly commandeered Nichol Street Ragged School until it could complete its own purpose-built schools in the area. First to be built, in 1875, was New Castle Street Board School (now Virginia Primary School, near the present junction of Virginia Road and Hocker Street). Four years later, the infant school was opened by the board just 75 metres away, on Nichol Street, replacing the old ragged school

27 Rochelle Street Primary School from Arnold Circus.

28 Rochelle Street Infant School, boys' entrance.

on a site that is now sandwiched between Club Row and Rochelle Street. Originally called Nichol Street Infant School, it would later become part of an enlarged Rochelle Street School (see below). The school had room for 363 pupils in a building that was unprecedentedly well built and well appointed, featuring cross-ventilated classrooms with large windows, cloakrooms, lavatories and staff-rooms. It also had a covered rooftop playground: an innovation that would become a feature of many of London's board schools, hemmed in as they were by terraces and workshops, with little space for street-level playgrounds.

The quality of the new school board buildings was in part a recognition of the need to avoid the unhealthy conditions of existing schools, and in part a deliberately symbolic gesture: an easily readable, indeed didactic, statement in bricks and mortar 'which was intended to be comprehensible to both ratepaying public and the public which daily used the buildings'.[11] Edwin Chadwick, former secretary of the Poor Law Board and author of the influential 1842 *Report on the Sanitary Conditions of the Labouring Classes of Great Britain*, warned in 1870 that 'if the schools that were about to rise in every district in England were built on a bad principle; if they were of unhealthy construction; if they were so constructed as to be unsightly inside and outside, they would miss half their national usefulness'.[12] Robson, the London School Board's chief architect, who designed both the Nichol Street and the New Castle Street schools, told the Architectural Association in 1872 that 'a school should appear like a school, and not like a monastery, a town hall, or a set of almshouses'.[13] Board schools, he wrote in 1877, should be 'sermons in brick'.[14]

The point was clearly taken by Arthur Conan Doyle. In his short story 'The naval treaty' Sherlock Holmes notes the way in which London's board schools were not only local landmarks, standing out in high relief against a general background of cramped terraced housing, but also manifestations of Victorian faith in education as the path to national progress:

> 'Look at those big, isolated clumps of buildings rising up above the slates, like brick islands in a lead-coloured sea.'
> 'The board-schools.'
> 'Lighthouses, my boy! Beacons of the future! Capsules with hundreds of bright little seeds in each, out of which will spring the wise, better England of the future.'[15]

Charles Booth, in *The Life and Labour of the People in London* (1889), had also noted the significance of board schools looming over London's poorer neighbourhoods:

> In every quarter the eye is arrested by their distinctive architecture, as they stand closest where the need is greatest, and each one 'like a tall sentinel at his post', keeping watch over the interests of the generation that is to replace our own ... Taken as a whole they may be said fairly to represent the highwater mark of the public conscience in this country in its relation to the education of the children of the people.[16]

There was also an important symbolism in the architecture of board schools. It was widely recognised that the Gothic styles favoured by denominational schools were inappropriate to the spirit of the new school system, their religious connotations at odds with a cornerstone of the 1870 act, which required school curricula to be entirely secular. The progressive middle-class supporters of board schools favoured Domestic Revival styles, especially Queen Anne, which was held to suggest both art and enlightenment: the 'sweetness and light' of Matthew Arnold's famous essay on culture.[17] The result was a distinctive cityscape of school buildings of red brick with white sash windows, brick pediments, ribbed chimney stacks, hipped roofs, wooden cupolas, fanlights, terracotta detailing and ornate gables. The Nichol Street and New Castle Street schools, early examples of Robson's work, were pared-down versions of the Queen Anne style that became emblematic of London's 447 board schools, distinctively secular in appearance.

The cost of providing such 'beacons of the future' did not sit well with everyone. An anonymous pamphlet published in 1876 complained that 'The London School Board, owing its very existence to this Act, has already, by its extravagant expenditure, raised the rate to about fivepence in the £ … an extravagance which must at once be curbed.'[18] The sentiment was countered by reformers like Charles Booth, who argued that 'It was necessary to strike the eye and hold the imagination. It was worth much to carry high the flag of education, and this is what has been done.'[19] And the London School Board itself noted that

> The policy of the School Board has almost always been to give these buildings, as public buildings, some dignity of appearance, and make them ornaments rather than disfigurements to the neighbourhoods in which they are erected … it is the policy of the Board, while studying in the first instance suitable arrangements for teaching, not to set aside the dignity and attractiveness of buildings which the Board have always felt should be a contrast to their poor surroundings.[20]

In the early 1890s, the schools of the Old Nichol were the only buildings left standing, as the slum was razed and the streets realigned to accommodate the LCC's first municipal housing project, the Boundary Street Estate.[21] From its foundation in 1889 until 1907, the LCC was dominated by Sidney Webb's Progressive Party, an alliance of radical Liberals with some Fabians and socialists. They took full advantage of the 1890 Housing of the Working Classes Act, targeting the Old Nichol, which was promptly declared a slum in 1890 by the medical officer of health for Shoreditch. This allowed the LCC to announce a clearance scheme for the Old Nichol on grounds of public health. It prompted fierce opposition from the district's major landlords,

29 Clearing the Old Nichol. Rochelle Street School is in the centre of the photograph.

including the Chandos Estate and Baroness Kinloss, who had inherited property from the descendants of John Nichol. Both claimed to support the LCC scheme in principle, but – surprise – wanted their own property exempted. Meanwhile, the LCC could not find developers who would pay the market price for the land and take on redevelopment of the cleared site. Reluctantly, the LCC decided to accept responsibility for redevelopment, creating London's first public housing project.

The Boundary Street Estate was a landmark in terms of both urban policy and urban design, revolutionary in its provision of facilities for residents,[22] and it brought a new community of immigrant families who would rely on the district's board schools to assimilate their children into the mainstream of British working-class life. The master plan by Owen Fleming, the LCC's architect in charge, envisaged a picturesque urban village featuring a central open space laid out as an ornamental garden, with seven tree-lined streets radiating from it. Altogether, the estate consisted of 1,069 tenements, housing 4,566 residents. Twelve pubs were swept away by the scheme, with no provision for replacements. Meanwhile, in 1899, the board schools were enlarged. The rebuilt New Castle Street Primary School found itself facing Virginia Road, and so it was renamed Virginia Primary School. An additional primary school was built next to the infant school on Nichol Street, a two-storey building for 624 pupils, with separate entrances for girls and boys. It was connected to the infant school by a joint boundary wall and a caretaker's house; and together they became Rochelle Street School.

Legal constraints on subsidising rents meant that the costermongers, matchbox makers, hawkers and petty criminals who had occupied the Old Nichol before clearance were displaced into other districts, unable to afford the rents the LCC was obliged to charge. The incoming tenants of the new estate were the 'quiet poor', as Charles Booth called them: cigar makers, clerks, cabinetmakers, tailors, shoemakers, nurses and uniformed railway workers. More than 75 per cent of the households were Jewish, the majority of whom had fled the pogroms of Ashkenazim in Russia and Poland, many of them still speaking only Yiddish. Among the children who attended Rochelle Street School were Louis and Bernard Winogradsky and Charles Clore. After arriving from Odessa, the Winogradskys had Anglicised their name to Grade. Louis attended Rochelle Street between 1914 and 1919. He had a gift for figures, and won several scholarships, after each of which a half-day school holiday was announced in recognition of his prowess. He recalled that 'This did wonders for my popularity. It also brought a certain pride to the Winogradsky home and gave my mother something to boast about for months.'[23] Bernard, the younger brother, was just two years behind Louis at the school. Both, having been assimilated into British life through Rochelle Street School, embarked on careers in showbusiness, Bernard changing his last name to Delfont to avoid being confused with his brother Louis (who preferred to be called Lew). Both eventually became hugely successful impresarios and directors of media companies. Lew became Baron Grade of Elstree; Bernard became Baron Delfont of Stepney. Charles Clore, meanwhile, went on to become one of the richest men in Britain, after establishing a financial and real estate empire. He was an early exponent of takeover bids, gaining control of large public companies by direct approach to shareholders, without necessarily consulting company directors.

Most of Rochelle Street School's pupils, of course, went on to more mundane careers, many of them staying on as part of a community that, between the world wars, was steadily assimilated into British ways of life, yet subject to persistent anti-Semitism. Shoreditch and Bethnal Green, along with the rest of the East End, were unable to attract the new engineering and light manufacturing industries of the 1920s and 1930s that needed large uncluttered sites near arterial roads. This left East Enders to find traditional employment in the docks, in the furniture and rag trades, or as part of the army of service workers who served London's wealthy population. Although there had been a general rise in income, with a shorter working day and improved literacy, many still lived in a state either close to or in poverty. A nine-volume *New Survey of London Life and Labour*, undertaken by a team from the London School of Economics between 1928 and 1935, replicated Booth's methods with a street survey. It documented the persistence of poverty throughout the area, including the Rochelle Street School catchment area, where between 10 and 20 per cent of the households surveyed were living below the minimal standard of living used by Booth in his survey forty years before. Anti-Semitism was also persistent, coming to a head in 1936, when Oswald Mosley and members of his British Union of Fascists organised a march from Tower Hill in the direction of Bethnal Green and Shoreditch, with the aim of intimidating Jewish populations en route. It was famously halted at Cable Street by an overwhelming number of local residents – Jewish and non-Jewish – sympathetic trade unionists, anarchists and socialists.

Rochelle Street School was closed during the Second World War, but escaped damage. It was reopened in 1951 by the LCC as a school for children with learning difficulties, and eventually closed in 1976. By that time, postwar economic recovery and the progressive reforms of the welfare state had softened the harshness of East End life. Nevertheless, the Boundary Street community retained close-knit family ties and a spirit of mutual self-help that was documented in a landmark study of *Family and Kinship in East London* by sociologists Michael Young and Peter Willmott, who found that between a third and a half of the residents had relatives in different flats within the same block of the estate.[24]

But the stability and cohesiveness of the estate was disrupted by the right-to-buy policy of the Thatcher administration.[25] This coincided with a tide of gentrification that spread eastwards from the northeastern corner of the City after the 'Big Bang' of financial reform in 1986. The privately owned flats within the estate became increasingly sought after, commanding high prices when sold on. But around two thirds of the flats have remained as social housing, and a residents' group has fought to resist any move to hand over the estate to a housing association. The Jewish population has largely moved to other parts of the city, and the newest arrivals are Bangladeshi immigrants. The estate as a whole was designated a conservation area in 2007, and contains thirty-five Grade II listed buildings and elements, including Virginia Primary School, Rochelle Street School and School House, its iron railings and playground wall. As a result, the physical integrity of the estate is assured: listed buildings may not be demolished, extended or altered without special permission, and consent is required even for minor work, such as replacing railings or felling trees.

Today, the estate stands on the edge of a booming Shoreditch economy that has brought a degree of retail gentrification to streets where, until relatively recently, many of the storefronts were boarded up. Rochelle Street School has itself become part of the cultural economy of the area. The school's bike shed has been converted into an upscale restaurant, Rochelle Canteen, while the primary school building has become an arts and media complex that hosted British designer Giles Deacon's London Fashion Week show in 2008 and whose tenants now include an architecture studio, a fashion designer, a jewellery and handbag designer and consultant, a historic buildings consultancy, two photography and film agencies, a graphic designer, an advertising and branding consultancy, a media relations consulting firm, a wellness studio, a product design studio, a textile design studio, a contemporary art gallery and a 'multi-disciplinary creative' studio. The infant school building contains an architecture studio and a firm that provides event production services to the arts, fashion and cultural industries. A building complex that was a frontier outpost of educational and social reform in a desperate slum has become a microcosm of the capital's post-industrial economy in a gentrified neighbourhood.

8 Christ Church, Turnham Green

THE streetscapes of London's nineteenth-century suburbs are dotted with the spires of Anglican churches: something that may seem unremarkable, consistent with what we understand of the piety and propriety of Victorian middle-class society. In fact they were largely a response to the social and political threats and uncertainties set in motion by urbanisation and industrialisation. In particular, Victorian church building was in large part the product of a determined attempt by the establishment and its official Anglican Church to counter the increasing secularism and nonconformism of the fast-growing metropolis. In the early decades of the century, the established Church of England was struggling to maintain not only its congregations, but also its secular authority. Christ Church, Turnham Green, was one of more than 200 new churches planted across London as part of an aggressive campaign by the bishop of London, most of them subsidised by the government.

For centuries, the parish system and the personal influence and control of the clergy had been an effective framework for the maintenance of both religious adherence and social order. The Church exerted a strong grip on society, the parish system effectively operating as the principal agency for local governance, with the vestry having responsibility for the relief of the poor, apprenticeship schemes, schools, the upkeep and lighting of roads and the removal of nuisances. In alliance with local squires, the clergy were heavily involved in the maintenance

30 Christ Church, Turnham Green.

of law and order, appointing parish constables and serving as magistrates. The political strength and social authority of the Church of England were palpable and potent. But the Church was also corrupt and authoritarian, and by the beginning of the nineteenth century, with a more literate and better-informed population served by newspapers and scandal sheets, it was increasingly seen to be so. Senior clerics lived lives of luxury and were effectively landlords – and in some cases slumlords – to vast tracts of British cities, especially London. Nepotism, sinecures and dodgy financial practice seemed to the broader public to be taken for granted, priced into the system, while public trust and respect for the Church as an institution had steadily ebbed the more it had become part of the British political establishment. For many, the Church was perceived as the morally coercive arm of the ruling elite.[1]

Anglican clergy meanwhile lost their professional monopoly as public opinion-formers to a predominantly lay intelligentsia drawn from the ranks of authors, publishers and scientists. Social change, political radicalism and progressive ideas fostered the growth of religious pluralism and nonconformity: 'a bewildering array of theological beliefs, political associations, and class connections'.[2] The nonconformists' target markets were the growing ranks of the lower-middle classes, for whom they offered not only spiritual support, but also an arena of socialisation and education with the prospect of social mobility. Meanwhile, the traditional Anglican parish system simply broke down in the face of the masses of people from diverse backgrounds who now lived in the metropolis. In addition, the Church of England's establishment meant that the creation of a new parish church needed an act of parliament before it could be built, whereas nonconformists could set up wherever they could find space and build a chapel. By 1821, dissenting chapels already outnumbered Anglican churches by a comfortable margin. Between 1810 and 1820 only 152 new Anglican churches were constructed, while more than 15,000 non-Anglican places of worship were built. In the following twenty years, a further 18,000 non-Anglican places of worship were built, compared with less than a thousand by the Church of England.[3]

Together, the church-building efforts of Baptists, Congregationalists, Moravians, Methodists, Presbyterians, Quakers and Unitarians chipped away at Anglican church attendance. Many in the Church of England hierarchy evidently could not see what was happening, clinging to an imagined past, in which the Church was indispensable to keep social order and stability, with a compliant and respectful populace. Their assumption was that hundreds of thousands of people were absent from worship, simply having 'lost the habit' of attendance amid the dislocations and distractions of intensifying urbanisation. Their worry was that others might also lose the habit as they moved out to working-class and middle-class suburbs, where there were simply no churches to attend. Turnham Green was a case in point. Situated beyond Hammersmith on Chiswick High Road, the hamlet around the common had grown by the 1830s into a ribbon of homes, with a few speculative terraces already developing behind. The parish church, St Nicholas, was down by the Thames, with the open country of Chiswick House Estate in between. It was just a matter of time before the westward spread of the metropolis caught up with Turnham Green, bringing a new suburban community with no church to attend and no minister to shepherd them. It was a situation that was repeated all around the metropolis.

Together with concern over working-class irreligion and lower-middle-class nonconformism, the prospect of losing middle-class suburbs energised various elements among high-church Anglicans and their middle-class followers. One way or another, their reactionary efforts pushed Anglicanism to an evangelical stance. The Religious Tract Society was an early example, along with the 'Hackney Phalanx', an influential group focused on the need for new churches that would uphold Anglican orthodoxy.[4] The 'Clapham Sect', led by William Wilberforce, provided a moralistic rationale for suburban living, teaching that city life was fundamentally corrupting and that family life and nature were the only legitimate bases for 'Christian contentment'. Their lay membership, along with other influential supporters, lobbied the government to support the established Church in a programme of church building along the lines of the 1711 act that had established a Commission for Building Fifty New Churches, funded by a duty on coal coming into London. With Anglican leadership and clergy well represented in a parliament under Tory control,

> The crisis thrust on the Church by the growth and concentration of population was thought by politicians to be so urgent as to justify, for virtually the first time in history, grants of money from parliament – and large grants at that ... In 1818 parliament gave the Church a million pounds, and another half million in 1824, to build churches in parishes of at least 4,000 inhabitants where there was Church accommodation for fewer than 1,000 worshippers.[5]

A Church Building Commission was established, with powers to subdivide parishes, to award parliamentary grants for church building and to oversee their design. These 'Commissioners' churches' were intended to be supplemented by private donations. To this end, the Society for Promoting the Enlargement and Building of Churches and Chapels was founded in 1818 and incorporated by an act of parliament in 1826.[6] The Commissioners established a building committee to approve designs for the churches built with the government subsidy, but the requirements were not restrictive, except that the new churches were to be recognisably Anglican and, with economy as a priority, to have a minimum of ornamentation.

31 Aerial view of Christ Church, Turnham Green.

In London, Charles Blomfield, bishop of London between 1828 and 1856, launched his own fund, the Metropolis Churches Fund, to supplement funding from the Church Building Commission and the voluntary effort that was already under way under the auspices of the Incorporated Church Building Society. 'Drawing an unflattering analogy with the building of fortresses to assert English control in Ireland, he believed that "building churches throughout the kingdom is something like the occupation of a conquered land".'[7] During his tenure he built more than 200 new churches. Christ Church, Turnham Green, was one of them, consecrated by Blomfield in July 1843. The church cost £6,900, towards which the Commissioners contributed a grant of £500. Given a prominent site on the common as the focal point of the new parish, the church provided a picturesque, village-like touch to the emerging suburb. Attendance soon reached an average of more than 400 for both morning and evening services on Sundays. By the turn of the century, after the church became the garrison church for the Army and Navy Furniture Repository (just across from the Green on Heathfield Terrace), attendance regularly reached nearly 600. An Anglican bastion had been secured.

The architects were George Gilbert Scott and William B. Moffatt. Scott would go on to become one of the nineteenth century's most illustrious and influential architects, whose designs included the Albert Memorial, the New Chambers at Lincoln's Inn, the Foreign and Commonwealth Office (Chapter 9), the Midland Grand Hotel at St Pancras Station (Chapter 11), the University of Glasgow's main building, and more than ninety churches and numerous parsonages and vicarages that contributed to the dominance of High Victorian Gothic styles in religious buildings in nineteenth-century suburban streetscapes. Christ Church was built in Early English style, with an octagonal spire topping a square tower. The body of the church is faced in knapped flint, with limestone dressings and tall, narrow, pointed ('lancet') windows. The spire is clad in red and black brick, presaging the fad for polychrome decoration that became a hallmark of High Victorian Gothic architecture. Nikolaus Pevsner felt that Christ Church was 'rather gloomy', but that it showed that Scott was 'already a competent if uninspired performer'.[8] The Scott family blog also gives the church a mixed review:

> Christ Church is quite unusual for this date for making an attempt to give itself a more medieval surface texture: disguising any use of stock brick with flint and Bath stone dressings. A good idea, but Scott goes a bit over the top and dresses the entire building in it, including the spire. This makes the steeple look rather awkward, like a nervous young clerk in a pinstripe suit at their first day in the office.[9]

The design of Christ Church reflects the moment when church building transitioned from a practical campaign to an evangelical crusade. The Church Building Commissioners had been concerned first and foremost with the practical priorities of providing capacity in the right places at modest cost. Design oversight was directed primarily at the latter, rather than stylistic issues. Some Commissioners' churches were Gothic in style; others were in Greek, Romanesque, Italianate or hybrid designs. The critique was that the Commissioners' churches were 'bad architecture serving a hollow religion'.[10] Meanwhile, the diminishing secular authority of the Church had stimulated further reactionary responses. One was the emergence in the early 1830s of the so-called Oxford Movement, whose approach to Christian worship – the liturgy – was known as Tractarianism after their ninety dogmatic 'Tracts for the Times' that advocated a return to early Catholic doctrines in the Church of England. The Ecclesiological Society, formed in 1839 as the Cambridge Camden Society, was equally doctrinaire in linking traditional medieval liturgy with church architecture. According to the 'science' of their doctrine of 'ecclesiology', new churches should be designed in a historically faithful Gothic, so as to symbolise their continuity with their roots in the medieval Catholic past. A.W.N. Pugin, an architect, critic and public intellectual, was widely influential in propagating the idea that unadulterated copies of fourteenth- and fifteenth-century architecture represented the best and truest Gothic design, and therefore the most appropriate setting for a more traditional liturgy.[11] Commissioners' churches were ridiculed by Pugin and the purists of the Ecclesiological Society, and 'Commissioners' Gothic' became a term of derision among the cognoscenti. Another public intellectual of the time, John Ruskin, emphasised the importance of medieval Gothic style for what he saw as an art of communal togetherness, created by a morally superior age that respected honest work and condemned capitalist usury. Rather less dogmatic than Pugin, his *Seven Lamps of Architecture* (1849) and *The Stones of Venice* (1851) advocated the abstraction of Gothic elements from a wider range of precedents:

representing the essence of the style, rather than merely copying past examples.

Christ Church, Turnham Green, was one of the first Commissioners' churches to earn the praise of ecclesiologists. Scott was newly sympathetic to Pugin's reasoning and the passions of the ecclesiologists when he and Moffatt were awarded the contract for the church. He recalled that in 1841

> I saw somewhere an article by Mr Webb, the secretary to the Camden Society, which greatly excited my sympathy ... and I wrote to Mr Webb and subsequently saw him on the subject ... Mr Webb took advantage of the occasion to lecture me on church architecture in general, on the necessity of chancels, &c., &c. I at once saw that he was right, and became a reader of the *Ecclesiologist*.[12]

The first volume of the *Ecclesiologist* featured a positive review of Christ Church, praising it especially for its tower and spire, which were considered 'peculiarly excellent, and worthy of any ancient architect'.[13] It was not long, though, before the issue of the relevance of Gothic design took on wider significance, with claims that it symbolised English tradition and moral rectitude, as well as religious probity. Scott, along with Pugin and Ruskin, had made Gothic architecture part of a nationalised discourse of history and imperial power, alongside other important signifiers, such as landscape painting, Union flags and the national anthem, all of them mobilised to give tangible form to abstract 'national' values.[14]

Today, the symbolism of the church and the nuances of its design have less to do with ideas of moral rectitude and national identity and more to do with idealised notions of 'heritage'. Similarly, the idea of the church as a bastion of Anglicanism has been rendered irrelevant within an increasingly secular and multicultural society. Across London there has been a steady loss of Anglican churches, as congregations have shrunk and church buildings have been deconsecrated and sold off for conversion to residences, cafés, antique furniture stores, music venues and rehearsal spaces, or simply demolished. Almost half of the more than 400 'struggling' and closed Anglican churches in England date from the Victorian era and the Church of England's campaign of planting churches in new suburbs.[15] Christ Church, however, has maintained a viable congregation, partly through its location in what became a comfortably middle-class district, and partly through its strategic amalgamation with St Alban's, a kilometre (half a mile) away on Acton Green Common.

III

VICTORIAN LONDON 2: HEART OF EMPIRE

THROUGHOUT the nineteenth century and well into the twentieth, London was the most populous metropolis in the world. It was the hub of a mercantile empire, well on the way to becoming the first 'world city', occupying a nodal position within networks of trade, influence, production and consumption that were global in extent.[1] By 1914, a quarter of the earth's surface and over a fifth of its population were governed from Westminster and Whitehall. Workshop London had been put into overdrive by the 'New Imperialism' that began in the 1870s, as European states scrambled to extend empires and secure markets and raw materials in Africa, Asia and the Middle East. The imperial project was supported by advances in trans-oceanic shipping, railway networks, machine tools, agriculture and food processing, and, not least, military hardware.[2] Eric Hobsbawm's classic work on *Industry and Empire* detailed the intricate interdependence between British industrialisation and imperial expansion.[3] The period between 1870 and 1914 saw the ascendancy of London as a self-consciously imperial capital, the principal motor of a global economy that was underpinned by the imposition of peace under *Pax Britannica* and the maintenance of the stability of the pound sterling as the world's currency.

London's imperial status was reflected across the built environment in various ways: in its financial quarter and docks,

 Detail from 'Stanford's Library Map of London and Its Suburbs', 1877.

its state offices and commercial buildings and its streets and monuments. Public art and architecture in London 'together reflected and reinforced an impression, an atmosphere, celebrating British heroism on the battlefield, British sovereignty over foreign lands, British wealth and power, in short, British imperialism'.[4] But at the same time, it was largely an uncoordinated jumble of disparate monuments and public buildings. Enormous and impressive as London was, this did not reflect its status as the world's greatest imperial metropolis. Comparisons with the grand squares, sweeping avenues and boulevards of continental capitals were uncomfortable for many observers. The essayist Frederic Harrison complained in 1892 that 'London, with the grandest river of any capital in Europe, with a rich and glorious history, with boundless energy, wealth and culture, suffers itself to be put to shame by Paris, Berlin, Vienna, Rome, Chicago and New York.'[5]

There were good reasons why London did not seem to be punching its weight in terms of monumentality and Grand Design. Until 1889 and the creation of the LCC, the metropolis had no overall government capable of conceiving and administering large-scale projects of any kind. The Square Mile of the City was literally a law unto itself – 'London's own Vatican'[6] – while Westminster possessed only a vestigial form of government, and elsewhere administration lay in the hands of county magistrates and parish vestries. Localism consistently undermined metropolitan-wide projects, as ratepayers – less concerned with the condition of London than with their own neighbourhoods and personal pocketbooks – objected to the additional taxes they would have to pay to fund what today would probably be called vanity projects. Parliament was also somewhat constrained, with London's electorate significantly under-represented and the majority of provincial MPs ill disposed to vote for schemes to improve or embellish the metropolis at the regional taxpayers' expense.

In any event, London was overwhelmingly a commercial city. This allowed some commentators to advance a broader interpretation of its relative lack of a monumental cityscape: as 'a statement against absolutism, a proud expression of the energies and values of a free people'.[7] London had other claims on world-city status, mostly in terms of its 'whirlpool of activity', rather than fine public buildings.[8] The great railway termini – Euston, St Pancras (Chapter 11), Marylebone and Liverpool Street north of the river; Waterloo and Victoria to the south – were constant hives of activity, disgorging passengers from the ports of Liverpool, Bristol, Southampton and Glasgow, as well as from other towns and cities around the country. In terms of commercial activity, the streetscapes of the City – the banks along Lombard Street that financed enterprise and trade in every corner of the world, Lloyd's Shipping Register offices in Fenchurch Street that insured world shipping, and the rebuilt Royal Exchange on Cornhill with modern office spaces dealing with information by telegraph from all parts of the globe (replacing the old interior 'walks' designated for merchants specialising variously in East Indian, Irish, Baltic, Spanish, North American and other trade) – were an implicit expression of imperial London. The 'heart of empire' was arguably here, with Mansion House and the Bank of England joining the Royal Exchange at Bank Junction.[9] Downriver from the City, the Thames warehouses and docks had become the 'nexus of empire',[10] a global commodity entrepôt where the world's sugar, tea, coffee, cocoa, spices, textiles and minerals that had been financed, insured and traded through City offices and on City trading floors were warehoused, distributed or reshipped for export, along with the specialised products of workshop London: furniture, scientific instruments, electrical apparatus and machine tools.

Across town, the West End and the suburbs had their own commercial manifestations of empire: a concentration of steamship company offices, including Cunard, P&O, Royal Mail Steam

Packet Company and White Star Line, on Cockspur Street, for example. More overt were the West End's department stores, positioning themselves at the centre of a world of trade and consumption with spectacular displays of goods, using techniques that had been introduced by the World Expositions: staged representations of ancient Arabia, Egyptian tombs and Japanese gardens. In Bayswater, William Whiteley's ('The Universal Provider') had by 1875 expanded into a row of neighbouring buildings that effectively constituted a department store. The following year, Bon Marché, London's first purpose-built department store, opened in Brixton. Other landmark stores followed, including Bourne and Hollingsworth, D.H. Evans, Marshall and Snelgrove and Selfridges along Oxford Street; Harvey Nichols and Harrods (Chapter 12) in Knightsbridge; and Arding and Hobbs in Clapham.

Meanwhile, London was not, of course, entirely without grand and monumental public buildings, some of them overtly imperial in character. None was more spectacular than the Palace of Westminster, rebuilt in High Victorian Gothic to Charles Barry's designs, assisted by A.W.N. Pugin, between 1835 and 1860 after the old parliament complex had burnt down. Parliament Square was redeveloped as an appropriate setting for the kind of statuary befitting an imperial power. Trafalgar Square, at the other end of Parliament Street, was laid out as a more explicitly imperial space, dominated by the iconic column commemorating the great naval hero Lord Nelson, each side of its plinth depicting one of Nelson's famous victories. Four great black lions, symbols of British might sculpted by Edwin Landseer, guard the column. Before the end of Victoria's reign, four additional statues stood in the square, commemorating George IV and three imperialist generals: Sir Charles Napier, who fought the Peninsular campaign with Wellington; Sir Henry Havelock, who suppressed the Indian Mutiny; and Charles 'Chinese' Gordon, of Khartoum. Not far away on the Victoria Embankment was Cleopatra's Needle, an obelisk 21 metres (68ft) high and weighing 180 tons, with two large sphinxes at its foot. It was widely construed (at least in Britain) as a token of Egyptian obeisance to British imperial power. Another highly charged monument was the bronze statue of Boudicca and her daughters in a two-horse chariot, sponsored by Prince Albert and installed on Westminster Bridge across from the Houses of Parliament.

Prince Albert arguably did more than anyone else to put London on the map as an imperial capital. He was the driving force behind the Great Exhibition of 1851, which produced the first urban megastructure, the Crystal Palace, to house the exhibits.[11] The exhibition was conceived by Prince Albert to symbolise Britain's commercial and industrial supremacy, while stimulating British manufacture and design. After the Crystal Palace had been dismantled from its Hyde Park site and carted off to be reassembled in Sydenham, the profits from the exhibition were used to seed the creation of what became known as 'Albertopolis', across from Hyde Park in South Kensington. There, the Natural History Museum, the South Kensington Museum (later renamed the Victoria and Albert Museum – Chapter 10) and the Imperial Institute were created as sites of imperial display on a par with the British Museum in Bloomsbury.

For its part, the national government contributed a series of offices along Whitehall. Increasing state involvement in various aspects of the economy and environment, as well as Britain's expanding empire, meant that new government departments were created and existing ones greatly expanded and reorganised to accommodate the growing civil service. The first to be completed were the Foreign Office and the India Office, in 1868 (Chapter 9). Great importance, and much debate, surrounded their design: Britain was the leading world power, and offices dealing with foreigners had to remind them of that. When the administration of London itself finally came under the jurisdiction of a single, powerful entity, the LCC, there was further impetus to at least give the city the streets its status demanded.

The Aldwych and Kingsway scheme, masterminded by LCC planners, was opened in 1905, a deliberate statement of civic pride. The crescent of Aldwych was built to take the route of the Strand around the historic church of St Clement Danes, while the Kingsway ran north from the centre of the crescent to Holborn. The Kingsway was London's widest street to date, 'thoroughly modern in spirit, not least because a tunnel for electric trams ran beneath it ... [while] Aldwych's location on the royal route from the palace to St Paul's made it suitable for buildings associated with the empire'.[12] Australia House, built in 1913–18, was the first of the large Dominion headquarters in the area; it was joined by New Zealand House in 1916 and India House in the 1920s. Canada and South Africa, meanwhile, set up overlooking Trafalgar Square, close to another imperial project, this time masterminded by the central government after the death of Queen Victoria to commemorate Britain's rise to greatness under her reign. A massive monument to Victoria on Constitution Hill in front of refaced Buckingham Palace served as the terminating vista at the head of a newly widened Mall, a processional route running along the northern edge of St James's Park all the way to Admiralty Arch (Chapter 13), which links the whole ensemble to Trafalgar Square: 'the single most significant and self-consciously imperial reworking of urban space in London's history'.[13]

9 Foreign and Commonwealth Office, Whitehall

THE Foreign Office Building in Whitehall is the product of a pivotal moment in the history of British governance and diplomacy. Economic growth and increasing global influence following victory in the Napoleonic Wars in 1815 required a significant increase in the capacities of bureaucratic administration, with London fast becoming the seat of a growing civil service with new powers and responsibilities. By mid-century this was being reflected in the built environment. The Foreign Office Building was designed in the late 1850s, when Britain was arguably at the height of her national and geopolitical self-confidence – if not quite of her imperial extent. By 1868, the Foreign Office and India Office had moved into the new building, followed by the Colonial and Home offices in 1875, when additional space had been completed. The complex became the nerve-centre of British diplomacy, as civil service mandarins docketed, indexed and deciphered communications from around the world. It was designed to function as a workplace for the mandarins and their staff, but to look like a palace fit for cabinet members to host titled foreign dignitaries and for the government to stage events important to Britain's statecraft. This led to the Foreign Office Building representing another pivotal moment – this time in the history of architecture – as it became the focus of a furious 'Battle of the Styles' that went well beyond aesthetics

33 Foreign and Commonwealth Office, detail of west elevation.

and matters of personal taste to become an expression of the tensions implicit in mid-century British society.

The symbolic cultural meanings and political baggage attached to the furore over its design have been forgotten, except among students of architectural history. Meanwhile, the transition to a post-colonial era and Britain's dwindling super-power status have modified the meanings and weakened the potency of the original imperial symbolism of the building. It has become taken for granted amid the ensemble of government buildings in Whitehall, a 'filler', relatively speaking, among iconic landmarks that include the Houses of Parliament, Westminster Abbey, Downing Street, Banqueting House, Horse Guards and Trafalgar Square. The uniform Parliament Street frontage and long King Charles Street elevation of the Foreign Office Building are impressively massive and suitably embellished, but uninspiring. Pevsner damns the building with faint praise: 'a most competent piece of High Victorian design … swotted-up Cinquecento'. The west elevation is more handsome, and has the advantage

34 The Foreign, India, Home and Colonial Offices in 1866.

of being able to be viewed at a proper distance, from St James's Park. With a square pavilion at one end, a projecting façade with two tiers of arcading near the other, and a tower topped by a belvedere storey joined to the projecting façade by a curved return, it is, as Pevsner concedes, 'eminently picturesque'.[1]

The building had been a long time coming. After the creation of the Foreign Office in 1782, the foreign secretary and his staff had been accommodated in a series of six town houses that had been cobbled together along Downing Street, with an overspill annex in a couple of buildings nearby. Plans for a purpose-built facility were discussed in the 1830s, but decisions were put off because the government was preoccupied with the need to rebuild the Houses of Parliament. The issue was revisited in the early 1850s and new plans were commissioned. The need for a new building was underscored in 1852, when the foreign secretary's ceiling fell in just after he had left his desk. But the following year, the Crimean War diverted attention away from the issue once again. Meanwhile, collapsed ceilings notwithstanding, the need for new government offices had become acute. A near-exponential increase in communications was coming through the Foreign Office, all pre-dating the development of the overseas telegraph system. A growing staff and expanding stacks of paper records were spilling out into rented space around Whitehall. 'The government', commented *The Times*, 'lives in lodgings.'[2] Edmund Hammond, the permanent under-secretary, was energetic in lobbying for a building capable not only of accommodating the necessary staff and records and allowing for ease of internal circulation, but also of providing additional space for formal receptions, meetings and dinners. Eventually, in 1856, the government invited designs for new Foreign Office and War Office buildings. Lord Palmerston, who had just become prime minister, decided on an open architectural competition divided into three parts: one for a site plan for Whitehall offices; a second for the design of the elevations for the Foreign Office;

and a third for the design of the elevations for the War Office. The competition judges introduced an additional caveat: that no one entrant could win more than one part of the competition.

The emphasis on elevations immediately set off a free-for-all about the desired appearance of the buildings. As Anthony Sutcliffe observed, 'the reduction of architecture to simple elevations meant that even the most ignorant could hold an obdurate and raucous opinion (the "gentleman's club effect")'.[3] The emerging professional field of architecture had no canonical aesthetic, and differing interpretations and opinions abounded. Debates about design routinely drew in enthusiastic amateurs, leaders of industry, newspaper editorials, an increasingly opinionated public and, now, politicians. Nevertheless, the debate was regarded as a side show by the majority of Londoners: the working classes were totally uninterested, while the middle classes, by and large, were against the building on grounds of public expenditure; if they were interested in the issue at all, they simply wanted the building to be serviceable.

The competition was a mess. Having three separate elements and three different winners was all but guaranteed to produce designs that were mutually incompatible. It produced a saga of great length and complexity before a design was eventually approved. The events have been described and analysed in detail by historians.[4] It was, observes Bernard Porter, 'an entertaining story involving a rigged competition, a prejudiced old peer (Lord Palmerston), a spineless and avaricious architect (George Gilbert Scott), [and] a hint of scandal ...'.[5] From more than 200 entries, the jury identified a dozen or so finalists, before selecting the winners. Palmerston did not care for the results and appointed James Pennethorne, the government's official architect, to produce new designs in neoclassical style. In 1858, Palmerston lost power and a parliamentary select committee, chaired by the Conservative MP (and president of the Ecclesiological Society) Alexander Beresford Hope, recommended that a different architect be appointed: someone sympathetic to Gothic designs. George Gilbert Scott, a finalist in the original competition, was given the commission. It was around this time that the plans for the War Office were ditched in favour of the India Office, established in 1858 to take over the governing of India from the East India Company. This resulted in Scott having to collaborate with the former East India Company architect Matthew Digby Wyatt. Then Palmerston, back in power in 1859, stubbornly rejected successive neo-Gothic designs submitted by Scott until, at last, the architect gave in and submitted a neoclassical design to Palmerston's taste.

The Battle of the Styles was a skirmish in broader nineteenth-century culture wars. But within the pro-Gothic camp was a deep split. Older and more conservative and upper-class elements preferred the symmetry, cleaner lines, clear rules and 'orders' associated with neoclassical architecture, understood by its advocates as representing Enlightenment rationality. Counterintuitive as it may seem now, the pointed arches, lancet windows and ornate decoration of neo-Gothic design was the preferred aesthetic of younger, more progressive factions and, more broadly, of the rising middle classes. Following the writings of John Ruskin, the progressives were advocates of continental variants of Gothic design, because of their richness and flexibility. This view was at odds with the backward-looking Gothic 'copyism' advocated by A.W.N. Pugin and the Ecclesiological Society: a view that had earlier been adopted by George Gilbert Scott in approaching his many church commissions, such as Christ Church, Turnham Green (Chapter 8). Like many others, though, Scott later allowed himself to be persuaded by Ruskin's more liberal approach to Gothic design. Having met Ruskin in Venice and read *The Stones of Venice*, Scott 'was now fully committed to the excitement of a new rich, eclectic European Gothic style, and was, in principle at least, unprepared to work in any other style'.[6]

Each of the contending styles carried complex webs of association that were dragged into the Battle of the Styles. The claims, counter-claims, contradictions and inconsistencies of the arguments have been laid out in detail by Porter and others. Many of the arguments were specious: on behalf of Venetian Gothic, for example, was the claim that since it expressed the city-state's fifteenth-century commercial greatness, it could be seen to stand for Britain's commercial dominance in the nineteenth century. Gothicists claimed that Classical architecture, rooted in Athens and Rome, was inherently foreign, and therefore unsuited to a building associated so closely with British national identity. Gothic was championed because it was more 'English'; but the Gothic finalists in the competition, including Scott's design, 'were all covered with Flemish, French, Lombardic and even Byzantine features'.[7] At one point the argument descended into a debate as to whether a Gothic or Classical style was better for admitting light and for the circulation of air. A more decisive factor was the addition of the India Office to the project.[8] It was appreciated that 'people from India might not fully comprehend the subtleties of the Gothic or Byzantine style. They would expect to see something which resembled "a political palace"',[9] and that 'Classicized style was a forceful generator of imperial symbolism. Palaces from Diocletian to Louis XIV made and sustained this tradition.'[10]

In 1858, the final report from Beresford Hope's Select Committee on Foreign Office Reconstruction specifically set aside the issue of style. 'The committee decided that the style did not significantly impact upon the price of the building, the presence of light and air, or even neighbourhood coherence (as the site was between the Gothic Houses of Parliament and the Italianate Horse Guards Parade).'[11] This left Palmerston free, on returning to office, to coerce Scott into submitting a neoclassical design in Italianate style. The plans were finally approved by the government in 1861. It was to be a massive complex planned

35 Foreign and Commonwealth Office, King Charles Street elevation.

around courtyards, the main one entered by triple archways from both King Charles and Downing streets. The Foreign and India offices, facing St James's Park, were completed by 1868; two new quadrants housing the Home and Colonial offices were added in the 1870s, aligning their façade with Parliament Street. The façade itself was relatively restrained, but since it was, after all, Parliament Street, it was given an allegorical group of figures on the parapet. Victoria herself is the centrepiece of the composition, posing as a Roman empress seated upon her throne, the British lion and unicorn at her side. Representations of Knowledge and Power (the Book and the Sword) symbolise the means by which Britain would maintain control across the globe. Inside, there was a sharp differentiation between public and working spaces. The latter were plain and functional, but with a state-of-the-art network of bells, messenger boxes and speaking tubes. Even more plain and functional were the rooms on

36 Grand Staircase of the Foreign and Commonwealth Office.

the two upper floors for thirty-six servants, resident clerks and night messengers and their families. Public spaces, on the other hand, were conceived by Scott to be a 'drawing room for the nation', and had to be suitably impressive. The Grand Staircase leading to the Foreign Office staterooms is certainly designed to impress: a cavernous space covered by a barrel-vault ceiling and a central dome which depicts the sun and the signs of the zodiac. Surrounding the sky are twenty female figures representing some of the geopolitically important countries at the time. The staterooms – the Cabinet Room, Dining Room, Conference Room and the Secretary of State's Office – were decorated with generous use of marble, gilding, granite and mosaics, with coffered ceilings and majolica plaques on the walls.

Although the Foreign Office was the most powerful and politically important occupant of the complex – the reason it has given its name to the entire edifice – the India Office quadrant was paid for by Indian taxpayers. Under the budgetary discretion of the secretary of state for India (rather than the Treasury), and with Matthew Wyatt having a strong hand in the design partnership, both the interior and the exterior were more lavish. Outside, there were statues of the heroes of British India, as well as sculptural figures symbolising the animals, rivers and regions of the sub-continent. Inside, the Gurkha Stairs were adorned with statues of former governors-general, while the Muses' Stairwell was topped with an octagonal glass lantern. The centrepiece was the India Office Courtyard (later renamed the 'Durbar Court'), a lavishly decorated space surrounded by galleries and covered with a glazed roof.

Over time, the staterooms were not cared for in the way they might have been, gradually becoming a bit shabby and then, during the First World War, distinctly beaten up when they were occupied by the Contraband Department. In 1925, they were used to host the official signing of the Locarno Treaties, drawn up in the hope of reducing geopolitical tension in Europe.

37 Durbar Court, Foreign and Commonwealth Office.

The Cabinet Room, Dining Room and Conference Room were renamed the Locarno Suite. Other important occasions followed, but during the Second World War the staterooms were beaten up again, occupied by the Cyphering branch of the Communications Department. It got even worse after the war, when civil servants were crammed into makeshift cubicles under false ceilings. Keith Hamilton quotes a letter published in *The Times* in 1946, its author

> outraged at the 'slovenly squalor' of the entrance hall, 'dimly lit by a single naked bulb, littered with packing cases, dispatch boxes, and cups of tea', and at the 'squalid' room occupied by the News Department, its floor without carpets, its windows without curtains, its otherwise bare walls rendered in a 'sickly green distemper', and its furniture consisting of an iron bed with a few grubby blankets and some decrepit desks and chairs.[12]

The building's occupants changed as Britain adjusted to the realities of postwar diplomacy. The India Office was dissolved when India won independence in 1947. The Foreign Office promptly expanded into the space. The Colonial Office gradually morphed into the Commonwealth Office, and a single Foreign and Commonwealth Office was established in 1968. In 2020, it was renamed the Foreign, Commonwealth and Development Office. Meanwhile, the building itself was caught up in another 'battle of the styles', this time between Modernism and conservation. Persuaded by the evangelical enthusiasm of Modernist planners and architects, the Conservative minister for public building and works, Geoffrey Rippon, commissioned Leslie Martin, designer of the Royal Festival Hall, and Colin Buchanan, an influential planning consultant, to draw up a scheme for the wholesale demolition and redevelopment of the entire Whitehall complex between St James's Park and the Thames Embankment.[13] They concluded their study in 1965, setting off several years of debate over whether to demolish the government offices, gut them but leave the façades, or simply refurbish them. It was part of a much wider public debate surrounding the tensions between modernisation and conservation that involved other London landmarks, including the Royal Albert Hall, St Pancras Station, the London Coal Exchange, St James's Theatre, Euston Arch, the Army and Navy Club, and the entire district of Covent Garden, scheduled to make way for a series of office towers, wide roads and aerial walkways.

As with the rationale for the Foreign Office Building in the first place, the case for its demolition rested primarily on the need for space and efficiency. The 1965 plan produced for the government by Leslie Martin and Colin Buchanan advocated not only the demolition of the Foreign Office, the Treasury and several neighbouring buildings, but also the transformation of Whitehall itself into a 'Grand Axis' running up to Trafalgar Square through a redeveloped Covent Garden, and on as far as Bloomsbury.[14] Advocates of demolition and redevelopment were anxious to signal the emergence of a new Britain through modern government buildings. John Silkin, Geoffrey Rippon's successor, argued that the existing 'nondescript' structures would 'not be missed'. Sir Alec Douglas-Home, secretary of state in 1970 as the debate rolled on, favoured the notion of rebuilding within the existing façades, 'making use of all the present wasted space in the courtyard'.[15] On the other side of the debate, the Victorian Society and other activist groups did their best to popularise the case for preservation. In the end, neither side won the argument: the projected cost of the wholesale redevelopment of Whitehall simply led to an impasse. Meanwhile, the Foreign Office Building had been listed as a Grade I protected building, and in 1976 the government found a few million pounds to refurbish the Locarno Suite and the Grand Staircase. By the mid-1980s, London was becoming much more significant than ever before as an international tourist destination, and the value of the Whitehall and Westminster streetscape ensured its survival. The Foreign Office Building was given a £100 million restoration that took seventeen years.[16] When the work was completed in 1999, the Portland stone exterior, blackened by a century of pollution, was returned to a luminous off-white along with the rest of the ensemble of government buildings along Whitehall, the backdrop both to national pageant and to the movement of tourists between Westminster landmarks. Most of Scott's and Wyatt's interiors were painstakingly restored to their original appearance, along with the murals that decorate the Grand Staircase, completed in 1921, soon after the Versailles Treaty, by the well-connected artist Sigismund Goetze. The murals were designed to illustrate the origin, expansion and triumph of the British Empire. The final panel, 'Britannia Pacificatrix', shows Britannia acknowledging other nations, flanked by her standard bearers – white adult males representing the British Empire (including Australia in a bush hat). Africa is portrayed in the corner of the panel as a naked boy carrying a fruit basket. Altogether, an awkward example of imperial symbolism and ideology with which to greet visiting dignitaries in the twenty-first century.

1837
1901
ART
ALBERT
VICTORIA AND
ALBERT MUSE

10 Victoria and Albert Museum, South Kensington

THE Victoria and Albert Museum is a massive complex, most of it assembled in fits and starts over the second half of the nineteenth century, culminating with the construction of the frontage along Cromwell Gardens between 1899 and 1909.[1] The façade, in the characteristic South Kensington combination of red brick, Portland Stone and terracotta detailing, is a symmetrical composition with two domes and a tower either side of a Grand Entrance, with elaborate sculptural embellishments, topped by a tiered three-storey octagonal structure. Running along the entire length of the façade is a sequence of niches, each with statues representing a distinguished British painter, craftsman, sculptor or architect. The niches and statues continue around the corner, along Exhibition Road, where the building terminates with another dome. A colonnade then follows the building line to the Henry Cole wing of the museum, originally built for the School of Naval Architecture (it was later allocated to the Royal College of Science).

The heart of the complex, the inner quadrangle, was created piecemeal between 1856 and 1884 as the museum added buildings around the first permanent

38 Grand Entrance to the Victoria and Albert Museum.

block, the Sheepshanks Gallery, which still stands on the eastern side of the quadrangle. Each of the blocks facing the quadrangle is richly decorated with terracotta, mosaic and tiles in what is broadly Italian Romanesque style. The northern block is the most striking, with a triangular pediment featuring a mosaic that depicts Queen Victoria handing out laurels at the Great Exhibition of 1851. To her right, Science and Invention are represented by a steam locomotive and a printing press, while to her left the Arts are symbolised by a bust, a palette, brushes and canvas, a classical column and a violin. The bronze entrance doors echo the dual theme, with Humphry Davy, Isaac Newton and James Watt in bas-relief on one side and Bramante, Michelangelo and Titian on the other.

Museums were one of the great institutional enterprises of the Victorian age, part of the metanarrative of national progress carried forward through a variety of movements and institutions: public libraries, art galleries, mechanics' institutes, mutual improvement societies, exhibitions, schools and universities, as well as museums. For the growing lower-middle and middle classes of Victorian London, museums provided a novel mixture of education and diversion. Victorian museums were entirely new kinds of spaces that allowed – even fostered – the self-conscious performance of identity, including class identity: allowing people's dress and public comportment to be made visible to one another in a controlled setting (and incidentally providing perfectly innocent locales for rendezvous). Victorian museums functioned variously as

> emblem, as historical event, as institution, as image, as practice … [as] a 'master pattern' that illuminates the ideological workings of Victorian society and literature … Victorian society constructed museums, celebrated and criticized museums, attended museums, worked in museums, wrote about museums, and collected in homage to museums.[2]

39 Sketch of the Victoria and Albert Museum, 1909.

Today, the entire V&A museum complex covers more than 50,000 square metres (12½ acres) and houses more than 4 million objects in its 145 galleries and labyrinth of corridors. It has become an important stop for international tourists, as well as an important element in London's 'experience economy', a key element of the cultural quarter that includes the Albert Hall, Imperial College, the Royal College of Music, the Royal College of Art, the Royal Geographical Society and the Natural History Museum, as well as the V&A. As such, the V&A has had its share of blockbuster exhibits, several of them building on London's

'Cool Britannia' image of the 1990s. The V&A has become a brand image in its own right, because of its ability and willingness to commodify its collection. Meanwhile it has also become known for a curatorial policy that often subverts the original meanings of objects, inviting visitors to question traditional perspectives on the roles of art and design in society.

This is all a far cry from the original aims and intentions of the museum's founders, which were to straightforwardly advance the interests of British manufacturers by establishing a museum as a didactic experience, providing the public with a means of education and instruction in science and the industrial arts. In the wake of the Great Exhibition of the Works of Industry of All Nations of 1851 it had become clear that Britain was losing ground in terms of its capacity to produce innovative and marketable consumer products:

> While Britain's dominance in canals, roads, and railway construction was indisputable, its manufactured designs were a source of national embarrassment ... British designs were criticised for being far too lavish and ornate, inappropriate to the purposes of the objects they adorned.[3]

The new museum would incorporate its own schools to teach useful skills and instruct the broader public in practical matters of design and taste. It was an implicit snub to the connoisseurs of fine art and to their aristocratic patrons; and at the same time a nod to the needs and interests of industrialists (for better product design and a mass market primed to value good design) and to the aspirations of the middle classes (social mobility and respectability through the acquisition of symbolic cultural capital). From the start, admission was free on Mondays, Tuesdays and Saturdays, while the museum's art schools were open until 9 p.m., enabling working-class artisans to work by day and study for improvement by night.

The Great Exhibition, conceived and promoted by Prince Albert, had done more than anything else to sharpen the mid-Victorian appetite for innovations in technology and design. Six million visitors to the exhibition – equivalent to a third of Britain's entire population at the time – had meanwhile generated a significant profit (approximately £180,000; equivalent to £32 million in 2023) that Prince Albert and his circle saw as an opportunity to invest in a continuation of the project. Albert's vision was for a permanent cluster of institutions, including learned societies, schools and a university, devoted to encouraging the application of science and art to industry. He persuaded the exhibition commissioners to purchase 35 hectares (86 acres) of market gardens south of Hyde Park, to be developed as a multi-institution 'College of Arts and Manufactures'.[4] The concept was promptly nicknamed 'Albertopolis'. In 1857, the South Kensington Museum (which would evolve into the V&A) was established on part of the site as an omnibus museum of art and industry. It was effectively a condensation of the Great Exhibition and the founding element of Albertopolis.

Henry Cole, the director of the Great Exhibition, was tapped by Prince Albert to become the general superintendent of the new museum. With limited funds and a pressing need to accommodate a collection of items that had been purchased from the exhibition commissioners, the first building was a temporary iron structure that became known as the 'Brompton Boilers' (after the nearby neighbourhood of Brompton and the resemblance of the building's barrel-roofed galleries to a series of boiler rooms). Meanwhile Cole hired an engineer, Francis Fowke, to design and supervise the construction of permanent buildings. First out of the ground was the Sheepshanks Gallery, named after the donor of a collection of paintings. The economic role of the museum was made clear in the first *Guide to the South Kensington Museum*, published for the museum's official opening in 1857. The Great Exhibition, the *Guide* noted, 'taught that art is the parent of design, and that design is the essence of successful manufactures'.[5] The didactic role of the museum was reflected in its institutional home. Unlike the British Museum or the National Gallery, which had independent boards of trustees, the South Kensington Museum was a department of government, an adjunct to the Board of Trade. Through the Board of Trade, the museum acquired a large art school and the offices of the Department of Science and Art, which controlled government art and design education through a network of art schools throughout the country. In the early 1870s, the government rolled up several existing educational institutions into the Royal College of Science, giving it a new building next door to the museum. A few years later, the prominent biologist T.H. Huxley ('Darwin's Bulldog') was persuaded to move to South Kensington to help plan and develop what became the City and Guilds College, which opened in another new building just across Exhibition Road, before being merged with the Royal College of Science in 1907 to form Imperial College.[6]

Non-Western objects were prominent in the museum from the start. The South Court, opened in 1862, was set aside for the display of 'Oriental' collections. The intention was to provide examples of good design for British manufacturers and artisans, but the exhibits also sowed the seed of Orientalism in British culture, asserting the 'otherness' of Indian, Chinese, Japanese and Persian objects and their cultural context, while simultaneously collapsing differences within the category of 'Oriental'.[7] Art historian Tim Barringer argues that from about 1870 to the mid-1880s the curatorial mission of the museum was overtly one of 'academic imperialism', characterised by an increasingly prominent assertion of scholarly and popular interest in, and authority over, non-Western objects and, by extension, the non-Western world. This, in turn, evolved into a period of outright imperialist triumphalism. Just as Britain was ascending to the height of its global power, the South Kensington Museum became a sort of

40 Victoria and Albert Museum.

41 Inner quadrangle, Victoria and Albert Museum.

imperial archive, its collections of colonial spoils exhibited to highlight British prowess.[8] The mood was set by the Colonial and Indian Exhibition of 1886, which was held in a collection of temporary structures designed in an Indian style and set up behind the Natural History Museum. It attracted 5.5 million visitors – almost as many as the Great Exhibition itself – to what was in effect 'a massive exercise in publicity for the imperial ideal and a bonanza of national self-aggrandisement'.[9] The success of the exhibition encouraged the government to create a permanent Imperial Institute on the site, in commemoration of Queen Victoria's Golden Jubilee in 1887.

Meanwhile the growth of the museum's collections, combined with an intensified popular sense of imperial vanity, made a strong case for some fine new buildings. In 1891 a competition was held for designs to cover the unused parts of the site facing on to Exhibition Road and Cromwell Gardens. It was won by Aston Webb with a tactful proposal for a building with silhouette and massing echoing that of the neighbouring Natural History Museum (on the other side of Exhibition Road). In May 1899, Queen Victoria laid the foundation stone of what was henceforth to be called the Victoria and Albert Museum; it was the last public ceremony she performed before her death. Four years later, the V&A opened to great pomp and circumstance, witnessed by a crowd of 25,000. By the time the Grand Entrance and Cromwell Gardens façade were completed in 1909, it was clear that the primary focus of the museum was to be a dazzling repository of the material culture of empire, reinforcing the idea of London as a self-consciously imperial capital. The procession of objects from peripheries to centre 'symbolically enacted the idea of London as the heart of empire'.[10] The museum's collections relating to science were meanwhile passed along to other institutions, leaving the V&A to focus on art and design.

After the First World War, the leadership and staff of the V&A quietly and resolutely turned their back on the original mission of advancing the interests of British manufacturers and their aspiring middle-class market. The museum settled into an introspective phase, nourishing a public image of its curators as 'idle, disdainful officials ... who evidently regarded employment in the museum as an opportunity to escape from dreary jobs in the world of affairs into a calm environment where the self could be cultivated'.[11] Beyond their own connoisseurial interests, they geared their work not to the education of London's artisans, aspirational working classes or middle-class consumers, but to the interests of aspirational middle- and upper-middle-class collectors, antiquarians and aesthetes. The V&A became a magnet for readers of periodicals like *Town and Country*, *The Collector*, *Connoisseur* and the *Burlington Magazine*. Ironically, this came at precisely the time when radical new ideas about art and design were emerging from the Modern Movement, in particular from the Staatliches Bauhaus, a school established in 1919 in Weimar, Germany, that combined architecture, crafts and the fine arts. As contemporary artists and designers there and elsewhere grappled with the implications of electric power, telecommunication, internal combustion engines, aviation, radio, photography, cinematography and the dislocations of economic change and modern warfare, the V&A stuck resolutely to antiquarianism. The British government, though, recognised the continuing need to foster good design in the cause of economic competitiveness, and in 1931 the Board of Trade appointed a committee on art and industry (the Gorell Committee). Its report effectively wrote off the V&A as a useful influence.

The Second World War provided a clean break for the V&A, not least because its collections had been moved out for the duration, allowing a new director to reorganise them on their return. The postwar director, Leigh Ashton, did so, and in some innovative ways; but at heart he was himself a connoisseur of fine objects and paintings, and his new galleries 'presented their contents as Art, as masterpieces, reposing in all their purity and calm, speaking for themselves, and inducing a reverent mood of aesthetic contemplation'.[12] The focus on antiquarian interests and object-based research continued into the early 1970s under the directorships of Trenchard Cox and John Pope-Hennessy. But with the appointment of Roy Strong as director in 1974, the V&A became a latecomer to the landscape of 'Swinging London'. Strong brought an emphasis on fashion and an association with celebrity. He reintroduced craft and industrial design, inviting the Crafts Council to run a shop in the museum selling contemporary crafts, and collaborated with Terence Conran, founder of the Habitat stores, on a new gallery devoted to industrial design (the collection subsequently became the Design Museum at Butler's Wharf, before relocating again to the site of the former Commonwealth Institute on Kensington High Street). Strong also organised exhibits to take advantage of public interest in the growing 'heritage movement' and oversaw the renovation of the museum's refreshment rooms, lecture theatre, 'cast courts' and entrance hall. He achieved notoriety, however, as the person who enthusiastically 'Thatcherised' the V&A, following the end of the consensus politics that had endured since the war. The spirit and purpose of the museum were thoroughly ruptured by Mrs Thatcher's ruthless ideological stance against state support for anything or anybody.

Under Strong's directorship, the V&A found itself subject to staff cuts, corporate-style exercises in benchmarking, best practices, total quality management, performance indicators, internal policy reviews and so on. Exhibitions were required to be self-financing, visitors were exhorted to make 'voluntary donations', galleries were rented out for corporate events, and the V&A itself was moved out of the government's direct orbit to become the responsibility of a board of trustees. A commercial firm, V&A Enterprises, was established to exploit opportunities for marketing and retailing. By the late 1980s, the change in culture was neatly captured by a Saatchi and Saatchi advertising campaign that boasted 'An ace caff with quite a nice museum attached'. As Elizabeth Wilson observed,

> The museum ... has been transformed from educational instrument to something approaching, in some cases, a branch of Liberty's ... Today the trip to the museum – or the art exhibition – is quite definitely organised to lead up to the final stop of the shop, where, in buying coloured postcards of your favourite paintings (to be sent to equally aesthetically aware friends on suitable occasions) you set the seal on your own good taste.[13]

As with many other museums, the museum shop became an important part of the experience for visitors, as well as an important source of revenue for the museum. The V&A brand was licensed to manufacturers such as the high-street clothing store Oasis, which produced garments 'inspired by' designs in the V&A archive. The net result is a blurring of the boundaries between the artistic and the commercial,

> between 'high' and 'low' art, between the old and the new, between 'proper' and 'commercial' art and craft, and between the museum experience as observational and hands-off and that which is experiential and commercial. A similar diffusion and boundary crossing continues in the museum's three restaurants. One could almost mistake the three restaurant halls – the Morris, Gamble, and Poynter rooms – for three of the museum's permanent exhibit rooms.[14]

Meanwhile, the V&A was spared the 'Guggenheim Effect' that saw many museums around the world employ celebrity architects to design striking and improbably shaped new structures to modernise and intensify their brand image (the reference here is to the Guggenheim Museum in Bilbao). It was not for want of trying: a proposal for National Lottery funding for an asymmetrical geometric building, 'The Spiral', designed by Daniel Libeskind, was eventually abandoned by the board of trustees after failing to receive funding from the Heritage Lottery Fund (though the V&A was successful in acquiring an iconic modern building for its new outpost in Dundee, designed by Kengo Kuma).

The overall outcome has been to reposition the V&A, along with the other tourist attractions of South Kensington and, indeed, the rest of the metropolis, as part of London's 'experience economy'. This has inevitably prompted a great deal of controversy and conflict, both internally and among the museum's stakeholders and its public. Disagreements and critiques of museum policies and curatorial practices have been ongoing since the late nineteenth century,[15] but in the twenty-first century they have involved new dimensions, framed around the likes of critical theory, literary theory, feminist theory and the recognition of the museum as an active agent of cultural production. Thus the V&A's role in the experience economy can be seen as part of what social theorist Guy Debord identified as the 'Society of the Spectacle',[16] where material culture is characterised by extravagant architecture, blockbuster shows, celebrity-laden events, and themed and simulated settings, all in support of commodification and consumption. For Debord, it amounts to a pervasive condition that serves to stupefy the populace. For the culturally aware curatorial staff at the V&A, it has been a challenge to be met by orchestrating radical forms of display that work to subvert the historically accepted meanings of objects; and through special exhibitions that address, directly or indirectly, issues of social justice and democratic citizenship. Segall and Trofanenko cite the example of the 2014/15 V&A exhibition of 'Disobedient Objects', such as makeshift teargas masks, pamphlet bombs and home-made drones designed to carry mobile phones to record police actions.[17] The curators of retrospective exhibits featuring David Bowie and Alexander McQueen, on the other hand, took a less direct approach, insinuating issues of sexuality, the female gaze, body image and queerness into representations of the respective artistic careers of Bowie and McQueen. Thus the museum becomes as much a site of cultural politics as, simultaneously, a platform for British culture and a place for middle-class visitors to top up their symbolic cultural capital.

11 St Pancras Station and Hotel, Camden

THE railway boom that began in the 1840s introduced dramatic new architectural elements to the city: grand stations, enormous railway hotels, bridges and viaducts. It all took place in an unplanned and unregulated way: a careless frenzy of railway mania, with different companies each developing their own network. In the process, the railways rewrote the geography of the metropolis. Following the recommendation of a Royal Commission in 1846, railway termini north of the Thames were to be allowed no closer to the centre of the city than New Road (the present-day Euston Road and Marylebone Road). Not surprisingly, the termini of railway companies with routes entering London from the north – Euston (for the London and Birmingham Railway), St Pancras (for the Midland Railway), King's Cross (for the Great Northern Railway) and Marylebone (for the Great Central Railway) – ended up being aligned along this boundary, as close as possible to the city centre. The railways forced their way into the city through slum districts, where the land was cheapest. Tracks and marshalling yards carved great channels through North London, creating a line of demarcation between more affluent suburbs to the northwest and working- and lower-middle-class

42 Renaissance St Pancras Hotel (former Midland Grand Hotel).

suburbs to the northeast. Islington, for example, which had been developed as an aspirational middle-class neighbourhood, quickly went out of fashion, the wrong side of a twilight zone of warehouses, workshops and railway infrastructure. South of New Road, the Great Estates were spared the disruption of the railways, but the inner suburbs to the south of the Thames were not. The railway companies were given unprecedented powers of compulsory purchase, and slumlords were only too happy to rid themselves of embarrassing, depreciated properties, while securing healthy compensation in return. Most of the displaced households had no alternative but to crowd into neighbouring districts, at higher rents.

At the same time, the railways were one of the great achievements of the Victorian age, a symbol of the Industrial Revolution and the means by which it was articulated: accelerating travel, trade and urbanisation, extending the geography of markets and supply chains, democratising travel and introducing a new experience of space and time to a broad population. London's railway termini

> played a prominent role in civic and political life, as arrival and departure points for royalty, visiting dignitaries and British troops. Stations accommodated important social rituals, such as funeral processions, and were associated with acts of remembrance including the placement of war memorials and the conduct of commemorative services.[1]

In terms of London's development, the fact that termini were strung out around the periphery of the city centre stimulated the development of the city's underground railway system, which had opened as the Metropolitan Railway in 1863, connecting Paddington station with Euston and King's Cross. Within twenty years it had evolved into the Circle Line, dramatically improving circulation around central London, including connections with mainline stations serving the Southeast and Southwest. By flattening slums and, as we saw in Chapter 6, enabling the development of 'Cockneyfied' suburbs through cheap workmen's fares, the railways relieved the pressure of numbers in the older inner-city districts, and so helped to lessen the probability of revolutionary unrest. Meanwhile, the streets around the termini attracted clusters of shops, bars, office buildings and hotels, creating thriving new commercial districts.

The grand hotels attached to the termini were an important new element of London life in their own right, 'public interiors' that were spaces of enchantment, luxury and freedom. In the mid-nineteenth century, London's grand hotels were among the few places that welcomed women and catered to their needs and sensibilities, while the hotels' dreamlike worlds of glamour and restless activity provided new arenas for the aspiring middle classes to develop a modern, cosmopolitan and mobile sense of themselves. The railways

> reorganised time and space and the experience of both ... Like the railway station itself, the terminus hotel was a gateway building – to the city, to travel, and to tourism ... It served as an epistemological threshold as well, allowing Victorians to see their world as new [and] more precisely, as *modern*.[2]

Charles Dickens noted in 1879 that 'one of the greatest changes in London during the last score or so of years is in the matter of hotels'.[3] Between 1850 and 1890, almost two dozen major London hotels opened, including Claridge's (1854), the Great Western Hotel at Paddington (1854), the Great Northern Hotel at King's Cross (1854), the Westminster Palace (1860), the Langham (1865), the Midland Grand St Pancras (1868) and the Savoy (1889).[4]

At St Pancras, both the station and the hotel were the apotheosis of their respective new building types and they were tightly

43 'From Pentonville Road Looking West: Evening' by John Scorrer O'Connor, 1884.

integrated, together representing 'the proud symbol not merely of the Midland Railway's ambition but of the whole railway age'.[5] The Midland Railway, established in 1844 by the amalgamation of three Derby-based companies, had a virtual monopoly of rail traffic to and from the East Midlands, including the important freight traffic of beers brewed in Burton-on-Trent. To secure a foothold in London, the company had initially contracted with the Great Northern line to use the station and goods sidings at King's Cross. But by the mid-1850s the company had resolved to build its own passenger terminus and goods yard, and began to buy up land in Agar Town, just west of King's Cross. At the same time, the company decided to extend its network northwards to Manchester, Carlisle and Scotland. To compete with the London and North Western's established west coast line and the Great Northern's east coast line, the Midland Railway's terminus had to be something special.

The company was granted the power to compulsorily purchase the necessary real estate through the Midland Railway

(St Pancras Branch) Act of 1866. At least fifty streets in Agar Town and parts of Somers Town were bought up, displacing as many as 32,000 people,[6] and subsequently requiring the disinterment of more than 8,000 bodies from the Old St Pancras churchyard, the St Giles cemetery and sundry pauper pits. Thomas Hardy, not yet the celebrated writer he would become, was employed as a young architect in the office of Arthur Blomfield, whose firm got the commission from the bishop of London to disinter a large number of graves from Old St Pancras churchyard.

Although the railway company had to compensate residents who had taken out long-term leases with the landowners – the Ecclesiastical Commissioners – weekly tenants could be evicted without compensation. Agar Town had consisted 'mostly of small tenements of the lowest class, named after one Mr William Agar ... an eccentric and miserly lawyer to whom the site was let on a short lease for building purposes, about the year 1840'.[7] The Regent's Canal ran through the district, attracting knacker's yards and bone-boiling and soap-manufacturing works, as well as potteries, brick kilns and workshops. By 1853, *The Builder* was moved to observe that 'No words would be too strong to describe the miserable conditions of this disgraceful location. The houses have been planted here without any thought of drainage, or of any other arrangement necessary for health.'[8] Its population was dominated by poor immigrants from rural Ireland. Charles Dickens, drawing casually on British prejudices of the time, described the district as 'our English Connemara'.

W.H. Barlow, engineer-in-chief to the Midland Railway, was given the job of designing the station. As his consulting engineer Barlow selected Rowland Ordish, who had worked with him in developing the initial calculations for the structure of the Crystal Palace. They had the advantage of learning from London's existing terminals, in particular the importance of maximising space in the train shed for traffic purposes, 'unembarrassed by columns or other impediments', as Barlow put it.[9] The example of the Great Northern Railway's hotel at King's Cross, offset from the station, underscored the desirability of integrating the new station hotel into the functional operations of the terminus. Yet the Midland Railway's management had ended up with an awkward site, hemmed in by the Midland's own goods yard to the west, by the Regent's Canal to the north and east, by the King's Cross terminus and approach tracks to the east and by Euston Road to the south. In addition, Barlow and Ordish had to deal with two major challenges beneath the site, one above the other. The Fleet River (effectively a sewer encased in an iron pipe) had to be realigned, while the Metropolitan Railway's underground tunnel had to be excavated to allow the Midland to join up, via the underground tracks of the Metropolitan Railway, with the cross-London route of a southern ally, the London, Chatham and Dover Railway, thereby allowing coal to be hauled directly from the Midlands to the South London suburbs and the Southeast.[10]

Barlow decided to take the railway tracks over Regent's Canal, meaning that the station itself would have to be built on a pedestal more than 5 metres (17ft) above street level. It was a significant engineering challenge that Barlow was able to turn to advantage, creating an undercroft beneath the pedestal that could be used for freight storage (barrels of Burton ale, as it turned out), while enjoying direct access from the adjacent roads on either side. The pedestal, which had to carry the weight of the tracks, trains and platform infrastructure above, was supported by more than 700 cast-iron columns and set on a grid of iron girders. This grid, in turn, was key to overcoming the sideways thrust of the truss of curved iron ribs that carried the glass roof of the train shed. Sprung directly from the edges of the pedestal and tied into its floor grid of girders, the roof truss provided an unimpeded span of 73 metres (240ft); the structure was 210 metres (690ft) long and 30 metres (100ft) high at its apex. It was the largest enclosed space without internal supports in the world when it opened in 1868, a brilliant piece of engineering that

44 Interior of Midland Railway Station, 1865.

was considered by many to be one of the wonders of the world. It had cost £435,882 (equivalent to just £63 million today) and had taken 9,000 tons of iron, 60 million bricks and 80,000 cubic feet of dressed stone.[11] 'This was a building made possible by the railways, in every sense. Its materials came from far and wide – bricks from Nottingham, and stone from Ancaster, Mansfield and Ketton.'[12] The train shed served as a model for other landmark stations, including Manchester Central, Glasgow St Enoch, New York's Grand Central, the Victoria Terminus in Mumbai and the Palais des Machines in Paris. For London, it provided an iconic landmark that played into the capital's imagery of imperial power. Railway historian Jack Simmons wrote that 'There is no other building, in London or anywhere else, that embodies more precisely the achievement of mid-Victorian Britain.'[13]

Inside the station, waiting rooms were segregated by sex and ticket class. The platforms, though, were an extension of public space, allowing the classes to mix and mingle. The station attracted news vendors, shoeshine boys, bookstalls, refreshment rooms and, before long, machines selling sweets, postcards, matches and other sundries, and weight and height measuring machines. J.B. Priestley coined the expression 'Pancrastination' to describe the experience of loitering at kiosks, buying newspapers and tobacco at St Pancras.[14]

When railway operations began in 1868, only part of the eastern section of the Midland Grand Hotel had been built. It was only in 1872 that the company could raise the capital to resume construction work on the hotel. George Gilbert Scott, at the pinnacle of his profession, was the architect. He had been one of eleven practitioners invited by the company to submit a proposal. His design far exceeded their brief, but the company's directors recognised the opportunity to build a hotel that would overshadow those of other rail companies in terms of size and luxury, and it won him the commission. Scott himself saw it as the perfect opportunity to exorcise the disappointment of giving up his Gothic design for the Foreign and Commonwealth Office (Chapter 9). His design was in over-the-top High Continental Gothic, suggesting what he might have done at the Foreign Office without Palmerston's interference. This was a time when Gothic 'had emerged as a dynamic, individualistic and contemporary style. No longer a slavish exercise in imitation, it became confident and optimistic, whilst also being edgy and exciting.'[15] Scott saw himself launching a great wave of Gothic building in London with his design. It drew on Gothic motifs from the Low Countries, France and the Veneto, as well as England, cribbing specific details from the Lakenhalle (Cloth Hall) at Ypres, the medieval Palais de Justice in Liège, the Palazzo Pubblico in Siena, the Palazzo Ducale in Venice, Westminster Abbey, and Winchester and Salisbury cathedrals.[16] The distinguished art historian Kenneth Clark suggested that it was the 'gorgeous fruit' of Scott's humiliation at the hands of Palmerston.[17] Scott, pleased with himself, famously felt the hotel to be 'too good for its purpose' as a mere commercial building.[18]

It Is certainly a striking and monumental building when approached from Euston Road. Its principal façade is set back and elevated from the road, with a curved wing that sweeps down to street level, where an arcaded porte-cochère offers access to the hotel. A ramp and forecourt provide the approach to the main façade for wheeled traffic. Two double-storey pointed arches pierce the ground floor of the building, one leading through to the station platforms and the other to the hotel. The hotel's forecourt entrance stands at the foot of a massive square tower with turrets and slender spires on each corner. At the other (eastern) end of the building is a 95 metre (310ft) clock tower in the style of the Palace of Westminster's iconic clock tower, Big Ben. In between, a sweep of red brick runs for more than 150 metres (492ft), the elaborately framed windows grouped vertically and decreasing in size with each storey. This visual spectacle is all down to Scott, but many of the fundamentals of his design were prescribed by Barlow, written into Scott's brief to ensure that the station and hotel would become an integrated package, both functionally and visually. Barlow's solution for the train shed predetermined the footprint of the hotel, the position of the station entrances and exits, and their elevation above street level. Scott was required to extend the Gothic language and idiom of the hotel façade to the interior of the station, including the booking offices, waiting rooms and the red-brick walls screening the train shed at street level. It helped, coincidentally, that the shed's roof trusses were slightly pointed at the top to give the structure extra strength, thus contributing a hint of the Gothic to a structure that was, for its time, decidedly futuristic. Meanwhile, Scott reciprocated by using exposed cast-iron riveted girders throughout the hotel interior.

When the hotel opened in 1873, what the guests noticed most about the interior was the flashy eclecticism of the décor, the luxurious coffee lounge, the granite trefoils and quatrefoils, pointed arches and decorative columns, the hydraulic 'ascending chambers' (two for guests, and two for servants and goods) and, above all, the Grand Staircase.

> Here is Scott's most complete realization of the grand hotel as an ideal stage for self-display, public presentation, and spectatorship. Rising three stories, flanked by gilded fleurs-de-lys on its walls, the sweep of the stairs follows the iron beams that meet at a ribbed vault, decorated by painted panels representing the seven virtues: charity, temperance, industry, chastity, humility, truth, and patience.[19]

45 Coffee lounge, Midland Grand Hotel.

The Midland Grand was an explicit exercise in hierarchy and social stratification. 'Like the gentlemen's clubhouses of the West End, the hotel was a space in which upper and upper-middle classes could consort without uneasiness, whether as guests or visitors.'[20] The fact that the hotel was set back and elevated above street level insulated guests physically and symbolically from the hoi polloi swirling around the terminus. Inside, true to prevailing class sensibilities,

> Spending on decoration and furnishings on the upper floors of the hotel was much more modest than that on the lower floors, reflecting the hierarchy of uses in the building. In the servants' quarters in the attics, furniture was made from deal (pine) japanned as oak. The third and fourth floors were decorated with furniture made from ash; on the second floor the furniture was 'of mahogany and black, parts being carved, incised and ebonised'; the first-floor rooms were furnished in oak; and the ground floor was furnished with 'the furniture of walnut & black wood relieved with gold'.[21]

For a while the Midland Grand was peerless in its elegance and desirability; but its glory days lasted less than thirty years. By the turn of the century it was considered 'unsightly';[22] Gothic architecture had lost its appeal and Edwardian Baroque was already being written purposefully into London's townscapes, domestic and commercial, public and private.[23] More to the point, the hotel's facilities were badly dated. Electricity had been installed in the late 1880s, but the corridors were still long, cramped and airless; the 300 guest rooms had flushing toilets, but there were only five bathrooms for guests to use, leaving an army of servants to scuttle around with tubs, bowls and towels. Scott's innovative fireproof concrete floors made remodelling a prohibitively expensive proposition. Strikingly progressive policies were the only affordable response to falling demand. In 1899, the hotel installed one of London's first revolving doors, divided into thirds, in order to provide enough space for women's skirts: 'a literalization of the grand hotel's welcoming of female guests through its doors',[24] and in 1902 it became the first British hotel to offer a Ladies Smoking Room. But the Midland Grand had already fallen into London's second tier when the Midland Railway company lost control of the terminus as a result of its merger in 1923 with the London and North Western Railway to form the London, Midland and Scottish Railway. Euston, just up the road, became the principal terminus for the new company, ensuring a steady decline for St Pancras.

The hotel was closed in 1935 and the building, renamed St Pancras Chambers, was used for railway company offices. The terminus and its rail services were taken over by British Rail in 1948, part of a wave of postwar nationalisation. Before long, British Rail began to plan for closure and demolition of the hotel as part of a modernisation scheme. The Victorian Society had been campaigning for listed status for the terminus since 1954, and when news leaked of British Rail's plans, the poet laureate, John Betjeman, rallied a group of art-world *prominenti* in support of the society's campaign. In 1967, ten days before the scheduled demolition of the hotel, the entire terminus was given Grade I listed status. The reprieve did nothing to halt the deterioration of the buildings. The hotel was finally vacated in 1985, after the building failed to gain a fire safety certificate. Empty and neglected, dusty and cobwebbed, rotting and begrimed, it blighted the entire neighbourhood. The local stretch of Euston Road lapsed into a scruffy mix of launderettes, burger bars, mini-markets, computer-repair shops and dodgy-looking pubs. The only professionals to be found in the area, as a *Wall Street Journal* reporter had it, were 'those engaged in the world's oldest profession, working in the suitably Gothic shadows' of the former hotel.[25] In fact, another set of professionals was also attracted to the vacant building. Film crews came to use the now-creepy Gothic interiors for a succession of movies, including *Chaplin*, *102 Dalmatians*, *Batman Begins*, *Richard III* and *From Hell*. The central staircase was used for the 1996 music video for 'Wannabe' by the Spice Girls, and in 2001 the exterior was used for location shots for *Harry Potter and the Philosopher's Stone*, standing in for the less dramatic-looking King's Cross Station, where the plot actually takes place.

Meanwhile the fortunes of the terminus were changing, as both the government and developers began to perceive the potential of the entire district. In 1975, the government decided to locate the new British Library on the site of the old Midland goods depot, just to the west of the station. In 1993, St Pancras was selected as the terminus for the Eurostar high-speed rail service through the new Channel Tunnel. The Eurostar ran from Waterloo until 2007, while the new owner of the station, HS1, spent £9 million preparing St Pancras: cleaning brickwork and repairing damaged areas, and adding a new flat-roofed shed at the northern end of Barlow's shed to accommodate the unusually long Eurostar trains. When the hotel building was put up for sale in 1998 it was snapped up by an American developer, Harry Handelsman, whose company, Manhattan Loft Corporation, specialised in converting old buildings to New York-style loft apartments. The government was alert to the potential for more widespread regeneration, having set up an Urban Task Force in 1997 under the leadership of the architect Richard Rogers to establish a vision for the physical and economic rejuvenation of the area. An easy first step was rebranding. Henceforth the industrial wasteland would be known as King's Cross Central. With no population to displace, no more local jobs to be lost, and several legacy structures from the railway era to lend character and authenticity, the Task Force made a persuasive case for the potential social and economic gains of a large-scale redevelopment strategy. Within a few years it had become the largest urban regeneration scheme in Europe.

46 Renaissance St Pancras Hotel after refurbishment, exterior detail.

It took almost thirteen years and around £800 million to renovate the station, but by the time it opened in November 2007 it was once again a spectacular landmark. The removal of layers of grime revealed the red-brick detail; the roof glazing was repaired to the original design; and the wrought ironwork was cleaned and repainted in its Victorian light blue colour. What was most impressive, however, was the way that architect Alastair Lansley and engineer Mike Glover opened up and reprogrammed the functional operations of the station by slicing through the old floor of the train shed and linking the undercroft – itself converted into rail and border control offices, an arcade of shops and more than a dozen bars and restaurants – to the station platforms. The undercroft, in turn, was linked directly to the King's Cross–St Pancras Underground station, providing London with a critical transportation hub: not only are there connections to Paris, Avignon, Brussels, Lille, Rotterdam and Amsterdam via the Eurostar, but there are also direct services to Heathrow, Gatwick and Luton airports and connectivity within the metropolis via six Underground lines (Circle, Hammersmith and City, Metropolitan, Northern, Piccadilly and Victoria).[26] In order to recoup the public money invested in the new railway infrastructure, the British government decided to privatise the entire line, including the operation of the stations at Ashford International, Ebbsfleet International and Stratford International, as well as St Pancras. The winning bid of £2.1 billion was from a Canadian consortium of pension funds.[27]

Harry Handelsman's canny investment in purchasing the hotel building was indirectly underwritten by the massive public investment in the station. His property company, together with London and Continental Railways and Marriott Hotels, restored the building at a cost of a further £200 million investment, under the close attention of English Heritage. Re-emerging as the five-star St Pancras Renaissance Hotel and conference centre, it is once again a truly grand hotel (one of more than seventy five-star hotels in the city: the greatest concentration of luxury hotels in the world). The upper floors, formerly hotel rooms and servants' quarters, have been converted into sixty-eight private apartments, including a £10 million penthouse, while additional hotel rooms have been added in a new five-storey extension behind the original building,[28] its façade a pared-down 'Gothic' that does little to deceive the eye as to its authenticity. The restoration of the hotel, along with the revitalisation of the station, has been an important element in the realisation of the vision of the 1997 Task Force. The derelict railway and canal-side lands to the north of King's Cross and St Pancras stations have been dramatically transformed, with the adaptive re-use of several legacy structures – including the Fish and Coal Offices, the Granary Building, the Coal Drops Yard, and the iconic guide frames of three gasholders – and the creation of public open spaces. Meanwhile, former brownfield sites have been redeveloped as mixed-use buildings and corporate offices, including the Google 'groundscraper' on King's Boulevard (Chapter 25).

HANS

12 Harrods, Knightsbridge

HARRODS department store is an imposing physical landmark and an icon of London as a shopping destination. The building itself, a trophy property several times over, not only serves as an advertisement and brand-image for the company, but has also given identity and definition to Knightsbridge as a distinctive retailing and residential district. When it was built, it symbolised London's position at the centre of world trade, a place where the finest products from the furthest corners of the British Empire could be purchased. The company's telegraphic address was 'Everything, London', its motto *Omnia Omnibus Ubique* ('Everything for Everybody, Everywhere'). Along with London's other early department stores – Whiteley's in Bayswater, Barkers in Kensington, Shoolbred's on Tottenham Court Road, Arding and Hobbs in Clapham, Harvey Nichols in Knightsbridge and Selfridges on Oxford Street – Harrods was disruptive not only to the retail industry, but also to social norms and consumer behaviour.[1] Department stores were pivotal in the articulation of a consumer society: diffusers of culture and lifestyle, as well as goods. They were also agents of female emancipation and social mobility, and microcosms of changing labour relations. Harrods itself eventually transcended its local retail functions to become a tourist destination

47 Harrods department store.

in its own right, known for superbrand luxury goods and select provisions, serving a mixture of affluent local residents, out-of-town shoppers and international visitors.

Throughout much of the nineteenth century there was a time-lag between the industrialisation of production and the modernisation of retailing. Shops generally remained small and specialised and shopkeepers traded independently, pricing their goods autonomously in the same way that stallholders and street market vendors had done for centuries. For their part, customers might window-shop; but to enter a shop was regarded as an explicit commitment to purchase something. Gradually, the growth in middle-class prosperity, the development of the railway-based distribution system and the emergence of wholesaling networks supported a rapidly expanding consumer economy that gave rise to an array of new building types: market halls, exchanges, bazaars and arcades.[2] In addition to being spaces of consumption, bazaars and arcades were new social spaces that provided settings for browsing, shopping and entertainment. The likes of the Soho Bazaar (1816), the Pantheon, Oxford Street (1834) and the Pantechnicon, Belgravia (1830) were big retail halls controlled by a single proprietor. Traders offering dry goods of various kinds were assigned counters or booths on galleried sales floors. To attract customers, they commonly featured diversions such as dioramas, panoramas, waxworks, optical illusions and magicians.

Arcades catered to a rather more up-market clientele, with small shops, rather than counters or booths. Protected from the rain and mud by the innovation of glass roofs, with gas lighting, and with cafés and restaurants where shoppers could rest and observe fellow browsers, they were magnetic in their attractiveness to more affluent shoppers. Among the earliest examples were the Royal Opera Arcade, St James's (1817) and the Burlington Arcade, Mayfair (1819). By the time the Royal Arcade was opened in Mayfair in 1879, shopkeepers across the city had

48 Drawing of Harrods in 1911, showing planned (but unbuilt) Coronation Tower.

moved indoors. The best shops occupied the same streets in the 1850s as they had done in the eighteenth century, but they were entirely different in appearance. The arrival of plate glass led to a wave of shop window replacement, with embellishments in brass, wood mouldings and mirrors. The use of iron beams allowed for a window frontage extending along the entire ground floor of many shops, while cast-iron frames allowed some to have glazed façades over several storeys. Drapers were prominent in these developments: 'they offered a broader range of cloths, employed more assistants and their shops were built on an ever grander scale, filling a number of adjacent plots'.[3] The most successful drapers began to expand their range of goods to include furnishings, furniture, carpets and fancy goods, and to organise their stock into departments – often spreading into neighbouring properties or erecting spacious new premises to accommodate the extended range of goods. Department stores were able to exploit both economies of scale and economies of scope, and offer set pricing, rather than negotiated sales.[4]

Harrods department store grew slowly over the course of the second half of the nineteenth century, from a one-room shop with two assistants and a messenger boy to a grand emporium with a staff of hundreds. The original shop facing the Brompton Road had been purchased in 1853 by Charles Henry Harrod, a wholesale grocer and tea merchant from the East End. Knightsbridge had a poor reputation at the time, but the Great Exhibition, across the road in Hyde Park, had prompted the first shoots of gentrification. Harrod's son, Charles Digby Harrod, recognised the potential of the district and bought the shop from his father in the early 1860s. By 1867, he and his family were running a shop with five assistants and a new storefront with a plate-glass window, and by the late 1870s their staff was approaching a hundred shop assistants. The growth was accommodated by gradually acquiring adjacent properties. By 1883, the staff complement had reached nearly 200, with a paternalistic managerial structure organised into separate departments that included 'groceries, provisions, confectionery, wines and spirits, brushes and turnery, ironmongery, glass, china, earthenware, stationery, fancy goods, perfumery, drugs, etc. The provision department was the leading feature of the Stores.'[5] Later that year a devastating fire virtually burnt out the store, but it was hastily renovated and Charles Harrod continued to expand the business, introducing innovations such as free delivery of goods, pay desks separate from service counters, and an early-version escalator in the form of a conveyor belt (with an attendant at the top equipped with smelling salts and a snifter of brandy). In 1889, Harrods became a limited company, and the board of directors, enjoying a boom in trade, decided that it was time to rebuild the entire site to provide premises 'of very substantial character'.

Harrods acquired additional neighbouring properties along the Brompton Road and commissioned C.W. Stephens as their architect. He had undertaken previous design work for Harrods and had worked for both the Belgravia Estate and the Cadogan Estate, designing ornate Queen Anne-style apartment buildings on several streets in the immediate vicinity of Harrods. The redevelopment of the store took place in incremental stages between 1901 and 1905, by which time it occupied an entire block, with each façade approximately 150 metres (492ft) in length. The long Brompton Road frontage gave Stephens the opportunity to design a building that was palatial in scale. All four sides were faced in pink-buff terracotta, supplied by Doulton's factory in Lambeth. The upper floors of the signature façade on the Brompton Road are an elaborate mixture of Baroque and French Second Empire (Cherry and Pevsner: 'majestic and flamboyant').[6] Above the three central bays is a pediment filled with a figure of Britannia attended by cherubs larking among cornucopias; and above that an octagonal Baroque dome with terracotta ribs, dormers and

49 Harrods department store.

lunettes. At street level, an impressive run of nineteen plate-glass display windows, interrupted only by two of the store's entrances, is given scale and proportion by a series of gently arched windows featuring Art Nouveau-style tracery. At first, the store occupied the first two floors, with income-generating flats ('Hans Mansions') above, accessed from entrances on Hans Road. The most expensive flats were massive, with fifteen rooms each. Before long, however, they fell victim to the store's success: by 1912, the need for more retail space led to the conversion of some of the flats on the Brompton Road frontage, and by 1927 the whole building was in commercial use.

The store's interiors were designed to be opulent and exclusive, with only the finest, richest materials. There was Travertine, Breccia and Carrara marble; Ancona walnut, mahogany, satinwood and oak fittings; ornate plasterwork on the ceilings and the capitals of the many interior piers and columns; Art Nouveau frescoes and mosaic flooring. The bakery was given a floral frieze and an ornate plaster ceiling with mouldings of female figures, flowers, fruit and medallions. The walls of the Meat Hall were adorned with murals of decorative ceramic tiling, plaques of stylised birds and fish, and frescoes of hunting scenes and trees. The ladies' fashion departments featured elaborate French Rococo plasterwork with Art Nouveau detailing on ceilings, columns and walls, while the Gentlemen's Lounge was done out in 'Tudorbethan' style, with carved oak panelling, a fireplace with a stone Tudor arch and a carved frieze with gryphons and scrollwork. And so on.

By 1912, Harrods had been to all intents entirely reconstructed, recognisable as today's building (though the elevations to Basil Street and Hans Crescent were partly rebuilt in the 1930s and the interiors have been serially refreshed). 'With its great breadth, imposing height, elaborate internal design', it represented 'a new urban monumentalism ... the icon, an embodiment of newness and modernity, which has come to define our sense of

50 Egyptian Hall, Harrods.

51 The seafood counter in Harrods' Fresh Market Hall.

what constituted a real department store.'[7] Harrods became an attraction for visitors from the provinces and the suburbs, 'and had the same sort of cultural resonance as railway stations and other festival sites such as fairs, exhibitions and sports stadia'.[8] Just as today, many visited without any real intention of buying, merely to gawp at the display of opulence and be able to relate the experience to their peers.

Harrods principal market was London's emerging petite bourgeoisie, which was still in the process of establishing a distinctive culture and identity for itself. Writing about American department stores of the same era, Alan Trachtenberg concluded that they 'stood as a prime urban artifact of the age, a place of learning as well as buying: a pedagogy of modernity'.[9] The same could be said of Harrods in the context of London's evolving social landscape: helping to fill the petite bourgeoisie's cultural uncertainties by linking status and good taste firmly to consumerism. The tricky part was that the affordable 'luxuries' offered by department stores were mostly mass produced and therefore inherently lacking cachet or distinction. In response, department store owners created 'a kind of spectacle out of the store, a spectacle which would endow the goods, by association, with an interest the merchandise might intrinsically lack'.[10] It meant that attending to the customer experience was critical.

For Harrods, this began with its big shop windows, with dioramas of upscale domesticity featuring carefully selected products. Inside, 'Goods were no longer hidden from view but were openly displayed on stands, showcases and glass cabinets, aided by clever lighting and strategically placed mirrors.'[11] The whole store took on a theatrical character, with sophisticated arrangements of merchandise 'staged' in exotic settings or presented in unexpected places. Drawing on the successful precedents of London's bazaars, shoppers were drawn in using techniques that had been introduced by the Great Exhibition, with displays of goods from around the world set amid representations of ancient Arabia, Hindu temples, Cairo markets, Turkish harems and Japanese gardens. The sense of the spectacular was underscored by the store's claim to be able to supply anything and everything. Harrods 1912 mail-order catalogue ran to 1,500 pages, with illustrations of more than 15,000 items.[12] The store's ability to fulfil special orders – aeroplanes, made-to-order yachts, pet elephants – was well publicised, enabling regular customers to associate themselves, albeit indirectly, with the truly wealthy. Luxurious facilities and personal services for shoppers were, meanwhile, another important part of the package. There was a banking hall, a Georgian-themed Grand Restaurant, a tea room, a ladies' hairdressing salon and spacious ladies' club rooms in neoclassical Adam style where female shoppers could rest and recuperate. Harrods services included life insurance, property sales, theatre tickets, railway and steamship reservations, and storage of clothing and personal effects.[13] Shoppers could spend all day in the store and have all their needs attended to in style.

More generally, department stores created new, modern identities for both middle-class and working-class women, by providing a space in which both had agency – the working-class woman as saleswoman, the middle-class woman as shopper.[14] The relative safety and cultivated propriety of department stores represented an important new space for middle-class women, an anonymous setting into which they could safely venture without chaperones.[15] The restaurants and tea rooms 'added another dimension to the experience and could become a destination of their own for groups of women to meet and socialise. Tea rooms acted as a sort of feminine counterpart to male urban spaces like the saloon or men's club.'[16] As such, stores like Harrods have been credited with initiating a broader cultural shift towards female emancipation. This did not prevent the store's large plate-glass windows being targeted by suffragettes in 1912 in their campaign to get the vote for women. And while the physical spaces of the department store were liberating for middle-class women, the home-centred consumerism of the sales floors helped to inculcate the stereotype of women as good mothers and good housekeepers, 'thus reinforcing the existing border within the growing middle class between working males and non-productive females'.[17] Misogyny soon came into play as well: the stereotype of the female shopper as lacking in self-control. 'Women's so-called "natural" role as consumers had a dark side: the medical diagnosis of kleptomania played on notions of women as irrational and at the mercy of their hormonal and emotional impulses.'[18]

Perhaps the most important aspect of class and gender relations instigated by Harrods and their immediate competitors was the creation of a new category of female employment, the shopgirl. Until the mid-1880s, Charles Harrod had refused to recruit women, believing that male staff would be more efficient and more reliable. But with the going rate of salaries for shopgirls just half or two thirds the rate for young male assistants, the Harrods workforce – window dressers, manicurists, bank tellers, waitresses, etc., as well as sales staff – steadily came to be dominated by women. By the turn of the century, the shopgirl had come to be identified in the popular imagination as a symbol of social change, representing mass consumption, metropolitanism and the possibilities of upward social mobility.[19] 'She is working class, unable to afford the latest fashions she sells, and yet she must know those styles thoroughly and speak the language of the middle class ... She represented the instability of class relations and the fluidity of public and private realms.'[20]

Running counter to conventional contemporary expectations about women's domestic roles and 'feminine' submissiveness, this was unsettling for the patriarchy. Many shopgirls ventured out into the city for leisure or simply to travel home after working late. The idea of single women out after dark was especially disconcerting to the Victorian mind. There was 'sauciness and immorality of the pavement among young girls', complained

Thomas Sutherst in 1884.[21] A mixture of masculine anxieties, prurient speculation and a few real examples fostered the idea of shopgirls being especially vulnerable to sexual exploitation and promiscuity. The shopgirl who capitalised on her good looks and sexuality for workplace advancement and social mobility was a common trope in contemporary musical comedies, films, magazine stories and plays. But at least while at work, Harrods shopgirls were subject to a strict and hierarchical managerial structure that was cushioned by a kind of benevolent paternalism, with a variety of staff social and sporting clubs, a staff newspaper and evening classes through which employees might gain the chance to move upward within the store's hierarchy. The sheer size of the store, however, led inexorably to the 'Americanisation' of store management along the lines that Gordon Selfridge had established in his Oxford Street store, following the principles of 'scientific management' developed by industrial process theorist and management consultant Frederick Winslow Taylor. To catch up, Harrods hired the newly established National Institute of Industrial Psychology after the First World War to transform the entire business process within the store into a rationalised system. 'In a word,' observes Laermans, 'they changed selling into an industry.'[22]

By the 1920s and 1930s, Harrods was firmly established as the flagship of a district that had itself become established as one of the capital's elite neighbourhoods. After the Second World War, the store was still held in high regard, but its glory had faded somewhat and its customers were constrained by postwar rationing. When the economy began to recover, Harrods faced growing competition from multiple chain stores. But it was still prestigious enough for it to become the focus of a fierce takeover battle, won in 1959 by the House of Fraser, a chain of suburban and provincial department stores, for whom Harrods was a trophy building. Fraser ran the Harrods store as a sort of supercharged version of its other stores (but retaining a strong residual whiff of Harrods' Edwardian snobbery), lowering its prices and capitalising on new market segments boosted by currency exchange rates and the Swinging London image. In line with international retailing trends, Harrods opened a boutique-within-a-store in 1967 to cater for the youth market – 'Way In', with dramatic lighting, pop music, prices in pounds rather than guineas, a separate street entrance and later opening and closing hours than the main store.[23]

The international economic recession of the mid-1970s that followed the quadrupling of crude oil prices by OPEC put paid to the steady growth of Britain's economy, but it triggered a radical change in consumer behaviour that played to Harrods' advantage. The system-shock of the recession prompted the baby-boom generation to shift its focus from radical idealism (that had been nurtured by the postwar settlement) to self-oriented materialism. A significant fraction of the boomer population began to save less, borrow more (taking advantage of credit cards), defer parenthood and generally surrender to the hedonism of lives infused with affordable luxuries: designer clothes, shoes and bags, expensive luggage, prestige watches and pens and such. Harrods came into its own again as a 'cathedral of consumption'. The ripple effect was felt along the Brompton Road and in nearby streets, such as Hans Crescent and Beauchamp Place, as Harrods, together with Harvey Nichols, attracted a flotilla of boutiques and designer clothing stores, all of them capitalising on London's new status as a fashion centre and international tourist destination.

Once again Harrods became a trophy property, this time at the hands of Egyptian billionaire Mohamed al-Fayed, who restored Harrods to private family ownership in 1985, just in time to take advantage of London's winner-takes-all neoliberal climate. Fayed introduced 'concept interiors' such as the Egyptian Hall and attracted flocks of wealthy customers, domestic and foreign. Particularly wealthy customers are able to take advantage of a discreet entrance at the rear of the store with lifts and escalators that take them directly to bespoke service in a large private viewing room on the top floor of the store. A sales staff of about 3,000 meanwhile attends to the needs of regular customers, with half as many again working in management and administration, maintenance, service and delivery. In 2010, Harrods became a trophy property for the third time, added to the real estate collection of Qatari Sheikh Hamad bin Jassim bin Jaber al-Thani, 'the man who bought London'. Other trophy properties owned or part-owned by al-Thani and his Qatar Investment Authority include London's Olympic Village, Heathrow Airport, the InterContinental hotel on Park Lane, Canary Wharf (Chapter 23), The Shard (Chapter 24) and the super-luxury apartment towers of One Hyde Park in Knightsbridge.

13 Admiralty Arch, Whitehall

ADMIRALTY Arch was the pivotal element in the development of London's royal ceremonial route from Buckingham Palace to St Paul's, linking the Mall with the Strand via Trafalgar Square and Charing Cross. It was built as part of a monumental ensemble that included the Queen Victoria Memorial, a spruced-up Buckingham Palace, and a widened and straightened Mall. Together, they were a physical manifestation of the nation's idea of itself at the moment when London had become the capital of the largest empire the world had ever seen. Admiralty Arch itself is 'among London's most distinguished and identifiable landmarks, and a very prominent example of the Edwardian Baroque tradition in British architecture'.[1]

For the first three quarters of the nineteenth century, London, with its mercantile roots and industrial complexion, had been generally indifferent to royal pageantry. But Queen Victoria's Golden Jubilee (1887) and Diamond Jubilee (1897) celebrations linked royal pageantry with empire just as the mood of the city was responding to a more expansive (and overtly jingoistic) imperial culture with its newly invented traditions.[2] When Queen Victoria died in 1901, the appetite for imperial symbolism and displays of royal pageantry reached a new pitch. The government quickly stepped in to establish a committee to consider how best to memorialise the queen (and, implicitly, to bolster the image and reputation of the monarchy under the playboy king – Edward VII – who had succeeded her). Step forward those among the intelligentsia and Tory press who had long complained that London appeared a poor second to Paris, Vienna, Rome, Berlin and even Brussels in terms of imperial grandeur. The time was ripe for London to acquire a set piece of urban design in triumphal style, incorporating a formal processional way.

The committee quickly decided that the national memorial should be in London, include a statue of the queen and be architectural in scale. Prime Minister Arthur Balfour, who sat on the organising committee, was an important advocate for 'some great architectural and scenic change'.[3] Another committee member, Colonial Secretary Joseph Chamberlain, was a strong advocate for having the scheme somehow express imperial unity. It was a persuasive argument, allowing the committee to decide that the colonies should bear some of the cost of the project. Within three months, it had settled on the site – in front of Buckingham Palace – and agreed on an outline plan comprising a wide space in front of the palace with a seated statue of the queen in the centre and a triumphal arch at the other end of the Mall, a fashionable tree-lined promenade along the north side of St James's Park. Five architects were invited to submit detailed plans. Aston Webb, whose high-profile commissions already included the Cromwell Gardens façade of the Victoria and Albert Museum (Chapter 10) and the Royal College of Science in Kensington, was announced as the winner. His successful entry included a semicircular *place* rather than a triumphal arch at the Charing Cross end of the Mall, having been advised that an arch would prove too expensive. Meanwhile, however, the Admiralty – busy expanding and equipping the navy in response to Germany's new naval laws – was keen to add to its new office space on Horse Guards Parade. By integrating Admiralty offices into an arch, the committee found a way to have the government pay for it. The entire vista along the widened Mall from the arch would be a memorial to Queen Victoria. 'By building a processional way, elevating the stature of Buckingham Palace, and enshrining the memory of Victoria, the memorial's planners inscribed the monarchy in a new way onto the landscape of London.'[4]

Webb's site plan was ingenious. His building consisted of a wing of offices on either side of a triumphal triple archway. The eastern and western façades of the office wings are curved, providing semicircular frontages facing, respectively, the seventeenth-century bronze equestrian statue of Charles I at Charing Cross, and the Mall with its vista to the Victoria Memorial. The asymmetrical curved frontages cleverly disguise the slight change of axis between the Mall and the statue, opening up the processional route from Buckingham Palace and providing an articulation with London's unintentional vista from Trafalgar Square down Whitehall towards the Palace of Westminster. At the same time, the scale of the Admiralty Arch building – it is four storeys tall and its concave frontages span more than 125 metres (410ft) – means that it acts as both a real and a symbolic barrier between the relatively calm and stately environs of the Royal Parks and St James's to the west and the bustle of Westminster and Covent Garden to the east. Dressed in Portland stone, the preferred facing for London's public buildings, it is Edwardian Baroque in style, the default architectural language of empire. Webb was himself 'an enthusiastic subscriber to the idea of developing an architectural style that would, he hoped, "be understood all over the world" as representing Britain's grand and noble achievements'.[5] Historic England describes the final product as 'Edwardian Mannerist Classicism'.

The three central arches of the building, two storeys in height, were furnished with huge ornamental wrought-iron and bronze gates, with the central archway initially reserved for royalty. These principal carriageways are flanked by two smaller pedestrian arches, and all five are separated by modified Corinthian columns. Above them is a windowless attic storey with a dedication to Queen Victoria in large bronze lettering. Pilasters with Corinthian capitals on the curved façade of each wing reinforce the building's neoclassical iconography, while its naval connections are signalled by stone figures of Navigation and Gunnery on the pedimented gable ends of the wings, which face the Mall. Edward VII did not live long enough to see the building completed, but it was ready just in time for George V's coronation in June 1911. With war looming, the Admiralty promptly moved in, installing a mixture of civil servants and naval officers, including the first sea lord and chief of naval staff, who was given an apartment in the north wing. During the course of two world wars and the ensuing Cold War, the building and its operations were an integral component of a tight-knit Whitehall complex that included the Old Admiralty Buildings, Admiralty House, the War Office, the Ministry of Defence and the Admiralty Citadel (a massive concrete Second World War bunker and air raid shelter, now an ivy-covered communications centre), as well as Downing Street. The ground beneath the complex is a warren of secret tunnels and passages, including, reputedly, one connecting Admiralty Arch to 10 Downing Street, more than a kilometre (half a mile) away. Admiral of the Fleet Sir Arthur Wilson was the first live-in sea lord to occupy the lavish apartment; others have included Lord Fisher, Earl Jellicoe, Earl Beatty and Earl Mountbatten. Winston Churchill, as first lord of the admiralty (the civilian head of the Royal Navy) between 1911 and 1915 and again in 1939–40, lived in Admiralty House on Whitehall, but worked in the Admiralty Arch building and wrote wartime speeches there. Ian Fleming, author of the James Bond novels, worked there in Room 39 as personal assistant to the director of the Naval Intelligence Division.

53 Admiralty Arch from the Mall.

While Admiralty Arch has to be understood as part of the Whitehall complex, it is even more important to recognise it as part of Webb's imperial ensemble. The Mall pre-dated its imperial role by 250 years, having been laid out along the edge of St James's Park as a tree-lined promenade for Charles II and his court. Webb widened the thoroughfare and replaced the avenues of trees on both sides. The distinctive red colour of the road surface cannot be blamed on Webb: it was repaved in the 1950s to give the effect of a permanent red carpet. For the Victoria Memorial, Webb designed an impressive monument: 2,300 tons of white Carrara marble piled 25 metres (82ft) high. Thomas Brock, who had already furnished statues of Queen Victoria for Bangalore, Belfast, Birmingham, Brisbane, Cape Town, Carlisle, Hove, Worcester and Carlton House Terrace, just off the Mall, was the sculptor – as indeed he was for the Gunnery and Navigation statues on Admiralty Arch. Pevsner drily notes that 'originality and daring must not be expected' of Brock,[6] but for size, ostentatious grandeur, allegorical symbolism and imperial swagger it was just what the public wanted, confirming Victoria as the maternal heart of the British Empire. It was widely referred to and understood as London's Imperial Memorial. Never again 'would London see such an overt and self-consciously imperial statement vis-à-vis architecture and urban master-planning as Webb's memorial to Queen Victoria'.[7]

A seated Victoria stares sternly down the length of the Mall, surrounded by allegorical figures and arrangements. Beneath her are personifications of Constancy and Courage. Behind and at the sides of the queen are sculptures representing Motherhood, Justice and Truth. The memorial is topped by a gilded bronze figure of Winged Victory and two sculpted eagles (which, according to Brock, 'since the time of the Romans have been symbols of "Empire"').[8] Around the base is a nautical-themed frieze with ships' prows, dolphins, mermaids and tritons; and the whole thing is surrounded by two semicircular marble fountain basins: 'an allegory of the sea which encompasses our island'.[9] Overlooking the fountains are figures representing the Army and the Navy (to embody Courage) and figures representing Art and Science. At the corners of the fountain basins are bronze sculptures of standing lions (representing Power) accompanied by representations of Peace, Progress, Agriculture and Labour. The overall effect 'was to transform the diminutive and dowdy Queen into an empress triumphant'.[10] Webb surrounded the memorial with a broad *circus*, with a semicircle of formal flower beds linking the *circus* to the Mall. Despite the large sums contributed by the colonies, their only overt representation took the form of elaborate Dominion Gates – stone columns and gilded wrought iron gates at the corners of the flower beds – Canada Gate leading to Green Park and Australia Gate on Spur Road, alongside St James's Park.

The backdrop to the whole ensemble was Buckingham Palace; but in comparison with the splendour of Admiralty Arch, the Mall and the Victoria Memorial, it was decidedly shabby. The palace's east wing, facing the memorial and the Mall, had only been added in 1847, but because it had been faced in soft Caen stone it had quickly blackened and deteriorated in London's heavily polluted air. As luck would have it, the memorial committee found itself with £60,000 of unspent funds (equivalent to nearly £9 million today) from public subscriptions for the memorial, and so were able to commission Webb, in 1912, to design a new façade for the east wing (Pevsner: 'a tasteful but insipid performance').[11] Webb was careful to retain the central balcony as a feature of the new façade, evidently encouraged by George V, who, like Edward before him, enjoyed public pomp and ceremony. The balcony was an important stage on which royalty could appear at moments of national crisis or celebration, waving at crowds assembled around the memorial. George had set the precedent after his own coronation in 1911 and wanted to be able to continue the performance.

Victory parades in 1919 and 1946 both passed through Admiralty Arch to reach the Mall and terminate at Buckingham Palace. But Queen Elizabeth's coronation in 1953 was the event that truly established both the invented tradition of balcony appearances by royalty and the primacy of Webb's processional way for important national occasions, such as the weddings of Prince Charles and Lady Diana Spencer (1981), Prince Andrew and Sarah Ferguson (1986) and Prince William and Kate Middleton (2011), the funeral of Princess Diana (1997), Queen Elizabeth's Platinum Jubilee (2022) and state funeral (also 2022), King Charles III's coronation (2023), the sovereign's annual Birthday Parade, and the Trooping of the Colour. Nevertheless, the semantic symbolism of the entire ensemble shifted significantly as the 'everyday imperialism' of the early twentieth century was displaced by the post-colonial sensibilities of the 1950s and 1960s.

By the 1980s, Webb's set piece had become less of a national reference point for British prowess and more of an item on the checklist of provincial and international tourists. At the same time, the symbolism of Admiralty Arch itself was inevitably debased, as the size of the Royal Navy shrank from 128,000 enlisted personnel in 1955 to fewer than 30,000 in 2020, with only twenty-one deepwater warships and ten submarines. The monumental building had become functionally unnecessary, as well as an unwelcome reminder of how weak British naval power had become in comparison with the past. The navy finally vacated its offices and the first sea lord's apartment in Admiralty Arch in 1994.

The building was refurbished in 2000 and occupied by Cabinet Office staff; but in 2010 it was put up for sale as part of the government's austerity drive to reduce Britain's debt after the 2008 international financial crisis. But in many ways the sale of the building was the end game of a broader sweep of privatisation of major national assets that had been initiated by the Thatcher administration in the 1980s and that included Jaguar, Rolls Royce, British Steel, British Petroleum, British Telecom, British Rail, British Airways, British Aerospace, British Gas, British Coal and Thames Water. By 2010, saleable government assets had been reduced to heritage real estate, such as Admiralty Arch. In 2012, Admiralty Arch was sold for just £60 million to Prime Investors Capital on a 250-year lease, and plans were agreed with Westminster City Council to convert the building into private apartments and a luxury hotel. In 2017, it was announced that the Hilton hotel chain would operate the property under its high-end Waldorf Astoria brand, and in 2022 the billionaire property developers David and Simon Reuben took over the lease. In addition to the five-star Waldorf Astoria hotel in the south wing, planned renovations include provision for several large private apartments (including a twelve-bedroom apartment valued at £150 million) and a private members' club in the north wing. Below ground, excavations have been carried out beneath Trafalgar Square to create a double-storey ballroom and event space, along with a swimming pool, spa and gym, with additional function rooms and event spaces underneath the Mall. In many ways, the building is emblematic of the way in which the institutional fabric of central London has been carved up, privatised and commodified.

UNDERGROUND
SANCTUARY.
"'Tis pleasant, through the loopholes of retreat,
To peep at such a world; to see the stir
Of the great Babel, and not feel the crowd;
To hear the roar she sends through all her gates
At a safe distance, where the dying sound
Falls a soft murmur on th' uninjured ear."
William Cowper.
THE SOONEST REACHED AT ANY TIME
GOLDERS GREEN
(HENDON AND FINCHLEY)
A PLACE OF DELIGHTFUL PROSPECTS

IV

METRO LONDON

THE twenty years of the interwar period were transitional between the rigidities of Victorian and Edwardian society and the radical changes of the postwar welfare state. It was also the period during which London became metropolitan in terms of governance and functionality, as well as in scale. As it grew dramatically in population and areal extent, so London became a seedbed for social change, characterised by increasing social mobility, the spread of consumerism and increasing levels of home ownership. The hedonism and consumerism of the Roaring Twenties were especially marked in London, carrying over into the 1930s, even as rural and industrial regions in the rest of the country experienced the worst of the Depression.

Meanwhile, the overcrowding and substandard housing of London's poorer districts were exacerbated by a general backlog in construction during the war and by the arrival of migrants from depressed regions in search of work. Public housing, combined with slum clearance, was to be the solution. The day after the Armistice in 1918, Prime Minister Lloyd George announced what came to be known as the Khaki Election, promising 'habitations fit for the heroes who have won the war'. A special study of the housing needs of working people had been commissioned in 1917 from the Liberal MP Tudor Walters, and his committee's report, published just as the war ended, led to the recognition that private enterprise would not be able to supply houses of sufficient quantity and quality at rents that working-class families

54 Golders Green, London Underground poster.

could afford. It paved the way for the Housing and Town Planning Act of 1919 and generous exchequer subsidies to local authorities for a crash programme of public housing. Women in the Labour Party meanwhile combined class and gender concerns in developing a social care agenda for the embryonic welfare state.[1] In London, the responsibility for housing and social welfare fell to the LCC, which had already established several pioneering inner-city public housing projects, including the Boundary Street Estate (Chapter 7). Following the recommendation of Tudor Walters' report to build as much as possible on cheap, undeveloped land on the urban fringe, the LCC's postwar housing policy was one of decentralisation, building 'cottage' estates of social housing on peripheral sites (such as the Downham Estate on the border between Lewisham and Bromley and the St Helier Estate in Morden), some even beyond the LCC boundary (such as the Watling Estate, near Edgware, and the Becontree Estate, the LCC's largest, with more than 27,000 homes built on cheap farmland between Barking and Dagenham). The LCC provided London with a county-wide government that was able to take a strategic approach not only to housing, but also to public utilities, transportation, education, health care and consumer protection. It was powerful, innovative and progressive, and its importance was symbolised by its new headquarters, County Hall, located almost directly across the Thames from the Palace of Westminster (Chapter 14).

Between 1919 and 1939, around 150,000 council homes were built in Greater London. But most of the new residential fabric was built by the private sector for owner-occupation. The feverish investment in speculative suburban housing estates – 'Metroburbia'[2] – was arguably so intense as to have starved other industries and other regions of capital. Altogether, there was an increase of nearly 50 per cent in the extent of urban land around London in the twenty-year period between the wars. Expansion took place in all directions, but especially in the northwestern sector, where in places the belt of interwar development extended for nearly 16 kilometres (10 miles). It was the growth of white-collar employment in central London, adding to the ranks of middle-income households, that did more than anything else to stimulate the development of these new residential suburbs. The population of clerical workers in Greater London increased almost three-fold over the course of the interwar period, while the number of people in the professions roughly doubled, as did the number of foremen, inspectors and supervisors. A massive expansion and reorganisation of the metropolitan transport system allowed them to commute to their jobs from the new suburbs. After the First World War, the Underground system extended its surface lines into suburban districts, in an attempt to attract additional passengers. By the early 1930s, the company's lines extended to new termini in Middlesex, Essex, Hertfordshire and Surrey. In 1933, the London Passenger Transport Board absorbed the entire system, together with all the independent and municipally operated railway, bus and tram services in the London area, thus providing an integrated metropolitan-wide system. Meanwhile, the merger of three railway companies into Southern Railway and the subsequent electrification of all its lines opened up an extensive new commuter hinterland to the south. By the outbreak of the Second World War, 2.5 million people were travelling by public transport across Greater London every day, keeping an estimated 250,000 people employed in the transport sector. In addition, increasing automobile ownership allowed developers to build profitably at greater distances from train stations and bus routes. With the mass production of simpler, smaller designs such as the Austin Seven (it had a seven-horsepower engine) the price of cars fell dramatically. Smaller cars were accessible to a much larger number of buyers and were popular in suburbia because their narrow wheelbases allowed them to be parked in the slender driveways at the side of semi-detached houses. The real cost of car ownership fell by over 40 per cent in the twelve years after 1924, and by 1939 there were half a million cars in the Greater London region.

Large quantities of land around London had become available for development at reasonable prices, as a result of falling agricultural prices and the break-up of landed estates, whose owners were unable to cope with death duties. The construction of new arterial roads helped to open up this land for building, while the government intervened to address the backlog of housing by providing cash to developers towards the construction of family homes. The putative intent was to provide for working-class households, but in practice it subsidised the sale of houses to middle-class buyers. Meanwhile, because of the rent controls that had been introduced during the First World War, building for owner-occupation was a much more attractive proposition for speculative developers than building for rent. Further government intervention came in the 1920s, in the form of tax relief on mortgage interest payments. Capital and finance were freely available from building societies, which had been flooded with money as people sought a safe haven for their savings after the financial crash of 1929. Suddenly cash-rich building societies were emboldened to drop their requirement for a deposit from 25 per cent of the purchase price to 10 or even 5 per cent, while extending mortgage repayment periods from fifteen years to thirty. House prices relative to incomes were lower than at any time before (or since), because the Depression had forced down the cost of both materials and unskilled and semi-skilled labour. On many of the larger estates, the cheapest semi-detached houses in the 1930s were priced at around £450 (equivalent to just £41,000 in 2023).

The result was a burst of ribbon development followed by a mushrooming of sprawl. Suburbanisation created a mosaic of speculative estates that engulfed pre-industrial village cores in the Home Counties, as well as London's Georgian exurbs and

Victorian and Edwardian suburbs. New suburbs surrounded railway and Tube stations, medieval churchyards, village greens, Jacobean manor houses and Georgian inns, while old market towns morphed into suburban shopping centres. Whereas Victorian and Edwardian suburban development had been dominated by compact, high-density housing and rectilinear street patterns, most of this interwar development was dominated by low-density garden suburbs, in which the semi-detached house was the predominant building type (Chapter 15). Curved streets and culs-de-sac were common, and houses generally stood further back in their plots, to give larger front gardens. The new suburbs were supported by hundreds of new local shopping parades, while consumerism and a retail revolution introduced national chain stores to suburban high streets. Changing patterns of recreation brought new cinemas, dance halls and cafés, along with new public houses with 'lounge' bars. Golf courses and tennis clubs appeared on the fringes of more affluent districts, while new bypasses attracted factories, petrol stations and huge roadside pubs.[3]

There were, of course, plenty of people who did not want to live in suburbia, or to have to commute into central London, while changing lifestyles meant that the extended families with domestic staff that had been characteristic of the Victorian and Edwardian middle classes were becoming a thing of the past. The growth of the metropolis drew in tens of thousands of single people, as well as many of these smaller middle-class households. The result was a proliferation of upscale mansion blocks, which offered an affordable and more flexible lifestyle in a fashionable format. Many were built near suburban Underground stations, while others, such as Dolphin Square (Chapter 16), appeared in central London. All offered the convenience of apartment living, with modern amenities in terms of heating, bathrooms and lavatories, and electric lighting. Many were quite luxurious, and at the top end of this new housing market were serviced flats, with their own social clubs, restaurants, tennis courts and swimming pools, as well as concierge services. Some offered twinned apartments: a large one for the main occupier and a smaller one for a servant. 'The servant problem solved', announced advertisements for Taymount Grange in Forest Hill.

Meanwhile, residential development of a much more mixed character took place around new or rapidly expanding industrial areas on or near the edge of the conurbation, as in the Lea Valley, Thameside and west Middlesex. By far the most important of the new industrial districts were in Northwest London, around Wembley, Willesden, Park Royal, Perivale and Greenford, and the most striking feature of London's new phase of industrialisation were the corridors along the Great West Road and Western Avenue, where many of the larger manufacturing firms – notably American-owned multinationals such as Firestone, Gillette, Trico and Hoover (Chapter 17) – built showpiece Art Deco buildings. Altogether, the 1920s and 1930s represent a relatively brief but critically formative period in the development of the metropolis.

THE
COUNTY HALL

14 County Hall, Lambeth

ONCE a symbol of metropolitan civic pride, the repurposed County Hall now stands as an uncomfortable reminder of Global London's free-for-all commercialism. As the headquarters of the London County Council (LCC) between 1922 and 1965, and then of the Greater London Council (GLC) between 1965 and 1986, it was a manifestation of London's independence and metropolitan identity. In its heyday it was the administrative centre of a powerful municipal government with a reputation for progressiveness and efficiency across a broad spectrum of urban affairs. By the late 1930s, the LCC had responsibility for town planning, building regulations, public housing, state schools and colleges, adult education, parks and open spaces, sewerage and drainage systems, hospitals and asylums, the fire brigade and ambulance services, public assistance, social services for children and the elderly, and a wide range of regulatory functions, including licensing of places of entertainment. Today, the building is occupied by hotels and tourist attractions.

Established in an era of idealism and social reform, the massive building on its prominent riverside site reflected the self-confidence of London as an important international commercial, manufacturing and financial centre in its own right. Unlike most other great cities

55 County Hall, Lambeth, detail.

of the world, London had not grown from a single commercial, ecclesiastical or administrative centre, nor had it been laid out to an overarching plan. Rather, London's growth had gradually converted a scattering of villages and parishes into mini-towns, which in turn grew into specialised districts – each with distinctive physical, economic and social characteristics – within a single functional metropolitan fabric. London became, famously, a 'city of villages'.[1] The political and administrative legacy was a multitude of independent districts. The creation of the LCC and, later, the GLC provided London with political and administrative cohesion and the chance, at last, for a unified, strategic approach to urban affairs. But across six decades, the buoyant municipal socialism of the LCC and GLC was a thorn in the side of Conservative governments at the national level, with County Hall an unwelcome visual reminder across the Thames from the Palace of Westminster. Margaret Thatcher's government put an end to the annoyance by peremptorily abolishing the GLC, leaving the metropolis divided and conquered, with no overall framework for metropolitan policies, effectively defenceless against the unwanted side effects of market forces and the competing and often conflicting policies of London's constituent boroughs.

London's administrative challenges have always run deep. The City of London Corporation was established in the city's ancient commercial core in the eleventh century, and it has fiercely guarded its rights and privileges ever since, even as the metropolis has grown around it. Immensely wealthy and powerful, it has always remained beyond the authority of parliament. Its interests are largely those of City banks and financial companies, and it is inherently undemocratic: votes in twenty-one of its twenty-five electoral wards are allocated to business corporations, rather than individual residents; the bigger the business, the larger the share of the vote. Beyond the City there was no central authority to oversee the development of essential services, nor was there any authority to take control in emergencies, such as epidemics or fires. As London grew and expanded, the need for basic municipal services, such as paving, water supply and street cleaning, was addressed piecemeal by parish vestries and ad hoc administrative bodies, smothering the capital in complexity and inefficiency. Twenty years after other British cities had been granted a reformed system of local governments elected by local ratepayers (the Municipal Corporations Act of 1835), *The Times* complained that London was 'rent into an infinity of divisions, districts and areas … Within the metropolitan limits the local administration is carried on by no fewer than 300 different bodies, deriving powers from about 250 different local Acts.'[2] The parish of St Pancras alone had twenty-one paving and lighting boards and nine hundred unelected commissioners.

> Even single streets were divided, often longitudinally, and paved and cleaned at different times under different jurisdictions … Sewerage and main drainage were administered by eight Crown-appointed commissions with no less than 1,065 honorary commissioners. Building regulation, since 1844, was vested in a Metropolitan Building Commission employing fifty-two surveyors appointed by the JPs in quarter sessions, whilst water supply was in the hands of the eight private companies. Large public works projects, such as sewers and roads, were often carried out by central government agencies … The metropolis was in a state of total chaos.[3]

In 1855, the capital's plethora of local boards was reduced to just thirty-eight, with the Metropolitan Board of Works (MBW) given responsibility for local by-laws, road building and improvement, sewer construction, and building regulations and plans. The MBW subsequently took control of the London Fire Brigade and acquired powers to create parks and open spaces and to take over and demolish insanitary housing. But it steadily became corrupt and inefficient, unfit for purpose. The board

> consisted of small-business and professional men; it was part-time and unpaid, and members often saw life from their own narrow perspective. It was almost inevitable that they should blur the distinction between private interest and public responsibility. The end came in a series of scandals concerned with the disposal of surplus land, which made it easy for its staff to make corrupt deals.[4]

The key reform came with the Local Government Act of 1888, which created a new national administrative geography of counties and county boroughs. The LCC was one of the counties.[5] In 1899 the London Government Act replaced the vestries with twenty-eight metropolitan boroughs as administrative subdivisions within the LCC. London's new boroughs transcended the traditional insularity of the vestries, but established a new geopolitical framework for the metropolis that reinforced its polycentric geography. The attendant flush of local civic pride and competitiveness among the boroughs saw the appearance of new town halls, police stations, fire stations and civic amenities across the landscape.

The LCC, meanwhile, set about planning its own flagship building. The boardroom and office accommodation that the LCC had inherited from the MBW in Spring Gardens, off Trafalgar Square, was cramped in size and widely regarded as insufficiently distinguished in appearance. Finding a site of sufficient size and centrality for a new building was not easy, but by 1906 the LCC had acquired a total of 2.2 hectares (5½ acres) on the south bank of the Thames, next to Westminster Bridge. The site's previous owners – Lambeth Borough Council and the Ecclesiastical Commissioners – had tenants that included a Crosse & Blackwell factory and miscellaneous workshops, stables, wharves and houses. By 1908 the LCC was ready to hold a competition for the design of its new headquarters on the cleared site, specifying a preference for an 'English Renaissance' style. As with many of London's important public buildings, the competition provoked a great deal of commentary and discussion, often heated. A plain scheme was attractive to members of the Municipal Reform movement, with their anxiety not to be seen to be extravagant; but everyone else recognised that the building had to be able to hold its own in comparison with the City of London's Guildhall and the larger town halls that had recently been erected in provincial cities.

Ralph Knott, a twenty-nine-year-old assistant in Aston Webb's office, won the competition, beating ninety-eight other entries, including submissions by leading architects of the day, such as Edwin Lutyens, Aston Webb and Reginald Blomfield. Construction began in 1912, but was interrupted by the First World War; the building was officially opened by King George V in 1922 (though construction continued into the 1930s).[6] 'Now London has, at last, a building in which its governing authority will be housed worthily,' observed the *Westminster Gazette*.[7] The *Workers' Dreadnought*, edited by Sylvia Pankhurst, was less impressed:

> London's County Hall is a building of costly grandeur. We admire fine architecture, we know that wealthy modern civilization is capable of producing still greater and more beautiful structures than this without undue effort. Nevertheless, one thinks of the 'delightful members' terrace' and the marble halls of the LCC's new residence with disgust, because one recalls London's many homeless families and its innumerable insanitary dwellings.[8]

When the unfinished building was opened, it had cost just over £4 million (equivalent to £187 million in 2023).

56 County Hall from the Victoria Embankment.

Knott's neoclassical composition in Portland stone stands on a plinth of grey Cornish granite. The best view of the building is from the Victoria Embankment, across the river (though the London Eye, a massive observation wheel, now rudely intrudes on the northernmost corner of the building). The middle range of this western façade is its principal feature: a broad colonnaded crescent, its ends squared off by six-storey pavilions with their own Ionic columns. On either side of the crescent are five-storey wings with a double-storey range of dormer windows set in a distinctive, red-tiled mansard roof that is punctuated by tall stone chimneys. It is all topped off with a copper-sheathed spire above the mid-point of the central crescent. This western façade is one of four blocks that form an approximate rectangle enclosing internal courtyards, with the council chamber placed at the heart of the building. The eastern façade lacks the colonnaded crescent and instead has an elaborate screen projecting slightly from the main body of the building, with ten Ionic columns and a central pedestrian doorway. 'Set between pavilions similar to those flanking the riverfront Crescent, it matches the Crescent in width, as Aston Webb suggested it should, to distinguish externally the "county hall" part of the building from the "county offices" part.'[9] The shorter northern and southern façades repeat the basic features of the administrative 'county offices' wings, except that the southern block, which faces the approach to Westminster Bridge, is punctuated by a great vaulted tunnel of stone arches that lead to the Members' Courtyard. Pevsner calls it 'frankly operatic'.[10]

The interior of the building was a physical manifestation of metropolitan bureaucracy, with more than 8 kilometres (5 miles) of corridors and hundreds of offices, access to which was carefully stratified according to the needs and status of different categories of 'black-coated workers'.[11] The size and decoration of the rooms allocated to the council's officers reflected the hierarchical structure of the bureaucracy. The architect, the chief clerk, the chief education officer and the comptroller all had large oak-panelled offices featuring elaborate chimneypieces.

57 County Hall, eastern elevation.

Their subordinates occupied successively smaller and less well-appointed spaces, culminating in offices with lightweight partitions, the walls of the corridors distempered in grey, with cream painted woodwork. The spaces occupied by elected members of the council were given rich treatment in neoclassical style. The Main Committee Room, with its central barrel-vaulted ceiling, featured large marble fireplaces with recessed carved oak surroundings, a carved acanthus cornice and a generous amount of plaster moulding. Other committee rooms were similarly fitted in neoclassical style, with elaborate red, yellow and white marble fireplaces, fancy oak panelling, and ceilings ornamented with scrolled heart bands and floral motifs in moulded plaster.[12] The women elected to the council were afforded especially fine surroundings, decidedly symbolic in view of the fact that the first women elected to the council had been debarred by the courts. In the 1889 elections, Charles Beresford-Hope challenged the right of Lady Sandhurst to sit as a member of the council on the grounds that she was a woman. Following a court case and an appeal, Sandhurst's election was declared illegal and Beresford-Hope took the seat for Brixton. After that, no women sat on the LCC until the Qualification of Women (County and Borough Councils) Act was passed in 1907, just as County Hall was being designed. Women were given their own entrance, a panelled hall with an inlaid marble floor that led up to cloakrooms and to the Lady Members' Room and a Lady Members' Visitors' Room, both finished in oak, with marble chimneypieces and panels of silk tapestry.

Architecture cognoscenti were in agreement that although County Hall was of no great architectural distinction, it was at least good enough to warrant their critique. They struggled to fit it into the accepted taxonomy of styles and lineages, describing it loosely as Edwardian Baroque or Free Classic. C.H. Reilly, himself a competitor in the design competition, observed that it 'belongs neither to the English classical tradition nor to the

English Gothic. If one had to assign it an ancestry one would say it came from the Low Countries by way of Mr Norman Shaw.' Knott himself said that it 'may perhaps be best described as a free treatment of English Renaissance'.[13] But Londoners were generally pleased with the building, glad to have a focus for the civic pride that attended the LCC's progressive policies. Herbert Morrison, leader of the LCC between 1934 and 1940, saw it as an expression of the power of municipal government and thought it brought an impression of modernity to public administration.[14] The popular press was uncritically enthusiastic, while *The Times* thought the building was 'in every way worthy of the great municipality which has grown up round the historic capital of the Empire'.[15]

For more than sixty years, County Hall was the nerve centre for facilitating, managing and reimagining London's development. The first LCC election, in 1889, had resulted in a majority coalition known as the Progressives, a group allied with the national Liberal Party, but including Independents, Radicals and Fabians. Following the example of progressive municipal administrations in Glasgow, Manchester and Birmingham, they placed great emphasis on the need for municipal enterprise, earning them the label of 'gas and water socialists'. Their platform introduced many of the elements of municipal socialism that were to transform the landscape of the metropolis in the interwar and postwar periods. One of the Progressives' first strategies was to buy out and eliminate London's private water companies. The LCC's impact on the physical face of London was immediate and decisive, as it launched a major improvement scheme, laying out Aldwych between 1902 and 1905, demolishing a web of old streets and carving out the Kingsway, with its underpass to take electric trams. By the outbreak of the First World War, the LCC's tram system was carrying 260,000 passengers a day. Other early infrastructure improvement projects included rebuilding six bridges over the Thames and constructing vehicular tunnels under the river at Blackwall and Rotherhithe, and pedestrian tunnels at Greenwich and Woolwich.

Meanwhile, the LCC had taken over the responsibilities of the London School Board (in 1904), giving it a major role in the everyday lives of Londoners throughout the metropolis. Other initiatives – especially the pursuit of a broad spectrum of social and cultural policies – were less successful. The evangelical moralism of the Radicals in the Progressive coalition had been expressed in a proliferation of regulations and inspectorates for everything from midwifery and the protection of infants and children to lodging houses, pubs, music halls, street markets, workplace health and safety, and public comportment in municipal parks and gardens: attempts to 'manage other people's lives', as Susan Pennybacker put it.[16] Such policies led to the erosion of popular support, and the Progressives were duly ousted from office in 1907, defeated by the Municipal Reformers, a conservative group that held office until 1934. As Elain Harwood noted, the Progressives had unwittingly rehearsed the same issues that led to the GLC's abolition in 1986.[17]

In 1934, the Labour Party won control of London and held on to power until the LCC was absorbed into the GLC in 1965; and Labour won three of the six elections to the GLC before its abolition in 1986.[18] County Hall's principal legacies from that period were in terms of housing and town planning. Concern over sprawl prompted the LCC to allocate £2 million over three years to assist the new metropolitan boroughs in the purchase of open spaces, offering to pay up to half of the cost of any land selected 'to provide a reserve supply of public open spaces and of recreational areas and to establish a green belt or girdle of open space lands not necessarily continuous, but as readily accessible from the completely urbanised area of London as practicable'.[19] The policy was attractive enough to prompt the passage of the Green Belt (London and Home Counties) Act 1938, formally empowering (but not funding) local authorities to buy land to keep it open as part of a green belt. It was too little, too late, and it was in any case sidelined by the outbreak of war. But it nevertheless established both concept and precedent for the planned redevelopment and management of postwar London.

The same concern over sprawl contributed to the LCC's move away from building social housing in the form of garden suburbs (though a more compelling factor was Labour voters' unhappiness at the prospect of being decanted to distant suburban council estates). Tenement-style council housing was rebranded by LCC architects in County Hall as 'Modern Flats'. The new orthodoxy was for compact estates of four- or five-storey blocks of flats, a formula that was to carry over to the council-housing boom after the Second World War. The Oaklands Estate in Clapham was the first of the LCC's 'modern' designs, with long horizontal access galleries and enclosed staircases with futuristic wrap-around corner windows. The largest was the White City Estate, built on the site of the Franco-British Exhibition of 1908, with 1,842 flats in forty-nine blocks, along with shops and sites for churches, clinics and schools. It followed the *Zeilenbau* principles of interwar German Modernism, with most of the blocks running in parallel north–south strips, with alternating bands of green space and service yards, so that most rooms received either morning or afternoon sunlight.[20]

During the Second World War, the LCC charged its chief architect, John Forshaw, with the job of collaborating with Patrick Abercrombie, professor of Town Planning at University College London, to prepare a strategic plan for the metropolis. Before the war was over, Abercrombie had published his own extended version; after the war, underpinned by the radical legislation of the incoming Labour-controlled parliament, it was to become County Hall's blueprint for reframing the metropolis. Abercrombie and Forshaw wanted to preserve the distinctive 'village' character of the metropolis, while simultaneously erasing slums, controlling sprawl and easing traffic congestion. The *County of London Plan*, published in 1943, was cleverly conceived to achieve all these objectives. Slums would be eradicated in a series of local comprehensive redevelopment programmes. The Luftwaffe, of course, had already made a start on the clearance phase. A hierarchy of new roads and highways was proposed – not only to relieve traffic congestion, but also to give definition and shape to the communities they separated, with a green belt about 8 kilometres (5 miles) deep, separating the existing metropolitan region from an 'Outer Country Ring'. City-dwellers and suburbanites would all have access to this green space by way of riverside walks, footpaths, bridle tracks, green lanes, bicycle trails and parkways. Finally, a series of ten New Towns, each accommodating between 30,000 and 60,000 people, would be established beyond the Outer Country Ring to provide new industrial spaces and accommodate a workforce of 'overspill' population from the thinned-out inner-London slums. Industry would be banned from inner London and encouraged to set up in the New Towns, so that they would be self-contained, and not simply dormitory towns.[21]

In the radical spirit of the welfare state established by the post-war Labour government, County Hall's Architects' Department was able to put London on the map as one of the world's leading centres of progressive public housing: a striking expression of what Owen Hatherley has called the 'Red Metropolis'.[22] The architects in County Hall were genuinely idealistic, many of them adhering to strong socialist – if not communist – ideals. They were famously split between fans of hard-line Le Corbusian high-rise solutions and those of the 'New Humanism' of Swedish welfare-state housing in Stockholm suburbs that had inspired them on their study tours. By the mid-1950s, public housing had become a political numbers game, with high-rise solutions preferred (and subsidised) by the central government. Over the next twenty years, County Hall's Architects' Department transformed London's townscapes, building and commissioning a mixture of mid-rise and high-rise housing projects, some of which, such as Alton West in Roehampton and Balfron Tower in Poplar, were instantly iconic – in architectural circles, at least. After the LCC's housing stock and building programme were inherited by the GLC in 1965, it embarked on an accelerated programme of high-rise and slab-block combination estates, along with a New Town-sized development at Thamesmead (Chapter 21), 16 kilometres (10 miles) east of County Hall.

County Hall's administration now covered an area of 1,595 square kilometres (616 square miles), compared with the 303 square kilometres (117 square miles) of the LCC's jurisdiction. The GLC had been created in response to the realisation that London had once again outgrown its existing local government framework and required a new metropolitan-wide authority to guide and coordinate its development. In the spirit of the times – it was the Golden Age of heroic urban planning[23] – its overall development strategy was based on a massive urban motorway programme, with three concentric motorway rings and inter-connecting spokes: broadly as envisaged by Abercrombie. It was met with strong grass-roots opposition in the form of a 'Homes Before Roads' movement. The Ringway scheme was abandoned in 1973, but the outer ring did go ahead and was duly opened in 1986 as the M25 orbital motorway, becoming a key framing element for Greater London, with its own distinctive landscapes, as chronicled in Iain Sinclair's *London Orbital*: 'opened in a spirit of jingoistic triumphalism, [it] rapidly declined into a service road for toxic landfill, somewhere to shift an earlier era's mess; the rubble of asylums and hospitals, munitions factories and firing ranges. The road gave access to new Legoland housing developments.'[24]

Meanwhile, even though many of the GLC's powers and responsibilities had been devolved to the enlarged and strengthened set of metropolitan boroughs within its jurisdiction, it remained both powerful and influential. Its policies and pronouncements were not always congruent with those of the central government, and things reached a low point over the first half of the 1980s, when the western façade of County Hall was used to hang huge posters featuring opposition slogans that could be seen from the Palace of Westminster. The Thatcher administration, irked by the GLC's social policies, argued against the case for a metropolis-wide authority, suggesting that it was an unnecessary layer of government, and therefore inefficient and wasteful. The GLC was duly abolished in 1986. When Tony Blair's Labour-controlled parliament reinstated a metropolis-wide administrative body in 2000 in the form of a mayoralty and a London Assembly – the Greater London Authority (GLA) – it was effectively a scaled-down version of the GLC, its reduced circumstances signalled by its rental of a modestly sized office building near Tower Bridge (the landlord was Kuwait's sovereign-wealth fund). In 2022, the GLA moved to the Crystal at the Royal Docks, an office and exhibition space it had purchased from Siemens' urban development division.

The abolition of the GLC left County Hall redundant. A 'residuary body' was set up to dispose of the GLC's assets, but the question of possible future uses for the iconic building, which embodied so much of the metropolis's identity, was contentious. Disagreements and legal manoeuvrings, including two public inquiries, were eventually resolved by a fudged ruling by the secretary of state that allowed for the possibility of commercial and residential uses. The building was then sold off for a fraction of its value to Shirayama Shokusan, a Japanese investment company that has presided over its redevelopment as a tourist complex. It is now home not only to two hotels (a budget Premier Inn and a five-star Marriott Hotel), a health club and several restaurants, but also to tourist attractions, including the London Sea Life Aquarium, the London Eye's booking office and visitor centre, a children's 'funscape' (Shrek's Adventure) and a kitsch horror show (the London Dungeon): Mrs Thatcher's revenge.

What had been established, in Herbert Morrison's words, as a 'workshop of administration'[25] and become emblematic of London's pioneering municipal socialism has swiftly degenerated into 'the only part of the South Bank where you will seldom see Londoners'.[26]

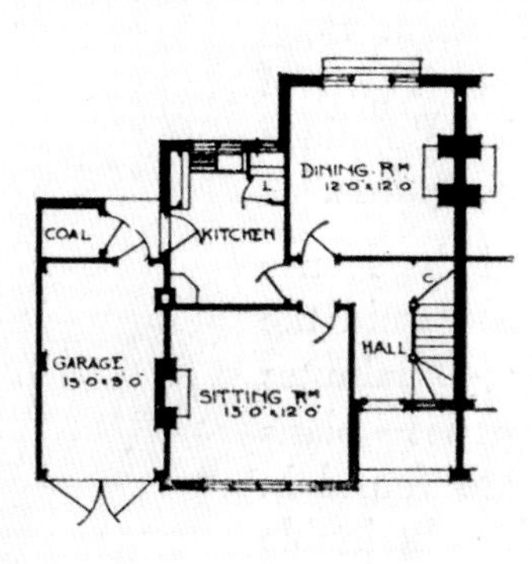

TYPE "A"

These attractive Semi-Detached Houses, each standing in a plot with frontage of 35 feet and a depth of about 125 feet have been erected in Woodside Close, facing a permanent open space and within 3 minutes' walk of station and a minute of the shops. Also in the corner of the Close and south of Railway fronting the Drive.

The properties are constructed in brick with red tile roof, white shingled elevation and oak half timbering.

There is a Built-in Garage with a covered way Coal Store. Tiled Kitchen. Leaded Glass Windows in Crittall Frames, Wired for Electric Light and ample number of Power and Gas Points. Tiled Bathroom with enclosed bath. Main Drainage.

An enlarged "A" type is also available in Woodside Close with the kitchen extended in line with the Dining Room rear wall and thereby also enlarging the first floor third Bedroom, the price being £900 Freehold.

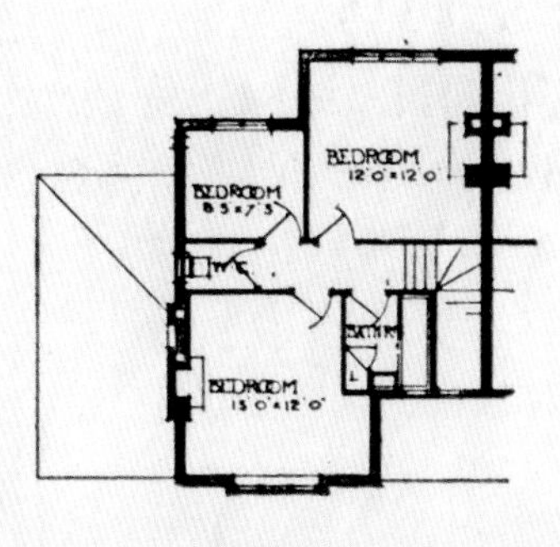

£875 FREEHOLD

TOTAL DEPOSIT £25

NO ROAD CHARGES

NO STAMP DUTIES

15 Dunroamin, Amersham

THE semi-detached homes on The Drive, The Green, Highfield Close, Woodside Road, Grimsdells Lane and Green Lane in Amersham were built in the 1930s, at the outer limit of London's Underground system. Examples of the stereotypical interwar speculatively built 'Dunroamin' semi-detached house,[1] they represent the high-water mark of interwar suburbanisation that, between 1921 and 1937, added a million and a quarter people to the area within a 40 kilometre (25 mile) radius of County Hall.[2] At the same time, the population of inner districts (as represented by the LCC area) declined by almost half a million.

This explosive centrifugal growth was the product of several intersecting factors. Suburbia's pioneer households came from an essentially new class of salaried white-collar occupations. They were enabled by easy loans and tax relief on mortgage repayments, and encouraged by the construction of new arterial roads, the availability of mass-produced motor cars, and the convenience of extended rail and Underground services. The builders and developers of suburbia, for their part, were assisted by the availability of cheap land and the relatively low cost of labour and materials. Home ownership was promoted by the government as a 'bulwark against Bolshevism': defending the property system by giving as many people as possible a stake in it, thereby defusing political radicalism. Developers, estate agents and local banks meanwhile promoted a narrative that cast home ownership as the normal aspiration for a respectable

58 Advertisement for homes on the Weller Estate, 1930.

family, something worth making sacrifices and going into long-term debt for. Few local authorities had acquired a professional planning staff in time for the ensuing suburban housebuilding boom. As a result, almost all this interwar growth took place without the benefit of land-use planning, spilling out across the countryside and snaking along arterial roads.

Influenced by garden-suburb ideals promoted by the likes of Raymond Unwin,[3] London's outlying suburbs represented a new pattern of building, with culs-de-sac, avenues and closes, rather than straight streets; and with semi-detached houses, rather than terraces of stock brick:

> There would be a neat front garden with perhaps a hedge and a formal flower bed, and a back garden with its own vegetable plot. Building styles harked back to bygone days: mock-Tudor houses with exposed wood beams on the outside and period metalwork details inside, or red-brick and clay tiles reminiscent of Jacobean times, or a pebbledash finish that gave the house a cottagey, stippled look.[4]

As the distinguished social historian F.M.L. Thompson noted, the new suburbs were the setting for the mass fulfilment of long-standing middle-class ideals of individual domesticity and group-monitored respectability. They were settings for the development of new ways of life that were marked by an increasing segregation of home and work, an intensified demarcation of public versus private worlds, and a sharpening of the distinction between male versus female roles.[5] Semi-detached suburbia also propagated a new and pervasive competitive consumerism, its houses and driveways effectively becoming giant display cabinets for consumer goods. Altogether, the growth of London's suburbs fundamentally changed the character of the metropolis within the space of just twenty years. Long-distance commuting became part of London life, with suburbia providing a mundane backdrop to the cosmopolitan bustle of London's central districts. It was variously pilloried, satirised and romanticised. For some, it was an escape from the noise, congestion and cramped rented accommodation of the city proper. For others, it was not so much an escape as an arrival: to a semi-rural idyll, to elevated social status and to a semblance of bourgeois privacy.[6]

Amersham's development as a commuter suburb was largely a product of the Metropolitan Line's real estate subsidiary, the Metropolitan Railway Country Estates Ltd (MRCE). By 1918, the Metropolitan Line ran from Baker Street in central London through Neasden and Wembley and out to Harrow, Pinner, Northwood, Rickmansworth, Amersham and Chesham, with a spur to Uxbridge. The MRCE was created to develop suburban estates within walking distance of the stations along the line, thus generating the highest possible volume of commuter traffic for the parent company. The result was 'Metro-Land': Northwest London's sector of semi-detached suburbia.[7] The MRCE's annual guidebook, *Metro-Land*, featured glowing descriptions of the villages and countryside along the way, special articles for ramblers, lists of local amenities, colour plates (a rarity at that time) of picturesque vistas with beaming homeowners surrounded by rolling countryside and, most important of all, a section that provided details of the purchase costs and utility rates of houses, the distance of new housing estates from the Baker Street terminus and the frequency of the train service. Most editions carried advertisements for the Abbey Road Building Society (later to become the Abbey National), a fast-growing new institution that helped finance the Metro-Land boom. *Metro-Land* magazine was very effective in propagating a seductive image of beautiful countryside that just happened to have plenty of new houses with every modern convenience. The reality, of course, was that the creation of Metro-Land destroyed the very thing – open countryside – that was supposed to be its chief attraction.

Many of the MRCE's developments were on 'surplus' land that had been acquired by the parent company in constructing its railway operations. Other railway companies were required by law to sell off land not required for railway operations, but the Metropolitan had managed to have clauses inserted in the 1885 Metropolitan Railway Act that allowed it to grant building leases on its surplus land. In Amersham, the MRCE had to purchase additional land, acquiring a 78 acre (31.5 hectare) site in 1929 from a family of brewers in Old Amersham (the Weller family) for £18,000 (equivalent to just over £1.4 million in 2023). Plans were developed for more than 500 houses, with a parade of shops closer to the station. By 1930 the first few streets had been laid out, and by 1931 purchasers were being invited either to acquire a plot and build to their own design, or to buy a completed house from one of the small range of designs – A, B, C or D – that had been developed by MRCE. The 'A' model was a two-bedroom semi-detached home constructed in brick, with oak half-timbering and a red tile roof. There were two reception rooms and a kitchen on the ground floor, and two bedrooms, a dressing room, tiled bathroom and separate toilet upstairs. The houses had leaded glass windows in fashionable metal Crittall frames, several power points and an integral garage. Advertisements in London newspapers asked:

> Why not live at Amersham? On the Weller Estate … amid glorious Chiltern scenery, yet only 40 minutes from Town. Delightful labour-saving residences available, offering every convenience and comfort. Good garden; liberal frontage; spacious garage. Without question the finest value available. 500 feet above sea level; 3 minutes to station; no road charges; no stamp duties.[8]

They could be purchased with a £25 deposit on the asking price of £875 (equivalent to £2,100 and £76,250, respectively, in 2023). They were featured prominently in the 1932 edition of *Metro-Land* magazine, along with the four-bedroom semi-

59 Type 'A' homes, The Drive, Amersham.

detached model 'B' (£985), the three-bedroom semi-detached model 'C' (£895) and the four-bedroom detached model 'D' (£1,200). Customers' varied preferences and budgets dictated that most of the curved avenues and short streets on the Weller Estate ended up with a mixture of models, providing a sense of individuality within what soon grew into a low-density development with the kind of village-style open spaces that characterise the mosaic of garden suburbs that carpet outer London.

Altogether, more than 2,300 houses were built in Amersham between 1921 and 1931, most of them contributing to the 'semi-detached suburbia' of outer London, but with some distinctively larger new detached houses in 'Stockbroker Tudor' style along Devonshire Avenue and Hervines Road, just to the west of the Weller Estate. Set in ample grounds, they are fragments of a 'Cocktail Belt' that is a manifestation of the fine-tuned segregation of social classes that characterises London's suburban geography. Cocktail Belt homes were typically the bespoke product of small local builders, but most of the 600,000 or so private-sector homes built across Greater London in the interwar period were produced speculatively by a booming industry that was itself transformed by the scale of demand.[9] The building industry was exceptionally easy to enter, since working capital was readily available and equipment needs were minimal. A large number of new speculative housebuilding firms came into existence. Some were created by estate agents or surveyors who seized the opportunity to become involved more directly in the suburban boom; other entrepreneurs had little or no previous connection with housebuilding and so were liable to find that ease of entry to the industry was matched by probability of exit. Rather quickly, the more successful firms became ever larger; by the mid-1930s, nine of the top ten UK builders were London based: New Ideal Homesteads, Henry Boot, Wates, Taylor Woodrow, Davis Estates, Wimpey, Richard Costain & Sons, G.T. Crouch and John Laing & Sons.

The inexorable logic of scale economies and standardisation led to homes designed around a 'universal plan' consisting of two-storey houses with two ground-floor rooms (a 'lounge' or sitting room and a dining room), a kitchen and entrance hall, and upstairs, three bedrooms, a bathroom and a toilet. The bathroom and toilet were typically above the kitchen, and the smallest bedroom was typically above the entrance hall. MRCE's Types A, B, C and D models were all variations of the universal plan. With such a dominant and ubiquitous basic configuration, consumers were left to establish their social status and express their distinction through the minor details of the house itself and its contents. They were served by popular magazines such as *Good Housekeeping* and *Woman and Home*, and by the annual Ideal Home Exhibition at Olympia in West Kensington, where the big firms exhibited mock-ups of fully furnished rooms and consumers were introduced to new products such as vacuum cleaners, electric irons, electric kettles, toasters and the Teasmade. Builders such as Laings, Costain and Wimpey would fully furnish a show house on each of their estates and supply the names of the stores from which the items could be purchased.

Developers did their best to avoid the dreaded uniformity that was characteristic of suburban council estates. If the semi-detached house built to the universal plan could be made to look detached, so much the better. The front doors of semis could be set at the two outer corners of the block, while hipped roofs could emphasise the separation of adjacent pairs. And while interior layouts might conform to the universal plan, exterior detailing could be finely differentiated to exploit marginal symbols of social distinction. Double-storey bays, tile-hung bays and decorative boundary walls easily lent themselves to minor variations, as did door and window treatments, building materials and finishes. In the hands of speculative builders, this often degenerated into sentimentalised and hybridised neo-Tudor and pseudo-Jacobean styles. The result was what cartoonist and critic Osbert Lancaster memorably characterised as 'Bypass Variegated'.

London's semi-detached suburbia has always attracted mixed reviews. Clearly there were hundreds of thousands of households that voted with their feet, suggesting that the speculative builders of the 1920s and 1930s had somehow got it right, and were attuned to the tastes of the British middle class and able to meet its physical, material, emotional and symbolic needs.[10] The novelist and prominent social commentator J.B. Priestley was positive – if somewhat supercilious – in his writing about suburbia, asserting that 'nearly all Englishmen are at heart country gentlemen' and that 'The suburban villa enables the salesman or the clerk, out of hours, to be almost a country gentleman.'[11] He praised the 'miles of semi-detached bungalows, all with their little garages, their wireless sets, their periodicals about film stars, their swimming costumes and tennis rackets and dancing

shoes', because they were 'essentially democratic'.[12] Similarly, J.M. Richards, an architectural critic, saw suburbia as the epitome of contented domesticity, 'each individual Englishman's idea of his home, except for the cosmopolitan rich, a minority of freaks and intellectuals and the very poor'.[13] Poet Laureate John Betjeman immortalised 'Metroland' in his postwar BBC documentary that romanticised the mundane landscape seen on a Tube ride from Baker Street to Amersham.

Others among the intelligentsia were alarmed by the accelerated urbanisation of the countryside and what they regarded as the cultural disaster of suburbia. Class antagonisms played their

60 Type 'A' semi-detached homes and 'D' detached home, Woodside Close, Amersham.

part. After all, the Berkshire, Buckinghamshire, Hertfordshire, Essex, Kent and Surrey countryside that had hitherto been the preserve of an aristocratic and upper-middle-class elite was now being invaded by the middle classes. Sprawling urbanisation came to be portrayed as the cause of rampant speculation, dreary streets and lifeless communities: a despoiler of the heritage (just *whose* heritage was only ever implied) of rural Britain. Patrick Abercrombie, who had founded the Council for the Preservation of Rural England in 1926 to campaign against sprawl and protect the symbolic value of the countryside (and who was soon to author the strategic plan for the County of London) described the semi-detached house type as 'perhaps the least satisfactory building unit in the world'.[14] The literati of the era took a similar line in describing suburbia, whether real or fictional. George Orwell wrote of 'labyrinths of meanly decent streets, all so indistinguishably alike, with their ranks of semi-detached houses, their privet and laurel hedges and plots of ailing shrubs at the crossroads'.[15]

Architects and planners were especially patronising, expressing thinly veiled contempt for the taste culture of the suburbs. Thomas Sharp, who was to become president of both the Town Planning Institute and the Institute of Landscape Architects, derided the 'drab, revolting neutrality' of suburbia in his polemic *Town and Countryside* (1932). Clough Williams-Ellis, an especially opinionated architect, authored a sustained attack on both sprawl and its inhabitants in *England and the Octopus* (1928):

> The spate of mean building all over the country is shrivelling up the old England – mean and perky little houses that surely none but mean and perky little souls could inhabit with satisfaction ... cultivated people of all classes must deplore what is happening.

He saw 'nothing at all noble or satisfying' in the suburbs: 'Whether bungalows or garages, teashops or villas, their nastiness is assured.'[16] In 1937, he collaborated with other influential figures, including John Maynard Keynes, G.M. Trevelyan, Patrick Abercrombie and E.M. Forster, to reiterate the message in an edited volume, *Britain and the Beast*. The beast, of course, was suburbia. What attracted less commentary at the time was the way that suburbia reframed London in terms of class and gender relations.[17] Drawing out middle-class households from central London had created a new social geography at the macro scale, broadly pitting the inner boroughs against the outer boroughs. At the same time, the suburban estates in the outer boroughs were incubators of the new concept of the suburban housewife, a domestic specialist chained not just to the kitchen sink, but to her new 'labour-saving' devices, while her husband commuted into central London.[18] For many women, though, the suburbs represented personal fulfilment and modernisation, not the limitation of options in neighbourhoods of sterile conformity.[19]

The critique of suburbia carried over into Abercrombie's 1943 *County of London Plan* and the foundational Town and Country Planning Act of 1947 that provided for strict land-use planning controls and the final realisation of London's green belt. As a result, the contiguous limits of built-up suburbia today lie roughly where they were at the outbreak of the Second World War, with the likes of Amersham cocooned within a band of rural landscape that is up to 30 kilometres (nearly 19 miles) in width. Although some housing developments, office parks, superstores and golf courses have been permitted as exceptions to local land-use restrictions in the green belt, the overall policy has effectively intensified London's house-price inflation problem, not only within the green belt itself, but also in more central districts and in villages and market towns immediately beyond the green belt. The principal social impact of the containment of suburbia has meanwhile been to preserve the status quo and comfortable lifestyles of more affluent ruralites and middle-class commuters – a particular irony, given the radical intentions of the 1947 act.[20]

DOLPHIN SQUARE

16 Dolphin Square, Pimlico

DOLPHIN Square is a complex of thirteen 1930s mansion blocks, each named after a famous British navigator or admiral. Located on the north bank of the Thames within a short walk of Westminster and Whitehall, it became synonymous with London's cosmopolitan elite: a mixture of the good, the great and the not-so-good 'living the bourgeois life of the late 1930s, with dinner dances, martinis, games of canasta, and the smoking of exotic cheroots'. Equally, it offered privacy 'for those attracted to a less conventional lifestyle'.[1] Its cosmopolitan character continued through the 1960s, when it became associated with 'Swinging London' and some of its more colourful characters. Along with London's other luxurious interwar mansion blocks, it was a precursor of new hyper-luxury developments, such as One Hyde Park in Knightsbridge and NEO Bankside in Southwark, and the spate of speculative luxury residential towers that are symbolic of the neoliberal political economy of Global London – Vauxhall Tower and St George Wharf, Lambeth, for example; Embassy Gardens, Nine Elms; and Amory Tower, 10 Park Drive and 10 George Street on the Isle of Dogs.

Mansion blocks were not a common element within London's nineteenth-century built environment. Most Londoners assumed that only poorer people – or

61 Dolphin Square, Grosvenor Road façade.

foreigners – lived in shared buildings. Queen Anne's Mansions, built in 1875 between Victoria Street and St James's Park, was London's first high-rise apartment building. Its innovative range of amenities – hot and cold water laid on at all hours, speaking tubes, an impressive coffee room with newspapers, a billiard room, a smoking room and a laundry – was geared to 'bachelors of means'. The experiment was commercially successful, and the developer, Henry Alers Hankey, stealthily extended the original ten-storey, 35 metre high (115ft) building to an unprecedented twelve storeys. Pevsner called it 'an irredeemable horror', and *The Builder* described the mansions as 'monster blocks of dwellings' and 'Babel-like structures'.[2] There was a good deal of debate as to the compatibility of such buildings with traditional notions of propriety and family life. Out of scale, Queen Anne's Mansions prompted the newly formed LCC to limit the height of new construction on established streets. But mansion blocks were an attractive proposition for developers planning to build in more expensive parts of town, where land was at a premium and building at high densities offered the prospect of reaping higher profits per acre. Queen Anne's Mansions had also caught the attention of London's upper-middle classes, and soon mansion blocks began to appear here and there in West London (though they were still sufficiently unusual that people referred to them as 'French flats'). Among the first of the big apartment buildings in this vein were Albert Hall Mansions and Albert Court in South Kensington, on land leased from the commissioners of the Great Exhibition of 1851.

Demand for apartment living increased significantly after the First World War. The extended families with domestic staff that had been characteristic of the Victorian and Edwardian middle classes rapidly became a thing of the past. Large town homes with servants' quarters fell out of favour, and well-appointed apartments provided, for many, an attractive option. This, incidentally, freed many working-class women from the necessity of taking care of other women's homes, and simultaneously destabilised some upper-middle-class women's sense of themselves as household managers.[3]

For the emerging young professional class and the tens of thousands of single people drawn to the metropolis, apartment living offered an affordable and functional format. The result was a proliferation of upscale mansion blocks. Some sprang up near Underground stations, some were to be found close to the expanding arterial road network, and others were shoehorned into more central sites, especially in the West End, Marylebone, St John's Wood and Maida Vale. Dolphin Square was built in Pimlico on a prime riverside site in a district that, by the 1920s, had become 'a mixture of shabby gentility and vice'.[4] In mid-Victorian times it had been a well-planned, desirable and healthy suburb, largely the work of Thomas Cubitt, a new sort of master builder, whose company was vertically integrated, with its own supply lines of building materials and an army of a thousand workers in permanent employment. He is best known for the development in the 1820s of the Grosvenor Estate in Belgravia in the classic Regency style of squares, streets and crescents aligned to overlook private gardens. In the 1840s Cubitt began to develop the southern reaches of the Grosvenor Estate, in Pimlico, having established a riverside builder's yard with a draw dock on land leased from Robert, Earl Grosvenor, the 1st marquess of Westminster. Cubitt's Pimlico development attracted comfortably off middle-class households, but its social geography changed with the resurgence of railway building and the opening of Victoria Station in 1860. The station's approach lines separated Pimlico from Belgravia, sending Pimlico into a state of middle-class desperation, as terraced homes were converted into lodging houses and commercial hotels. Cubitt's yard had meanwhile been leased to the War Department and became an army clothing factory.

When the factory closed in 1932, the site was ripe for redevelopment, Pimlico's proximity to Whitehall and Westminster having ramped up demand for its real estate, as the number of civil servants increased dramatically after the First World War. The duke of Westminster's Estate lost no time in seeking a buyer, but only the largest companies and investors had the capacity to purchase and develop the entire site. The challenge was taken up by American developer Frederick Fillmore French, buoyed by the success of his Tudor City development on New York's East Side. Drawing on that experience, French believed that it would take a self-contained enclave, insulated from the drabness of surrounding streets, to ensure the success of the project. But soon after commissioning designs, French was embarrassed by overstretched finances and the project was taken over by Costains, a development company in the process of diversifying its product line from semi-detached suburban estates to city mansion blocks.[5] Costains hired Stanley Gordon Jeeves as the architect: he had previously designed other large blocks of flats in London, including Claridge House, Mayfair, Latymer Court, Hammersmith, and Cranmer Court, Chelsea. Oscar Faber was taken on as the consulting engineer. Together, they produced a neo-Georgian design in red brick, with steel framing and reinforced concrete. Construction was completed in 1937, having taken a labour force of 3,000 to excavate some 200,000 tons of earth, erect 6,000 tons of steel, set 125,000 tons of concrete and lay 12 million bricks.[6] It was, at the time, the largest block of flats in Europe.

Indeed, the most striking aspect of Dolphin Square is its monumental scale. The street views of the complex are uncompromising and monolithic: 200 metre (656ft) stretches of sheer seven- and ten-storey walls in red brick, with regimented rows of neo-Georgian multi-paned, white-framed windows, punctuated only by grand entranceways: a triplet of double-storey archways on the Thames-facing Grosvenor Road and, on the north side facing Chichester Street, a double-storey colonnade in stripped Classicism style, with six square stucco columns topped by minimalist capitals. The eastern and western façades of the quadrangle, accessible only by service roads, are no less severe, even though they are broken up by a series of shallow, full-height bays. In the interior of the quadrangle, the bays become ten-storey wings projecting into a courtyard garden that features a dolphin-themed fountain.

Dolphin Square's 1,200 apartments were designed for a mix of affluent residents and professional and retired classes of more modest means. For the latter, there were 240 bed-sitting-room flats and 600 two-room apartments. These smaller apartments were also marketed by Costains to working members of the Establishment as a convenient and fashionable pied-à-terre. At the other end of the scale were thirteen five-room apartments, ten six-room apartments and three seven-room 'Windsor' suites that included an additional maid's bathroom and pantry. By early 1938, all 1,200 apartments were occupied. They were served by electric lifts and had central heating, a constant hot-water supply, 'scientific fitted kitchens' with a refrigerator, a telephone connected to a central exchange and provision for a

62 Dolphin Square courtyard and mansion blocks.

radio service. Heating and hot water were initially provided by coke-burning boiler houses, but in 1951 Dolphin Square joined Westminster Council's new housing estate, Churchill Gardens, in deriving its supply from Battersea Power Station by way of an innovative scheme that piped exhaust heat under the Thames. There was a large underground garage (which included a petrol station, servicing bays and car showrooms, as well as parking spaces for 300 vehicles) and an internal shopping arcade. A recreation centre featured eight squash courts, a swimming pool and a gymnasium. Other amenities included bars, a winter garden, a palm court, a restaurant (the Costains colour brochure of 1936 was illustrated with residents in evening dress), luggage rooms, a beauty parlour, a laundry depot, a theatre booking office, a children's centre and nursery, a library and a music room.[7] At the heart of the complex was a courtyard of 1.5 hectares (3½ acres) with themed gardens. In addition, there were thirty guest rooms that could be rented by tenants at a moderate charge to accommodate visitors. Residents also had access to a range of services, such as shoe cleaning, laundry, valeting, on-call errand boys, and the hire of private rooms for 'music, parties, art studies, etc.'.[8]

The square's first residents included a broad cross-section of people, from Whitehall clerks to politicians, writers, celebrities, military personnel and aristocrats. There were several members of parliament and more than sixty commissioned officers, including a vice-admiral, a major-general, two brigadiers and several colonels. Among the aristocratic tenants were Lord Burghley, a Conservative politician and Olympian; Lord Cottenham, a motor racing driver and MI5 officer, who campaigned for driving tests and compulsory insurance; Viscountess Snowden, a feminist and peace campaigner; the earl of Listowel, a Labour minister and author of *A Critical History of Modern Aesthetics*; and Lady Diana Mosley and her husband Sir Oswald Mosley, leader of Britain's fascist faction. One of Diana Mosley's neighbours, Maxwell Knight, another MI5 officer (who is believed to have been the inspiration for Ian Fleming's 'M' in his James Bond novels), had her arrested in 1940 and taken straight from Dolphin Square to Holloway Prison. Other notable tenants included Ellen Wilkinson, a pioneering socialist, anti-fascist and champion of the Jarrow marchers; film star Margaret Lockwood; and Ida Cook, a romantic novelist who used her Dolphin Square flat to take in refugees, having made several trips to Germany with her sister to help Jews escape the Nazi regime.[9] The security and anonymity of the square was particularly attractive to women living alone, which in 1937 was still unusual and inevitably gave Dolphin Square, along with some other interwar mansion blocks, a somewhat louche reputation.

War came along before the residents' community had really gelled. Proximity to MI5 headquarters and Westminster made the complex a target for both enemy bombs and government requisitions. The square's Grenville House wing was converted for the operations of General de Gaulle's Free French Movement; the garage became an ambulance depot; and there was a decontamination centre, a mortuary and three neighbourhood bomb shelters – 'one for snorers, another for non-snorers, and a third for pet owners'.[10] During the course of the war, the square was hit by thirteen bombs, which killed twelve people and seriously injured thirty-two. Soon after the war, Costains put Dolphin Square on the market and the complex was eventually taken over by a tenants' association, financed by Westminster City Council, which set up a housing association to manage the property on a non-profit basis. The roster of residents continued to reflect a cross-section of London's metropolitan elite. Politicians who lived in the square in the 1960s and 1970s included Hartley Shawcross (attorney-general in the Labour administrations of 1945–51, and chief British prosecutor at the Nuremberg war crimes tribunal), Lewis Silkin (Labour's minister of town and country planning, responsible for the key legislation that underpinned London's postwar planning strategy of New Towns, land-use controls and the green belt), and later Harold Wilson, David Steel, William Hague and Mo Mowlam. Celebrity tenants included the racing driver Donald Campbell; and actors and entertainers Ben Lyon and Bebe Daniels, Valerie Hobson, Vanessa Lee, Peter Finch, Arthur Askey, Tommy Trinder, Bud Flanagan and Roy Plomley. In the early 1990s, Princess Anne moved in for a while with her new husband, Captain Timothy Laurence, who had been assigned a position at the Admiralty.

Some of Dolphin Square's residents and their guests attracted a certain amount of notoriety that became part of the chronicle of 1960s and 1970s London.[11] Winston Churchill's daughter Sarah was remanded to Holloway Prison after being found drunk and disorderly in Lupus Street; not long afterwards she was evicted from the square for lobbing gin bottles from her window. John Vassall, an assistant private secretary at the Admiralty, lived in the square from 1959 until his arrest for spying for the Russians in September 1962. Call-girls meanwhile took advantage of the anonymity and transience of the square. As K.F. Morris wrote in 1995, 'There have been members of the oldest profession and there probably still are some highly gifted amateurs.'[12] Others were simply free-spirited women in the vanguard of the emerging 'permissive society' of 'Swinging London'. Two of them were central to the heady mix of sex, lies, drugs, espionage, moral panic and hypocrisy that captivated London and the rest of the country in 1963. Christine Keeler, who may or may not have been simultaneously in a relationship with John Profumo, the secretary of state for war, and Yevgeny Ivanov, a Soviet naval attaché and intelligence officer, lived in a Dolphin Square apartment rented by Mandy Rice-Davies, who was in turn connected to both William Waldorf Astor II (3rd Viscount Astor) and London's most notorious slumlord, Peter Rachman. The newspapers had a field day. In 1971, it emerged that Dolphin Square hosted a sado-masochistic service run by a woman named Sybil Benson, who on a good week claimed to make £1,260 (equivalent to £22,750 in 2023), even though she limited herself to six clients a day.[13]

There was nevertheless a feeling among older tenants that certain standards still applied within the community. Morris relates the story of one tenant who complained to the general manager that he had seen a couple engaged in sex on the courtyard lawn. 'Asked by the GM how he knew the couple were tenants he replied "Well, the man was wearing a dinner jacket".'[14] But the square's notoriety has persisted. *Vanity Fair* magazine noted in 2014 that 'There's a bleak certainty in British public life that whenever the words "sex scandal", "MPs", "establishment", and "cover-up" appear in pretty much any order, the name of a vast central London apartment block, Dolphin Square, follows soon afterwards.'[15] The article followed an allegation of a paedophile ring with membership in the square. Subsequently unproven, it nevertheless prompted a high-level police investigation with extensive national press coverage. The following year, the press also devoted much attention to a leaked video tape allegedly of sixty-nine-year-old Lord Sewel, wearing an orange bra under a studded leather jacket, snorting white powder with two prostitutes in a Dolphin Square apartment.[16]

The notoriety of a handful of Dolphin Square residents and guests likely had little to do with Westminster City Council's decision in the mid-2000s to wind up the Dolphin Square housing association and sell the property. The London real estate market had changed and the council was in the throes of controversial decisions over borough-wide housing policy. The square was sold initially to US property firm Westbrook, but the company's proposals to reconfigure apartments, demolish parts of the complex and add a new nine-storey building were strongly opposed by the Twentieth Century Society and eventually turned down by Westminster's Planning Committee. Westbrook sold the property in 2022 to French fund group AXA Investment Managers for a reported £850 million, with the prospect of a multi-million-pound refurbishment with a 'sustainability' theme underpinning an 'aspirational living environment'.

17 Hoover Factory, Perivale

EVER since the Hoover factory opened in 1932, it has been a landmark for commuters travelling in and out of London on the A40, which runs westwards from the Edgware Road via the Westway and Western Avenue towards Uxbridge. It is a reminder of the dynamic phase of London's interwar development: new bypasses with roadhouse pubs and new trunk roads carrying ever-larger lorries and ever-faster and more affordable cars. It is symbolic of the introduction of mass consumption of household gadgets and of the beginning of American corporate influence in British industry. It has become an icon of London's interwar industrialisation and a monument to the conservation movement of the 1970s. More recently, it has been caught up in a shift within the London region's economic landscape from manufacturing to retail, and in the wave of conversions of industrial spaces to upscale apartments.

The interwar period saw a new phase of industrialisation based on 'light' (that is, electrically powered) manufacturing using new production methods. The London region accounted for a disproportionate share of this new industry: of the net increase of 644 factories in Britain between 1932 and 1937, no fewer than 532 were in the Greater London area.[1] Many

63 Building No. 7, Hoover complex, detail.

were 'assembly industries' producing mass-market electrical consumer goods, such as vacuum cleaners, wireless and telephone apparatus, electric irons and electric fires; or light engineering, producing cars, aircraft, gas cookers, refrigerators and washing machines.[2] Freed from their dependence on congested railway yards and river- and canal-bank locations by electric power, new and improved roads and heavy-duty lorries, manufacturers were able to opt for cheaper and more spacious sites, building space-hungry 'daylight factories': large single-storey blocks with sawtooth roofing bays with north-facing glazing, concealed at the front by offices. The Victorian manufacturing belt of central, north and east London began to expand up the west side of the Lea Valley, while many small manufacturing operations were drawn to new industrial estates. The abandoned site of the 1924–25 British Empire Exhibition in Wembley, for example, attracted a cluster of factories, including Osram's light-bulb factory, Wolf Power Tools, Sunbeam Electrical Appliances and the General Electric Company's research laboratories.

The most striking development of new industry, however, was to the west, along the new trunk roads of Western Avenue (A40) and the Great West Road (A4). Both were laid out in the mid-1920s, and both ran through the open countryside of Park Royal, Perivale, Greenford, Brentford and Osterley, where there were plenty of large sites for modern daylight factories. A critical factor in the development of these trunk roads as industrial corridors came with the end of Britain's commitment to free trade, when the Import Duties Act of 1932 imposed a 10 per cent tariff (promptly doubled to 20 per cent) on manufactured imports from outside the Empire, making it a matter of urgency for European and American companies to manufacture their products in Britain. American companies, in particular, brought automation, assembly lines and attention to worker health and productivity. They also introduced American practices of scientific management, co-locating manufacturing and management in modern signature buildings. The Hoover factory was one of these, fronting what is now Fleetway Business Park on the north side of Western Avenue.

The Ohio-based Hoover corporation selected Britain's leading industrial architect, Thomas Wallis, for the project. His firm, Wallis, Gilbert and Partners, had emerged as pioneers in the design of daylight factories.[3] For many architects, the factory represented the challenge of the age: an opportunity to refine the idea of an uncompromisingly Modern building type, its purified geometry tied closely to a broadly unified system of ideology, technology and aesthetics. Wallis was not entirely convinced by this, influenced more by his association with the prolific and market-oriented American factory architect Albert Kahn and his Trussed Concrete Steel Company.[4] Kahn's design philosophy was to focus first on the imperatives of efficient mass production in relation to site planning and interior layout, then treat building façades as an opportunity for corporate brand identity, rather than as an exercise in geometry. Wallis's talent was to do just this, with stylish buildings embellished with eye-catching detail. As he observed:

> Colourful decoration is not money wasted. It has a psychological effect on the worker, if he is a good worker, and good workers look upon their business buildings with pride. A little money spent on something to focus the attention of the public is not money wasted, but is good advertisement.[5]

Among the factory buildings that he had designed before getting the commission from Hoover were the Firestone and Pyrene buildings, both on what would become known as the 'Golden Mile' of the Great West Road in Brentford.[6] They were both derivative of the Art Deco style that had been a sensation at the Exposition Internationale des Arts Décoratifs in Paris in 1925, a response to the hardships of the First World War and a celebration of French victory. Free of the ideological undertones of avant-garde Modernism, Art Deco drew on a variety of influences, including Moorish, Mayan and Egyptian motifs (Europe was in thrall to ancient Egypt at the time, Howard Carter having unearthed King Tutankhamun's tomb in 1922). Art Deco was soon adopted as the style of the Jazz Age, showing up in ocean liners and skyscrapers, picture palaces and night clubs, before blending with Streamline Moderne and appearing in the design of department stores, hotels, Underground stations and private homes.[7]

Wallis, Gilbert and Partners designed several separate buildings for Hoover on the Western Avenue site, all in Art Deco style – though Thomas Wallis himself avoided the term, instead simply calling his style 'Fancy'.[8] The main block facing Western Avenue ('Building No. 1') was the administration building. Set back from the road, with formal gardens and sitting areas in front, the façade is a striking array of fifteen double-storey bays flanked by taller staircase towers with quarter-moon windows. The metal glazing bars of the windows within the bays are a distinctive green colour and extend through two storeys, with green window blanks obscuring the first-storey floor plate. The windows are recessed into the body of the building, separated by stone columns with distinctive angular fluting, decorated with red, green and blue tin-glazed tiling. The central entrance, also recessed, is a flamboyant Art Deco-style statement (visitors only: staff had to use doorways at the foot of each staircase tower). The body of the building was rendered in 'Snowcrete', a cement with a brilliant white pigment that was common to many interwar factories, giving them a crisp, clean appearance – especially when floodlit at night – that helped to signify the contemporary image of the parent company. The Hoover building was given additional high-quality detailing in the form of Art Deco wrought-iron gates and railings and pyramidal concrete piers capped by ornate lanterns. Similarly, the interior of the administration building

64 Hoover building, Western Avenue, Perivale.

was designed to exude *à la mode* quality. The central entrance hall had colourful and elaborate plaster detailing, with recessed chromium-plated lamps flanking each door and terrazzo flooring edged with geometric patterns. David Thompson's description of the gents' toilets captures the intention to make a statement about innovation and stylishness:

> Green tiled walls with a solid black line near the top but the undoubted feature: two free-standing communal hand basins in the centre of the room. These are about a metre tall with a large circular basin and a central column topped with six taps equally spaced like the spokes of a wheel.[9]

As Hoover's production expanded, Wallis designed extensions to the production building to the rear of the administration block; and as the number of employees increased, it was decided that there should be a separate canteen and recreation centre ('Building No. 7'). This was built facing Western Avenue, immediately to the west of the administration block, to a design that slid

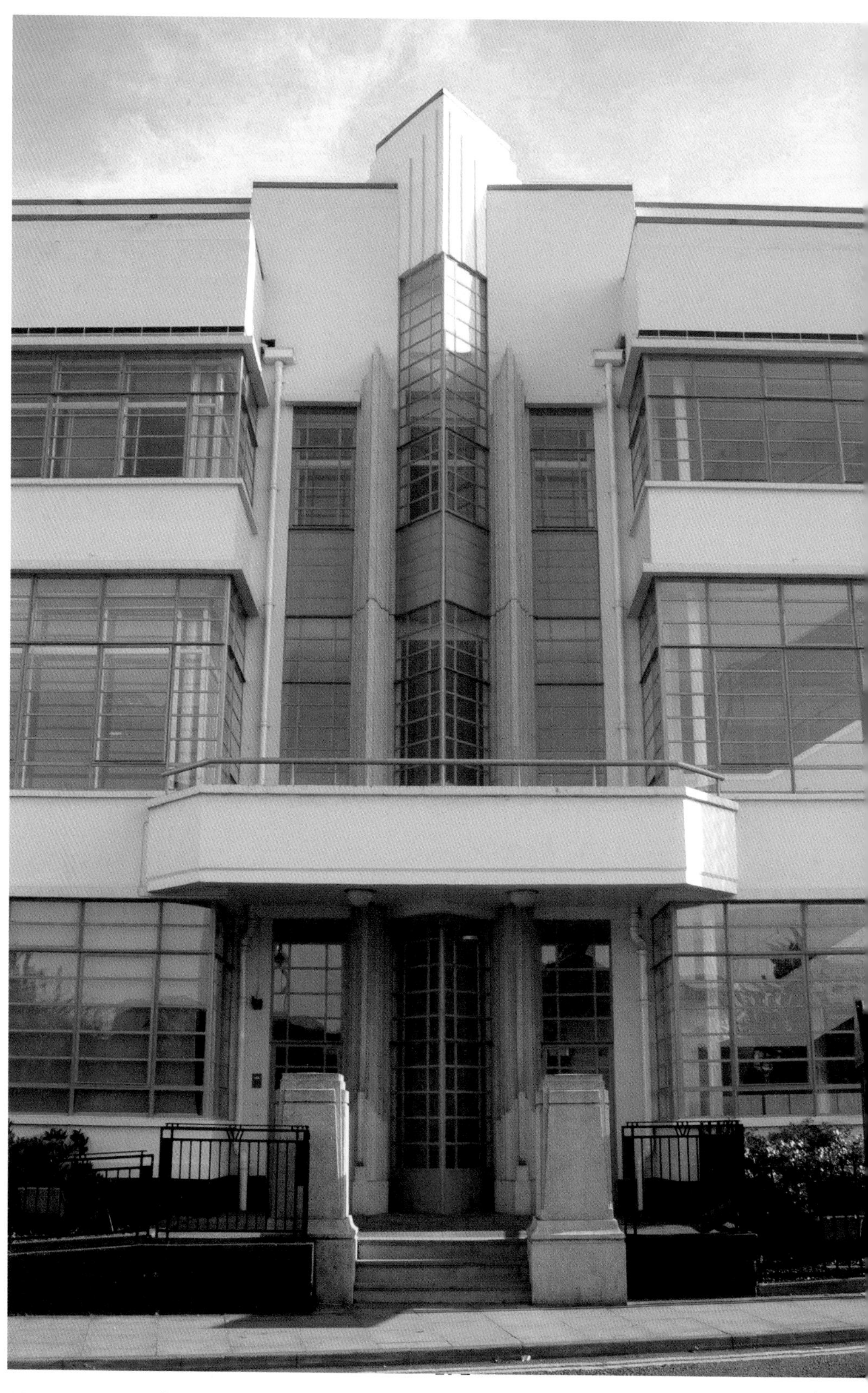

65 Building No. 7 (former canteen building), Hoover complex.

away from Art Deco towards Streamline Moderne. Completed in 1938, the cafeteria was on the second floor, with a fine view across to the fairways of Ealing Golf Club. The company's directors were provided with their own dining room and lounge on the south front of the first floor, with a dining room for senior management to the rear. On the ground floor were a print shop, a stationery store, a garage and a car wash. All in all, the Hoover complex was an exemplar of modern industrial facilities, an embodiment of the company's brand image and a symbol of the emergence of London's new manufacturing sector. It did not, however, endear itself to the avant-garde among architectural critics, for whom the accepted canon was now that of continental Modernism; or to traditionalists, for whom Modernism of any kind was distasteful.[10] Wallis's 'Fancy' design, incorporating Expressionist quarter-moon windows into an eclectic Art Deco palette, was generally belittled. It was ridiculed in a pettish poem published in the self-consciously avant-garde *Architectural Review* in July 1932, illustrated with a caricature of the administration block surrounded by personalities from the architect's office.[11] Pevsner snootily condemned the building as 'perhaps the most offensive of the modernistic atrocities along this road of typical by-pass factories'.[12] The building is now listed at Grade II* by Historic England: so much for architectural critics and theorists. The latest edition of Pevsner, edited and revised by Bridget Cherry, has meanwhile retreated, simply noting the building's 'particularly striking combination of white glazing and green trim', before damning it with faint praise as 'The most striking of all their [Wallis, Gilbert and Partners] West London buildings.'[13]

During the Second World War, the Hoover factory was repurposed to manufacture aircraft parts. After the war, production reverted to vacuum cleaners, as sales boomed with the emergence of what J.K. Galbraith called the 'Affluent Society'. By 1963, the factory, which was then being extended, employed more than 3,000 people.[14] But the global recession of the mid-1970s and the decline of the pound led to the withdrawal of several of London's key multinational manufacturing firms and the contraction of others. Hoover discontinued manufacturing at Perivale and moved its administration to Merthyr Tydfil in Wales, leaving the Perivale building empty. Firestone Tyres and Trico-Folberth wound down their operations on the Great West Road with a combined loss of almost 14,000 workers. By the mid-1980s, the deindustrialisation of the capital had led to the disappearance of around 100,000 jobs in just ten years. British Leyland closed its production lines in Southall and Park Royal with the loss of 3,500 positions; Westland shed 2,000 helicopter production jobs in Hayes; General Electric cut 6,000 posts at factories making electrical products in Willesden; Lucas shed 1,500 jobs in car parts from Acton; Delta Enfield Rolled Metals cut 1,000 engineering positions; and Thorn EMI shed 2,000 jobs at its electrical products factories in Hayes and Ilford.[15]

The industrial corridors along the Great West Road and Western Avenue joined the docklands as symbols of London's industrial decline. Edward Platt has described the painful decline of the communities along the A40 between East Acton and the Hoover factory.[16] While the corridor's industries were victims of structural economic change, the trunk road itself was a victim of its own success, unable to cope with the volume of traffic moving in and out of central London. The residential communities along the way, once part of semi-detached suburbia, were collateral damage: victims of congestion, pollution and poor planning. In the 1980s, households living along the road were threatened with eviction in preparation for a scheme to widen it. The area had declined sharply, with squatters living in some houses, while in others families clung to the suburban dream of the 1920s and 1930s, despite the traffic that poured past their front gardens. All were evicted by the authorities,

> who then smashed up perfectly good houses to make them uninhabitable. And then, in 1998, for political reasons, the Highways Agency changed its mind, abandoned the plans for more flyovers and underpasses and decided to increase capacity by less extravagant means. The evictions and demolitions had been largely unnecessary.[17]

The decline of West London's industrial corridors meanwhile highlighted the problem of finding sustainable uses for large, redundant buildings of architectural significance. The 1970s saw a surge of interest in conservation and the heritage of the built environment, as more and more of London's familiar streetscapes began to disappear.[18]

> As the supply of bomb sites dwindled from the late 1950s much development entailed the destruction of familiar landmarks. These included West End theatres and railway termini, targeted in the late fifties and early sixties by private developers promoting the replacement of an existing Victorian building by a supposedly more efficient successor.[19]

Sunday newspaper magazines published photo galleries of 'lost' buildings, including celebrated cases, such as the Coal Exchange in the City of London, demolished in 1962 for a road-widening scheme that was never realised. In 1974, the V&A mounted a provocative exhibition on 'The Destruction of the Country House'. Although it might understandably have been interpreted as a special pleading to middle-class museum-goers on behalf of an even more privileged class, the general response was one of shock at the scale of the loss of irreplaceable common heritage. The following year was officially European Architectural Heritage Year, and SAVE Britain's Heritage was founded as a media lobbying group. Meanwhile, the 'property machine' threatened more and more demolitions. Pevsner's snooty condemnation of the Hoover factory was cited by developers interested in demolishing the building in order to redevelop the 4.5 hectare (11 acre) site, while property conglomerate Trafalgar House got away with demolishing the Firestone factory by sending in the bulldozers over a bank holiday weekend, just days before it was due to be saved by being listed as a historic building. The ensuing outcry led to the formation of the Thirties Society (now the Twentieth Century Society) and prompted Michael Heseltine, then secretary of state for the environment, to undertake an urgent review of the process and criteria for listing historic buildings.

Just two months after the demolition of the Firestone building, the Hoover factory was one of the first to benefit from the subsequent expansion in the number of buildings deemed worthy of listing. It sat anointed but unused until 1989, when the Tesco supermarket chain purchased the site, having reached a compromise with English Heritage, whereby the factory building behind the main office building would be demolished to make way for the construction of a superstore with its own petrol station, while the main administration block, the canteen block and Wallis's eastern additions were preserved and restored. By this time, developers throughout London and Britain's larger cities had become adept at the conversion of nineteenth- and early twentieth-century industrial and commercial buildings. Building No. 7 was promptly leased to Warner Music for offices, before being converted into a restaurant and event venue serving Indian and Pakistani halal food. It took a little longer for a viable business plan for the conversion of the administration block to get the approval of English Heritage. In 2015, the building was purchased by IDM ('Invest, Develop, Manage') Properties, which contracted with Interrobang Design to convert the old office spaces into residential apartments, taking advantage of the building's distinctive – and now very marketable – Art Deco features. It has prompted a new-build gentrification project by build-to-rent specialist Amro Partners: construction of their 278-apartment Wiltern building, in pastiche Art Deco style, began in 2022 on the site of the Tesco petrol station behind the old factory.

V

POSTWAR LONDON

More than 80,000 dwellings in Greater London were destroyed or damaged beyond repair during the Second World War, most of them during the Luftwaffe's night bombing campaign between 1940 and 1941. The damage to London's fabric included hundreds of historically significant buildings. During the night of 29 December 1940 alone, four churches that had survived the Great Fire of 1666 fell victim, along with thirteen Wren churches that were either completely destroyed or severely damaged.[1] Because of the inaccuracy of German bombers, there was an unpredictability to the raids that made them all the more terrifying. By the end of the war, more than 20,000 people had been killed in air raids and another 30,000 seriously injured. Postwar recovery and reconstruction were hampered by shortages of timber and steel, and by the continuation of the strict building controls that had been imposed during hostilities. Meanwhile, bomb sites and old air raid shelters were used as children's playgrounds – some official, but mostly unofficial – until the owners found the means to develop them.[2] It was not until the early 1960s that the last bomb sites were built over.

The scars of war can still be seen, not only in shrapnel damage to the stonework of many of London's landmarks and monuments, but also in London's 'missing buildings' that have left silhouette traces on the walls of surviving neighbouring units, and in postwar constructions that incongruously intrude on older terraces.[3] Among the many sites left vacant by wartime

66 Advertisement for the 1951 Festival of Britain.

bombing was an extensive tract next to the Hungerford Bridge in Lambeth. This became the site of the Festival of Britain in 1951 – the centenary of Prince Albert's Great Exhibition. Most of the festival consisted of temporary pavilions, but permanent legacies included the Royal Festival Hall and the National Theatre (Chapter 18), intended as cornerstones of the 'Great Cultural Centre' envisaged by Abercrombie and Forshaw in their *County of London Plan* (1943).

The Festival of Britain had aimed to promote a feeling of recovery amid the exhaustion and deprivations that followed the conclusion of the Second World War. But most of London was in a sorry state throughout the 1950s. In addition to wartime damage and neglect, a century of pollution had made for a dark and dreary city. But there was nevertheless an entirely new sensibility among the populace. The complacent middle-class attitudes of the interwar period had been replaced by a 'postwar consensus': a determination to break with the past and a conviction that centralised planning – which had served the country well during the war – was necessary to forge a new, more prosperous, healthier and more equitable society. A Labour government swept into power in the summer of 1945 with a mandate to implement a comprehensive programme of civil reformation and social engineering that included the establishment of a 'cradle to grave' welfare state, the selective nationalisation of major industries and utilities, centralised economic planning, urban land-use planning, a commitment to affordable public housing and higher education, the development of New Towns, and the creation of green belts around large cities.[4]

It was a golden age for LCC and GLC architects and planners. Public housing was grafted onto the fabric of the metropolis on an unprecedented scale. High-rise building was still the exception through the mid-1950s, but the combination of slum clearance, the desire to limit sprawl and the high cost of land in central London, together with an unexpectedly high birth rate, resulted in an impossible arithmetic. There was no alternative but to build dense and build tall. The Conservative government in power after 1951 introduced significant subsidies for high-rise building, motivated in part by the prospect of keeping Labour voters in their inner-city constituencies. The net result was an inner-cityscape punctuated by system-built 'point blocks' and slab blocks of eighteen and twenty-five storeys, mixed with short terraces of four- and five-storey maisonettes.[5] Suburban council estates, where space constraints were less severe, featured fewer point blocks and were typically planned on the same principles that had influenced New Town design, based on the idea of a traffic-free estate organised around neighbourhood units, with a central pedestrian shopping precinct. Some of these new suburban council estates also adopted system-built designs, as at Thamesmead (Chapter 21), a vast development housing more than 30,000 people. As families were provided with these new council homes, their place in London's private rental sector was taken by new immigrant groups: Polish and Central European refugees from communism; Chinese who came via Hong Kong during and after the Chinese Civil War; migrants from South Asia escaping the horrors of Partition; and the 'Windrush generation' of migrants from the Caribbean, drawn to London to staff its growing service economy.[6] These groups would go on to play a pivotal role in forcing a public conversation about racial discrimination and the relationship between race and citizenship in the United Kingdom.[7]

By the late 1950s, Britain's postwar economic recovery had taken off, initiating the 'long sixties', a distinctive period of increasing prosperity, social mobility and cultural change that was especially marked in 'Swinging London'.[8] By the beginning of the 1960s, the real income of working Londoners was more than double what it had been before the war, and the welfare state began to morph into a consumer society. Property speculation flourished, encouraged by an influential government report,

Traffic in Towns (1963), which portrayed a futuristic 'two-level city' of motorway rings, giant flyovers, high-rise office and apartment towers, multi-storey car parks and pedestrian walkways.[9] A new cityscape began to emerge across central London, generating iconic buildings such as the Post Office Tower, Millbank Tower and Centre Point (Chapter 20). The heady economic and policy climate also brought forth several high-profile, large-scale proposals from the new alliance of developers and planners – notably those for Piccadilly Circus, Whitehall, Covent Garden, Oxford Street and Regent Street – that backfired, supercharging the emerging conservation movement by adding the voices of working- and lower-middle-class communities threatened by the proposals. One significant outcome was the Civic Amenities Act of 1967. This introduced conservation areas, an important policy instrument that has helped to sustain the distinctive character of London's built environment. It also invited the law of unintended consequences, accelerating, in turn, the social reconquest of inner London. Together with the Rent Act of 1957 (which made it much easier for landlords to evict long-term tenants and make older properties available for sale), conservation areas boosted the process of gentrification, as young professional households sought the character and convenience of less expensive housing in centrally located districts. Beginning in a few pockets of Chelsea and Kensington, gentrification spread north to parts of Notting Hill and North Kensington, Camden and Kentish Town, Barnsbury, Islington and Canonbury; and across the Thames into parts of Kennington and the Elephant and Castle.

The postwar economic boom meanwhile underpinned a remarkable social and cultural liberalisation that was driven by a baby-boom generation that had reached its teens by the early sixties.[10] The interdependence of economic, demographic, social, cultural and political change during the 'long sixties' in London has been thoroughly documented by John Davis in a wide-ranging and very readable history.[11] It was the spending power of Britain's youth that supported Swinging London's booming fashion, design and music businesses. Together with photography, modelling, magazine publishing and advertising, the new creative industries generated wealth 'for almost a quarter of a million Londoners, in the process giving London a new image, and its people a fresh sense of identity and vitality'.[12] This was most visible in the boutiques of the King's Road in Chelsea and Carnaby Street in Soho, and in the clubs, musical instrument shops and recording studios of Denmark Street (also Soho). But the signs of change were also evident across the city in high-street record shops and dance clubs and, not least, in 'mod' street fashions. It was all 'discovered' in the mid-1960s by American journalists, notably recorded in *Time* magazine's April 1966 cover story that introduced London as 'The Swinging City'. The collage on the magazine's cover included traditional London symbols, such as a red Routemaster bus and the Houses of Parliament, together with symbols of 'swinging' London: a Mini Cooper, Op-art fashion, the Who, Union Jack sunglasses and so on. The international cachet of Carnaby Street and the King's Road – and later, Abbey Road recording studios (Chapter 19) – meant that they were added to the itineraries of many tourists, along with the Tower and Westminster Abbey.

'Swinging London' was emblematic of a socio-cultural turn that, in the long run, was profoundly important – sowing the seeds of London's creative industries, hastening gentrification and regeneration, signalling new pathways of social mobility, and bringing a new, cosmopolitan dimension to urban politics and culture, for example. But the 1960s portrayals of Swinging London were stylised accounts that 'privileged the exotic over the routine, leisure over work, the centre over the periphery, producing a city portrait which was inevitably overdrawn'. They were 'based almost entirely on the West End, which was, for many Londoners, a place to visit rather than the focus of their lives'.[13]

Across the rest of the metropolis, structural economic change was taking its toll. Lack of competitiveness in a rapidly globalising economy, labour unrest and price inflation brought an abrupt end to the boom years of the 1960s. In October 1973, an Arab–Israeli war led Arab countries to impose an embargo on shipments of oil to the United States and other Western countries, and soon afterward OPEC quadrupled the price of crude oil. The subsequent shock to the global economic system laid bare London's long-term structural economic problems and turned the spotlight on the physical deterioration and social problems of inner-city districts. As the period of postwar economic recovery and growth came to an end, so did the speculative property bubble and the optimism and confidence that had sustained the golden age of Modernist urban planning.[14] Meanwhile, the quality of public services deteriorated, along with London's physical infrastructure, and increasing numbers of households found themselves trapped in run-down neighbourhoods with high rates of poverty and unemployment. Confidence and trust in local government was badly shaken by the 'bureaucratic aggression' associated with slum-clearance schemes and the GLC's controversial proposals for Piccadilly Circus, Whitehall, Covent Garden, Oxford Street, Regent Street and the Ringway system of concentric motorways. Nationally, the inability of Keynesianism (the operational policy framework of the welfare state, based on the importance of managing aggregate demand) to navigate global economic forces opened the way for the reassertion of market forces and the emergence of a radically different political economy. It was the end of the 'long sixties'.

National

18 National Theatre, Waterloo

THE foundation stone of the National Theatre (NT) was laid in 1951 by HM Queen Elizabeth (later the queen mother) on a site next to the recently completed Royal Festival Hall on the South Bank. It was the second such ceremony, George Bernard Shaw having done the honours in 1937 on a site in Cromwell Gardens, across from the V&A. At that time the NT was envisaged as part of 'Albertopolis', along with the V&A, the Albert Hall, the Royal College of Music, the Natural History Museum and the rest of the legacy of the Great Exhibition of 1851. But the necessary funding never materialised, and by the late 1940s there seemed to be a more compelling case for the NT to join the Festival Hall on the South Bank to form 'a grouped architectural composition' in at least partial fulfilment of the 'Great Cultural Centre' envisaged by Patrick Abercrombie and John Forshaw in their *County of London Plan* (1943). The LCC duly swapped the Cromwell Gardens plot for the site next to the Royal Festival Hall. For five months in 1951, the surrounding area, between County Hall and Waterloo Bridge, was used for the Festival of Britain, a centenary celebration of the Great Exhibition of 1851 and an attempt to demonstrate British contributions to global civilisation, while signalling the prospect of a bright and modern future. Soon after the closing

67 National Theatre.

ceremonies of the festival, the LCC decided that a better spot for the NT would be next to County Hall, on the site that had been used for the festival's Skylon and Dome of Discovery. The foundation stone was quietly moved 300 yards south. But funding once more became an issue: in 1955 drama critics Kenneth Tynan and Richard Findlater, despairing of the theatre's ever being built, staged a mock funeral beside the foundation stone. The new site next to County Hall became a car park.

In the early 1960s, the LCC and the central government agreed to share the capital cost of a national theatre building in London after an unlikely alliance between Home Counties conservatives and inner London socialists. Conservatives supported funding the NT as an ideological cultural totem, and wanted it in London, capital city of Commonwealth and Empire, to underscore its symbolic importance.[1] The intellectual fraction of the bourgeoisie was especially supportive, seeing itself as the principal element of a metropolitan audience. Socialists supported funding the NT so that the arts would be available to all in the same way that the welfare state provided access to health care, housing and education. The dissenters were also both conservatives and socialists, but from provincial cities, and they had no particular alternative to promote. By the mid-1960s, yet another site had been identified by the LCC, this time just downstream from the Waterloo Bridge – the queen mother is reputed to have joked that the theatre should be put on casters – and work finally proceeded on construction in 1969.

In parallel with the saga of site selection, a succession of architects had produced designs for the theatre.[2] The earliest was for a site behind the British Museum in Bloomsbury. In 1924, William Somerville won a competition organised by the British Drama League with a predictably neoclassical design. In 1938, Edwin Lutyens, having been given the commission for the site on Cromwell Gardens, also produced drawings in neoclassical style. When the site was switched to the South Bank, his preliminary design was for slightly plainer neoclassical elevations. After Lutyens' death, Hubert Worthington was appointed to succeed him as architect for the NT. His solution, in 1944, was an exercise in Imperial Classicism, with a riverfront elevation dominated by a huge pediment above a colonnade with Corinthian capitals. By 1946, Brian O'Rorke had been given the commission: his scheme, for the site adjacent to that of the Royal Festival Hall, was more modern, acknowledging the plans for its putative next-door neighbour. This was the building for which Queen Elizabeth had laid the unlucky foundation stone. When the location was switched to the old Dome of Discovery site, O'Rorke produced drawings for a combined theatre and opera house that were redolent of the stripped neoclassicism of interwar Italy and Germany: shockingly tone-deaf, so soon after the country had concluded its exhausting fight against fascism. O'Rorke's ideas were shelved as soon as the central government and the LCC had agreed on funding, and a newly formed governing board decided to recruit an architect from scratch.

In 1963, the board's Building Committee – an assortment of theatrical egos chaired by Laurence Olivier – appointed Denys Lasdun as architect. Lasdun himself had an ego robust enough to navigate the board's internal disagreements over the merits of a proscenium stage versus an open stage, and over the desirability of combining theatre and opera facilities on the same site. In the end, Lasdun went ahead with plans for three stages: a fan-shaped 'open theatre' (the Olivier), a proscenium theatre (the Lyttelton) and a small, flexible space (the Cottesloe, now the Dorfman) intended for programming new plays by lesser-known authors. The opera-house component, meanwhile, was dropped from the design programme. Lasdun's final design was stunningly Modernist, a complete break with all previous designs and conceptions of what a national theatre should look like. Construction began in 1969, eighteen years after the queen mother had laid the peripatetic foundation stone. It was not completed until 1976, having been delayed not only by the economic recession following the OPEC oil crisis and by the three-day week and rolling power cuts of 1973–74 (enforced to conserve electricity during an extended strike by coalminers), but also by technical challenges in realising Lasdun's design.[3]

Seen from across the Thames, the building is a monumental pyramidal arrangement of concrete decks, punctuated by blank flytowers (lift towers) and ventilation shafts. Lasdun himself described it as 'a sort of rocky outcrop of stratified concrete'.[4] Seen up close from the riverside Queen's Walk, the decks and balconies present a more elegant and detailed geometry, the horizontal planes emphasised by the linear markings left by the Douglas fir planking used for the concrete formwork. The effect is commonly referred to as Brutalism, a clever word-play on the French term for raw or unfinished concrete: *béton brut*. Lasdun disliked the term, preferring to emphasise the deliberate care taken in detailing the linear form of the building with the grain of the wood: not 'brutal' at all, he insisted. Lasdun's particular conceit was to claim that the NT was not a building, but 'an urban landscape'. His conception was for the theatre's foyers to be a seamless continuation of public space, and for the terraces to provide places for activities

> such as busking, dancing, music, steel bands, events, and so the building performs much the same function as the piazza … All these things help to break down the barrier between ordinary people going to the theatre and the past tradition that it was something only for the élite.[5]

Inside, Lasdun cleverly arranged the ancillary spaces around the auditoria to include large and fully equipped workshops, dressing rooms, restaurants and ample bars. Outside, broad terraces shelved over the river.[6] There was no attempt to apply decoration. As Lasdun himself put it, 'It is simply light, space, people, concrete.'[7]

The NT was accorded a special issue of the *Architectural Review*, the first building so honoured since the Royal Festival Hall in 1951. It was a reflection of the building's importance and of Lasdun's stature (as well as of the editors' ideological preference for heroic High Modernism). Lasdun's design had been very much of-the-moment when it was conceived. Modernist architecture was the logical aesthetic for postwar recovery: wipe-clean and futuristic, its claims to social redemption ready made in both practical and symbolic terms for the build-out of the fledgling welfare state. The purified geometry of Modernist aesthetics, it was believed, would ensure the democratisation of good taste.[8] Architectural cognoscenti remained enthusiastic when it opened in 1976, and the arts community was thrilled at the recognition afforded by association with a landmark building. The *Guardian*'s theatre correspondent described it as 'a superb piece of sculpture'.[9] More generally, 'it has also given rise to two "co-existent" forms of fandom and imaginative place-making, one focused on its theatrical status, and one focused on its distinctive brutalist architecture'.[10] It was listed by Historic England as a Grade II* building ('particularly important buildings of more than special interest') in 1994. But Londoners, by and large, did not like it. By the time the NT was completed, concrete Brutalism was irredeemably associated with the everyday Modernism of bleak tower blocks on social housing estates. The satirical magazine *Private Eye* alluded to it as the 'National Car Park'. The prince of Wales described it more ponderously as 'a clever way of building a nuclear power station in the middle of London without anyone objecting'. In 1989, a poll of *Observer* readers made the NT a runaway winner in the category of 'Worst Building' in Britain: readers compared it to 'a warehouse for tinned food' and a 'high security prison'.[11]

By the time the NT opened, the Hayward Gallery, Queen Elizabeth Hall and the National Film Theatre had been added to the South Bank arts complex, along with the Royal Festival Hall.

Meanwhile the out-of-scale (twenty-seven-storey) Shell Centre had been built on part of the festival site, behind the car park that had been occupied by the Dome of Discovery. The arts complex soon became synonymous with 'highbrow' arts, isolated in the midst of the South Bank's semi-derelict mixture of wharves, factories, decaying workshops and shabby Victorian housing. Further along the river, the oil-fired Bankside B power station had been built in 1952 in response to a critical shortage of electricity, casting a shadow effect on the surrounding area. With postwar economic recovery, modern social housing began to replace

68 National Theatre terraces.

Victorian terraces and tenements; but then deindustrialisation hit the riverside area hard, resulting in depopulation, social deprivation and dereliction. Dockside industries moved downstream, and warehouses were demolished. Bankside B ceased operations in 1981 as a result of increased oil prices and stood semi-derelict, a symbol of the Surrey riverside's plight. The GLC's response was to rezone the riverside for office and hotel development. Planners' strategies focused on the prospect of large-scale office development schemes, hoping to exploit the commuter hinterlands of Waterloo and London Bridge railway stations. But it only resulted in a series of undistinguished speculative buildings, while the local community's 'Coin Street Campaign' halted office development schemes in favour of providing affordable housing and opening up access to the riverfront for everyone to enjoy.[12]

One early improvement was the conversion of the car park in front of the Shell Centre into a landscaped park and garden in commemoration of the Queen's Silver Jubilee in 1977. The key improvement, however, was the creation of a continuous river walk, the Queen's Walk, in 1990. It immediately generated pedestrian traffic between Waterloo Bridge and Shad Thames, 4 kilometres (2½ miles) away (just beyond Tower Bridge), that encouraged both public and private investment along the riverfront.[13] The Oxo Tower Wharf building, just downstream from the NT, was redeveloped in 1996 as a mixed-use package of co-operative homes, retail design studios, restaurants, cafés, shops and exhibition venues. Further downstream, a replica of Shakespeare's Globe Theatre opened in 1997. Between the two, the derelict Bankside B power station was converted into the Tate Modern gallery, opening in 2000. These developments, along with others, encouraged speculative development.[14] The Surrey bank now had a certain cultural cachet, as well as potential river views. The Shell Centre building has been brought into scale by a surrounding cluster of five towers – Southbank Place – between twenty-one and thirty-seven floors tall, with a mixture of residential, retail, restaurant and office tenants. Further along the riverside are the forty-one-storey South Bank Tower, the fifty-two-storey One Blackfriars, and NEO Bankside, an ultra-exclusive complex of five residential pavilions of between six and twenty-four storeys, aimed at City bonus-day millionaires and the internationally wealthy.

The NT and the Southbank Centre now found themselves anchoring the western end of a 'string of pearls', with a footfall of more than 12 million visitors a year. Having been renamed the

Royal National Theatre in 1988, the NT was spruced up with the removal of staining and graffiti, while the road that had separated the theatre from the river was converted into a new public space, Theatre Square, for outside gatherings and performances. In 2006, the entire Southbank Centre completed a renovation that filled its terraces with cafés and bars; and in 2015 the NT undertook a further refurbishment, converting store rooms into bars and cafés. Lasdun's design for the NT finally came into its own as Brutalism and mid-century design began to enjoy a fashionable revival among some consumers. An 'open foyer policy' made the building accessible to the public all day, seven days a week, with free exhibitions, lunchtime concerts, education programmes, evening music performances, shops, bars and buffets. As architectural historian Barnabas Calder observes,

> the extensive foyers and terraces provide free indoor and outdoor space in which to eat a sandwich, talk to friends, read, listen to music, sunbathe, or just watch the world go by. They are used for exhibitions and a variety of casual, short-term arts events, and are enjoyed and exploited by people who have no intention of coming to a play.[15]

Along with the rest of the Southbank Centre arts complex, the NT has finally become an 'urban landscape'.

Abbey Road Studios
SIR
EDWARD
ELGAR
COMPOSER

19 Abbey Road Studios, St John's Wood

ABBEY Road (the B507) cuts through St John's Wood, a district of late Georgian and early Victorian villas, on its way between central London and West Hampstead. Most of the original villas along Abbey Road itself have been replaced by five- and eight-storey interwar and postwar mansion apartment buildings. Number three – Abbey Road Studios – is one of the few remaining late Georgian villas on this stretch of the road, set back behind a broad car park and fronted by a low brick wall topped by modern railings, with gateways at either end. From the street, the building presents a clean and unfussy façade of two storeys over a basement, with elegantly tall ground-floor windows set within moulded frames in stripped-down Italianate style. Steps lead up from the parking area over the basement lightwell to the front door, with its glass transom that announces 'Abbey Road Studios' in modestly sized lettering. The recording studios themselves are housed in substantial additions to the rear, along with part of the neighbouring building, number five.

For almost a hundred years, number three Abbey Road itself was unexceptional; but it was part of an entirely new kind of district, the prototype for

69 Entrance to Abbey Road Studios.

Victorian suburbia. St John's Wood's detached and semi-detached Italianate villas, set behind garden walls, 'offered the withdrawn seclusion and social homogeneity that its later imitators aspired to achieve'.[1] The district took its name from its medieval owners, the knights of the Order of the Hospital of St John of Jerusalem, a fraternity of military monks. After the dissolution of the monasteries, it stood for 300 years as a tract of the Great Forest of Middlesex under the ownership of the Eyre Estate, one of the Great Estates of the West End. Development began to appear only at the start of the nineteenth century, with the establishment of an orphan school, the opening of Lord's cricket ground and the Eyre Arms Tavern, and the construction of an army riding school. Suburban development began in earnest with the opening up of Abbey Road in 1824. The trustees of the Eyre Estate commissioned the architect Charles Tatham to guide development. The subsequent construction of broad avenues of detached and semi-detached villas in substantial grounds gave St John's Wood a distinctive character and established a new model of suburban structure that catered to privacy, the new touchstone of Victorian bourgeois sensibilities. New omnibus services made it unnecessary for the residents of the district to keep carriages of their own, and so developers were not required to include mews quarters. The result was an unprecedented degree of social segregation, the district's comfortably off residents separated geographically from service workers.

From the start, St John's Wood acquired a slightly bohemian and raffish character, as a result of the disproportionate number of academics, actors, architects, artists, musicians, novelists and philosophers who were drawn to the new district. In addition, a number of frustrated activists and intellectuals settled there after the failure of liberal revolutions across Europe in 1848 and 1849. Among the district's notable residents at one time or another were the future French Emperor Louis Napoleon, novelist George Eliot, actress Sarah Bernhardt, painters Edwin

Landseer, Lawrence Alma-Tadema, John MacWhirter (who built a great house and studio at 1 Abbey Road), W.P. Frith and Ford Madox Brown, poet Robert Browning, social philosopher Herbert Spencer, biologist and anthropologist T.H. Huxley, and political economist Friedrich Engels. Karl Marx lived on the southern fringe of the district at 41 Maitland Park Road. Painters and sculptors were particularly attracted to the larger villas in the district 'with ample spaces and big windows that guaranteed the type of light that artists needed for their compositions'.[2] As a direct consequence of the influx of artists, 'models started to arrive in the neighbourhood. Soon, they had invaded the streets and were circulating freely around the district looking for jobs that the numerous studios in the area could provide them with.'[3]

By the end of the century, St John's Wood had become London's most transgressive urban space, highly charged with a sexual and intellectual openness that was lacking in other districts. A local guide published in 1913 noted obliquely that 'there are certain people we cannot imagine living in the Wood, and there are certain other people we cannot imagine living anywhere else'.[4] The sequestered character of the district offered the possibility of privacy for unorthodox liaisons, and it soon acquired a reputation for tolerance in relation to mistresses ('heroines of passion and victims of propriety') and homosexuals, as well as for discreet and expensive vice. 'On being informed that the philosopher Herbert Spencer had gone to live in St John's Wood a bishop is said to have responded by asking "And who is the lady?"'[5] The southeastern part of the district was known for the residences of high-class prostitutes, 'who could sustain a middle-class life style' there.[6] Some of the streets were later renamed after their notoriety had become too great.

Number three Abbey Road was originally a nine-bedroom residence, Abbey Lodge, built in 1829. When it was converted into apartments in the early 1920s, one of the occupants was John Maundy Gregory, a political fixer who is best remembered for selling honours and who was implicated in the suspicious death of his platonic companion, Edith Rosse, who had lived with him in the Abbey Road apartment.[7] The building was purchased by the Gramophone Company in 1928 with the intention of transforming it into the world's first custom-built recording studio. The site was attractive because it was relatively close to central London, but away from the noise and vibrations of traffic and trains; and its back garden was large enough to accommodate extensive additions and renovations. Wallis, Gilbert and Partners were selected to design the studios, which opened in 1931 with a recording session for the London Symphony Orchestra, conducted by Sir Edward Elgar. By then, the Gramophone Company had merged with its arch-rival, Columbia, to form Electric and Musical Industries Limited (EMI).

> For the next three decades, the studio forged a name for itself as one of the premier recording spaces for classical music and opera, as well as hosting many popular artists of the era, including Glenn Miller, Fred Astaire, Marlene Dietrich, Dame Vera Lynn, Alma Cogan, and Judy Garland, plus various members of a radio comedy team known as The Goons, featuring an up-and-coming star by the name of Peter Sellers.[8]

There are three full-size recording studios, as well as numerous mixing, mastering and copying rooms in Abbey Road Studios. Studio One, the largest, with 12 metre (39ft) ceilings, was designed to replicate a concert hall capable of housing a full symphony orchestra. Studio Two is the size of a large suburban home, with 8 metre (26ft) ceilings; and Studio Three is large enough to accommodate small chamber groups or pop bands. The studios acquired an early reputation for innovation in recording technology and cutting-edge sound engineering, but it was a policy change that led to the studios becoming a landmark building of broader significance. In the late 1950s,

70 Administration building, Abbey Road Studios.

EMI made the studios and their staff available to artists who were not signed with EMI Records. Aspiring artists could now record a high-quality demo that might launch them into stardom. It coincided with the massive social and cultural shifts of the 'long sixties', in which music played an important role and where 'Swinging London' was the crucible of change. The 1950s vanguard of jazz clubs and coffee bars had morphed into a succession of distinctive youth subcultures, beginning with Teddy Boys and Teddy Girls, then Mods and Rockers. By the mid-1960s, the postwar baby boom meant that London's population was the youngest it had been since Roman times, with 40 per cent of the population under the age of twenty-five. Their impact on the economy and on social and cultural trends amounted to what some observers described as a 'youthquake'.[9] Teenage boomers were not only the first generation free from conscription, but also the beneficiaries of an economic boom, the availability of the contraceptive pill, the liberalisation of the law and increasing secularisation. As they entered the labour market and acquired money to spend, they expressed their new freedoms and generational identity through music and fashion. The 'Mersey Beat' notwithstanding, it was in London that innovation and creativity in music and fashion (and the associated businesses of photography and film) flourished. Although directly affecting only a few small parts of the metropolis – and involving perhaps just a couple of thousand principals – the effects of the work (and play) of the leading practitioners rippled through the entire metropolis and beyond, influencing dress, popular culture and patterns of consumption,[10] provoking a subset of counter-cultural movements,[11] and seeding the creative industries that eventually became a key element of London's post-industrial economy. All this also helped to break down the rigid class barriers that the city had nurtured for so long. Some of the most influential icons of 1960s music, fashion, literature and cinema – such as Mary Quant, Lesley Hornby ('Twiggy'), Roger Daltrey, David Bowie, Dave Davies, Mick Jagger, David Bailey, Helen Shapiro, Jane Birkin, Terence Stamp, Michael Caine, John Osborne and Harold Pinter – were famously from the 'wrong' parts of London.

Abbey Road Studios were catapulted into the iconography of the 'Swinging Sixties' when the Beatles decided to pose for an album cover by strolling across the zebra crossing directly outside the studios, and then naming the album after the road itself.[12] *Abbey Road* turned out to be the last album the Beatles recorded together; they had already recorded 190 of their 210 songs at the studios, including every album except *Let It Be*, and every single except 'Can't Buy Me Love', 'Hey Jude', 'Get Back' and 'Let It Be'. By the time *Abbey Road* was released in 1969, the studios had acquired an international reputation among recording artists. Throughout the 1960s and into the 1970s, musicians were still recording their work by playing together in the same room at the same time, the collective sound captured by microphones (rather than later digital recording technologies). The skilled and innovative technicians at Abbey Road Studios were able to produce a distinctive 'British sound' in this way.[13] Other artists associated with the 'Swinging Sixties' who made Abbey Road their creative home included the Hollies, Cilla Black, Gerry and the Pacemakers, the Zombies, Pink Floyd and the Alan Parsons Project. Abbey Road Studios did not have a monopoly – the Rolling Stones, the Who, Jimi Hendrix and Led Zeppelin, for example, tended to use the Olympic Studios in Barnes, West London – but it was Abbey Road Studios and the nearby zebra crossing that captured the public imagination. And more recently, a steady stream of artists – including Kate Bush, Radiohead, Oasis, Kanye West, Amy Winehouse, Florence + The Machine, Ed Sheeran, Lady Gaga and Adele – have added to the aura of the studios.

In the years since the 'Swinging Sixties', Abbey Road has become a tourist site and a place of pilgrimage, particularly for Beatles fans. A 1982 fan guide insisted that 'the true Beatlemaniac must go straight to the Abbey Road crosswalk. Nowhere else is more sacred.'[14] For a long time, staff at Abbey Road 'Somewhat stoically … refused to transform the complex into a formal tourist attraction'.[15] But in 2007, EMI was acquired by private equity firm Terra Firma, and in 2009 the company let it be known that it was planning to sell Abbey Road Studios. This provoked an immediate public outcry involving petitions, media campaigns and intervention by the National Trust.[16] By February 2010, the studio buildings had been given the protection of a Grade II listing by English Heritage; and for good measure, the zebra crossing was added (also Grade II) before the end of the year. Tourists probably find the street view of the building to be underwhelming; but they can make up for any disappointment by adding graffiti to the stone gateposts and low wall outside the parking lot (they are regularly painted over to accommodate the constant stream of visitors and their messages)[17] and by having

themselves photographed on the zebra crossing. Abbey Road Studios has become a marketable brand, with a licensed income stream that supports the economic viability of the studios themselves. A gift shop next door carries branded coffee mugs, fridge magnets, coasters, T-shirts, replica street signs and postcards, while a twenty-four-hour 'crossing cam' records and archives footage of posing visitors.

71 Graffiti on Abbey Road Studios' gatepost.

20 Centre Point, St Giles

STANDING thirty-four storeys high at the intersection of New Oxford Street and Tottenham Court Road, Centre Point was the most visible product of London's postwar economic boom. Completed in 1966, it had immediate symbolic importance as one of London's earliest speculative office towers, signalling the new vitality of the metropolis. *Building* magazine enthused that 'like the Beatles and Mary Quant, this building expresses the supreme confidence of sheer professionalism … more than any other building Centre Point made London swing'.[1] It had been designed for the property tycoon Harry Hyams by Richard Seifert and Partners in collaboration with LCC planners, who endorsed the development as part of their urban design strategy for the West End. In contrast to the boxy shapes and smooth glass curtain walls of most of its contemporaries around the world, the tower is lozenge shaped in plan – its principal elevations slightly convex, with narrow side elevations and a striking façade created by hundreds of pre-cast concrete units that give pattern and texture to the building. Pevsner, sticking as ever to architectural convention, thought it 'coarse',[2] even as it was regarded more generally as capturing the transgressive energy of 'swinging' London. Architectural qualities notwithstanding, Centre Point soon came to be a symbol of both greedy capitalism and the ineptitude of planners.

London's postwar office-building boom was the product of a combination of factors. Some 9 million square feet of office

72 Centre Point.

space had been destroyed in the Blitz, while many of London's surviving office buildings dated from the nineteenth century and were unsuitable for modern office work. As the economy began to recover, the service sector was particularly strong, adding to demand for new office space. London was especially attractive for the 'prestige' headquarters of American companies that were beginning to move in on European markets. For several years the demand for office space had been pent up, partly because of postwar shortages of materials, and partly because of a 'betterment' tax that had been introduced just after the war. The tax was based on the recommendation of the wartime Coalition government's Uthwatt Report, which argued that any increase in the value of land derived from a planning decision granted by a local authority and supported by public expenditure on infrastructure should be taxed. In the spirit of secular reformation that accompanied the founding of the postwar welfare state, the new Labour government imposed a levy on annual increases in urban site values ('betterment') to help pay for improvements to the urban fabric. But without the prospect of windfall profit it quickly became clear that developers were reluctant to make the first move in addressing the pent-up demand for office space. When the Conservatives regained control of parliament in the 1950s, they rescinded the betterment tax and lifted controls over commercial development. Harold Macmillan, the minister of housing and local government, flatly announced that the people whom the government must help are those 'who do things and those who create wealth; yes, the developers, big or small, the people who do things and who create work, be their sphere humble or exalted'.[3]

It set off a building boom that saw the construction of almost 25 million square feet of new office space before Harold Wilson's 1964 Labour government stepped in to control the overheated London property market, passing legislation that strictly controlled office-building throughout Greater London by way of a system of permits, while relocating about 50,000 civil service jobs to provincial centres such as Doncaster, Newcastle and Swansea. The intervening boom had been dominated by a handful of developers who had laid the basis of their fortunes during the later stages of the war and in the immediate postwar years, snapping up bombed-out sites and other potential real estate bargains. When the betterment tax was rescinded and building controls were lifted, they were sitting on sites of inestimable value, able to finance development by borrowing money for projects at a fixed cost while real estate values skyrocketed. The few individuals who had had the foresight and nerve to acquire London real estate before the boom – Joe Levy and his brother David, Harold Samuel, Charles Clore, Felix Fenston, Jack Cotton and Harry Hyams – became household names because of their sudden fortunes. As Oliver Marriott noted in 1967, 'they were men who happened to be in the right business at the right time and, given the profit margins in that business, could hardly fail to make money'.[4] By the 1960s, a full-fledged 'property machine' had become established, involving finance capital, the banking system, insurance companies, pension funds, property bonds, the taxation system and the planning system, as well as the property magnates themselves.[5] Developers stretched the system to its limits,

> borrowing short-term from the clearing banks for site acquisition and then taking out long-term mortgages from insurance companies. By squeezing planning permissions … out of often bemused planning committees and by taking full advantage of inflating office rents they could turn a derelict square of land into a goldmine in a matter of weeks.[6]

The planning system was in its infancy, staffed by engineers and architects, while the universities geared up to provide professional planning courses. London's inexperienced town planners faced the task of rebuilding the city while burdened with the hopes and expectations of the secular reformation that had placed them in the vanguard of change. They had to deal with plans and proposals from property developers that were unprecedented in scale, with serious implications for local communities and circulation systems. In practice, 'the urban planning regime which operated in Britain in the postwar decades furnished the development industry with precisely the conditions in which it flourished'.[7] LCC planners, in particular, were so enamoured with modern design and the possibility of heroic interventions that they were complicit with developers' proposals in broad concept, endorsing the 'rich fantasy life'[8] of developers' futuristic sketches. For the most part, LCC planners confined themselves to policing fire and safety requirements, the details of pedestrian and automobile access, and plot ratios (the legally permissible maximum floor area of buildings that could be put on a site of given size), so long as developers provided the big ideas and the financing.

It was Harry Hyams' secretive negotiations over plot ratios that made Centre Point possible. Hyams, 'the daddy of all developers',[9] was notorious for his ability to operate stealthily. As chairman of a publicly listed company, he was required by law to hold an annual meeting for the company's shareholders. For many years he chose 4.15 p.m. on New Year's Eve. Knowing that local landowners had been frustrating LCC plans to build a roundabout at the busy junction at the north end of Charing Cross Road, Hyams stepped in and bought up an entire package of land around the intersection. He then negotiated with the LCC to allow the plot ratio for the whole site to be applied to the smaller part that he wanted to develop. In return, he offered the LCC the land required for its roundabout and adjacent road improvements.[10] The idea sat well with planners familiar with classical urban design principles that encouraged locating prominent buildings at major traffic intersections. London would have a futuristic skyscraper punctuating the vistas along Oxford Street, New Oxford Street and Tottenham Court Road, and the LCC's highway engineers would have the roundabout they thought they needed. The final deal assigned the freehold of the whole site to the LCC, with Hyams securing the land he needed for Centre Point at a fixed rent of £18,500 per annum on a 150-year lease, along with permission to breach existing rules over maximum height and to build at twice the statutory five-to-one ratio of floor space to site area.

Hyams hired Richard Seifert and Partners as his architects. Seifert had a reputation for understanding the business side of things and for his ability to work hand in hand with both developers and LCC planners. His principal design partner, George Marsh, could then focus on the details of aesthetics and technical systems. Centre Point was built at a cost of £5.5 million (equivalent to £136 million in 2023) between 1963 and 1966. It was an innovative building in terms of its construction, using prefabricated concrete units lifted into position by an internally situated crane that rose in height with the building. In addition to the thirty-four-storey tower, the Centre Point complex included Centre Point House, a nine-storey block with retailing at street level and office and residential space above, with an enclosed bridge over St Giles High Street connecting to the tower. The geometric pattern of the tower's façade, accented by a zig-zag cornice and with distinctive geometric pilotis (piers) supporting the whole thing, was something of a sensation. Ernő Goldfinger, a prominent Modernist architect, described the tower as London's first Pop-art skyscraper. Seifert himself regarded it as his 'first exercise in sculptural form, to get away from glass and concrete boxes as such … Architecturally it has a greater strength about it than a glass building.'[11]

The gloss soon faded from the project when word got out that the completed tower stood empty in the middle of an economic boom – only because Hyams insisted on renting to a single tenant, and at an unrealistically high price. There was a simple commercial logic to this at the time: real estate values were rising so rapidly during the late 1960s and early 1970s that the capital appreciation of an empty building more than compensated for the loss of a fixed rental income. Furthermore, no rates had to be paid on empty property.[12] The book value of Centre Point quadrupled in just ten years, but meanwhile it became symbolic of the stereotype of shady and disreputable speculative developers. Hyams denied, at every turn, any accusation of purposely keeping the building empty, instructing his lawyer to fire off letters and threats of legal action to anyone who suggested the vacancy was deliberate. Meanwhile, the 'planning gain' in the original deal came to nought after Ernest Marples, minister of transport, changed the West End's road system, making Tottenham Court Road and Charing Cross Road one-way routes, and thus rendering the Centre Point roundabout unnecessary.

The very visible vacancy of Centre Point led to the uncared-for area beneath the link to Centre Point House becoming a haunt of vagrants and drug users, many of whom were homeless. The symbolism of the homeless gathering beneath an empty skyscraper was powerful. In January 1974, protesters managed to occupy the tower briefly, gaining entrance courtesy of two of their colleagues who had taken jobs as security guards for the building. The publicity around the homelessness issue prompted the launch of a charity, called Centrepoint, for homeless young people. Because the charity was widely believed to occupy part of the tower, homeless youths were drawn to it, and from there were assisted by the charity. Centre Point itself stood empty until 1975, when Hyams finally relented and leased the building floor by floor to commercial tenants – though it was never fully occupied.

73 Centre Point, detail.

The tower stood as a rude reminder of the influence of speculative developers and the ineptitude of planners until the 2000s, by which time Hyams and his fellow developers had faded from tabloid scrutiny and public memory. Meanwhile, the embarrassment of the roundabout had been eclipsed by a much more general dissatisfaction with the planning system, which had in any case been thoroughly emasculated by the Thatcher administration (and successive governments).[13] Mid-century Modernism had meanwhile begun to be more widely appreciated by affluent, design-aware households. Centre Point had been listed at Grade II by English Heritage in 1995, after the Ministry of Housing and Local Government extended the possibility of listing to all buildings more than thirty years old – ten years if the building was threatened – in the hope of preserving exemplars of Modernism amid rapidly changing property markets.[14] Finally, the high-end London residential property market had become a focus for new forms of financialised global investment. A new generation of property developers was quick to spot the potential of Centre Point, especially after the Underground station at Tottenham Court Road had been designated for a major upgrade to accommodate London's new Crossrail Line (now formally renamed the Elizabeth Line). Centre Point now enjoyed an even more significant strategic location, directly connected to both Heathrow Airport and the City of London.

In anticipation of the opening of the Elizabeth Line, part of the Tottenham Court Road area was designated an 'Area of Intensification' under the Greater London Authority's first *London Plan* in 2004 (then becoming an 'Opportunity Area' in the 2008 and subsequent plans). The construction of the Elizabeth Line required the demolition of a landmark music venue, the London Astoria; and as developers moved in, 'opportunity' meant that while the district was cleaned up, it also lost much of its character. Most of Denmark Street ('Britain's Tin Pan Alley', a distinctive strip of shops selling musical instruments and sheet music, interspersed with clubs and bars and with rehearsal spaces and agents' and managers' offices on the upper floors) has gradually been bought up by a single developer, whose leasing and redevelopment strategies have replaced the rough-and-ready vibrancy of the street with an ambience more in keeping with its neighbouring investments on Charing Cross Road next to Centre Point.

Centre Point itself, meanwhile, was acquired in 2011 by a private equity fund, Almacantar, for £120 million. The initiative was part of a new pattern of investment in the London property market that took hold after 2008, driven by private equity funds whose investors include wealthy individuals and families seeking to deposit their money in a relatively safe investment climate.[15] Almacantar proposed adapting the tower to take advantage of the booming high-end London residential property market, but first had to secure planning permission. Pointing out that the listed building was in need of major repairs and refurbishment, and that it was 'designed for an era of typewriters and telephones, secretarial pools and filing' and could not economically be converted to meet modern business needs, the company's planning application sought to convert the tower into eighty-two apartments, claiming that only a change of use to residential would generate sufficient returns to make redevelopment a realistic proposition. This invoked long-standing national planning legislation that required developers to provide between 35 and 50 per cent affordable housing in projects of more than ten homes. ('Affordable' in this statutory context is defined as up to 80 per cent of the local market rent, which in London's overheated property market is hardly 'affordable' for a very large fraction of the population.) Developers who feel their schemes are not commercially viable because of the obligation to provide affordable housing can submit a financial viability assessment explaining precisely why their profitability is threatened, and Almacantar duly argued that their financial projections could only be met if affordable housing were to be provided elsewhere. The eventual compromise included the provision by Almacantar of thirteen flats for Camden Council to let at social rent in White Lion House, nearby on St Giles High Street, on the site of a former pub, the Intrepid Fox.

This left the conversion of Centre Point tower – now called Centre Point Residences – to an undiluted luxury market, with a mixture of small one- and two-bedroom apartments with combined kitchen/living rooms (priced at between £1.8 million and £5 million), three-bedroom apartments with separate kitchens (£7.65 million), and a prestige two-storey penthouse apartment (five bedrooms with en-suite bathrooms, a reception area, kitchen, study, living and dining rooms with 5 metre (16ft) high ceilings, and a full wraparound outdoor terrace: £55 million).

All residents have twenty-four-hour access to a thirty-strong concierge team, a club lounge with a dining room, a cinema room, gym, spa and a 30 metre (98ft) infinity pool overlooking Oxford Street. When potential buyers began to make offers well below the asking price, apparently because of concerns about the economic implications of 'Brexit' and the possibility of tax increases on overseas investors, Almacantar took the remaining apartments off the market in 2018, rather than reduce prices. Eight months later, with demand again picking up – thanks in part to the vibrancy of the redeveloped St Giles area, with its big media companies, small consultancies and startups – the company decided to start marketing Centre Point Residences again. The opening of the Elizabeth Line in 2022, together with the development around Centre Point of an entertainment centre with an immersive walk-in exhibition space (the Outernet), a mixed-use development with a new theatre (Soho Place) and streetscape improvements – bicycle lanes, pedestrian walkways and a plaza – has made the intersection into something that LCC planners might have settled for when they were negotiating with Harry Hyams fifty years ago.

74 Centre Point, St Giles Square.

21 Penton House, Thamesmead

BRITAIN'S first residential tower block was The Lawn, completed in 1951 as part of the first phase of Harlow New Town, just outside Greater London. By the mid-1970s, more than 6,000 tower blocks had been built around the country. Almost all were municipal housing, and the majority were system built, using pre-cast components designed to minimise on-site construction work. Penton House was one of them, along with twenty other tower blocks in Thamesmead, a vast development housing more than 30,000 people on former marshland between Woolwich and Erith. Thamesmead was designed by LCC architects and planners to be the 'Town of Tomorrow',[1] and in many ways it was the culmination of the golden age of British town planning and urban design. Tower blocks brought Modernism to the urban landscapes of the welfare state,[2] physical manifestations of the postwar consensus that created the welfare state as the nation's settlement for the burdens of wartime duty and sacrifice. Affordable social housing was a cornerstone of the welfare state, along with health care, education and social security, providing the foundation on which a generation of working-class families could thrive, learn and give something back: the greatest expression of humanity through policy that British society has ever

75 Penton House, Thamesmead.

achieved. But even in their finest hour, London's architects and planners were forced to watch themselves fail. By the time the first families moved into Penton House, the shortcomings of industrialised high-rise housing had been dramatically exposed by the Ronan Point disaster (when the corner of a tower block in Canning Town, Newham, collapsed after a simple kitchen accident, killing four and injuring seventeen in 1968). By the late 1970s, the postwar municipal building boom was well and truly over, along with the credibility of Modernist architecture and planning. Tower blocks like Penton House had become the tombstones of the welfare state.

There had been an inevitability about high-rise buildings as the solution to the problem of a lack of decent, affordable housing that faced successive governments after the Second World War. The avant-garde of the architecture profession certainly needed little convincing: they had long been persuaded by Le Corbusier's argument in the urban planning project/exhibition *La Ville Contemporaine* (1922) that the key to modern urban design was to reduce the congestion and slums of city centres by building upwards. His high-rise Unité d'Habitation, built in Marseille in 1952, was widely admired in architectural circles. Informed opinion had coalesced around Modernism in the interwar period as a unifying system of technology and aesthetics, and a progressive response to the elitism of nineteenth-century bourgeois culture. Architecture and town planning were to be agents of redemption, the physical manifestations of social reform. Through functional design, modern materials and industrialised production, architecture and planning would finally improve the physical, social, moral and aesthetic condition of cities. An evangelical spirit carried over to postwar thinking: cities *should* be better places; they *could* be.

In 1955, the Royal Institute of British Architects held an influential symposium on high-rise flats, opened by Dame Evelyn Sharp, permanent secretary at the Ministry of Housing and

Local Government, who quoted a poem about the beauty of tall buildings. It was an encouraging sign for the design professions, but the real turning point was the Conservative government's realisation that the combination of its slum-clearance programme, its green-belt policy and the density limits specified by Abercrombie's Greater London Plan left no alternative but high-rise solutions. By now public housing had become a political numbers game. The government set a national target of 300,000 units per year, initiating a golden age of municipal building that was to last for twenty years.[3] The big builders promptly moved in, pitching their ability to solve the housing problem through economies of scale and using their close links with policymakers to aggressively lobby for high-rise system building, relying on their expertise in building technology to exclude local competitors.[4] By way of encouragement for high-rise local-authority building, the government introduced a schedule of subsidies in 1956 that gave councils more money per flat the higher it was from the ground: three times as much for a flat in a fifteen-storey block as for a ground-floor unit, for example. In 1961, Harold Macmillan's Conservative government established mandatory and relatively generous space standards for municipal housing and introduced incentives that encouraged the use of industrialised building techniques. The approach, relying heavily on system-built tower blocks, was endorsed by the incoming Labour government in 1964 and became an essential part of GLC housing policy from 1965. Labour's housing minister, Richard Crossman, pledged to build a further 500,000 homes by the end of the decade.

The desirability and effectiveness of Modernist architecture and urban design had been challenged as early as 1961 by American-Canadian urbanist Jane Jacobs, who reasoned that, left to planners, city landscapes 'will be spacious, park-like, and uncrowded. They will feature long green vistas. They will be stable and symmetrical and orderly. They will be clean, impressive, and monumental. They will have all the attributes of a well-kept, dignified cemetery.'[5] Others were quick to document the technical shortcomings of industrialised building systems, while newspapers focused on the challenges of high-rise living. Nevertheless, a combination of hubris and evangelical zeal enabled the design press and the professional design community to overlook uncomfortable evidence. More and more tower blocks were built. The GLC alone built 384 in the ten years between 1964 and 1974. The new London boroughs followed suit, and in all some 68,500 flats in blocks of ten or more storeys were built in Greater London over the same period.

Building sites were harder and harder to find, however. Ever since the late 1950s, the LCC had been looking for a site on which to relocate up to 100,000 Londoners from substandard housing in inner-city districts. Plans for a New Town at Hook, in northeast Hampshire, had to be shelved after objections that it would destroy thousands of acres of prime agricultural land and cause significant environmental damage to a fragile and historic landscape.[6] When the GLC finally secured a sufficiently large site on the south bank of the Thames between Woolwich and Erith, architects and planners were able to unleash their good intentions, unhindered by any such concerns. It was not a propitious location, with soggy land vulnerable to flooding, a nearby sewage works, and heavy, polluting industry on both sides of the river. The western part had belonged to the Royal Arsenal for hundreds of years and had ended up as a military tip, before being sold to the GLC. Much of the area was covered in up to 7 metres (23ft) of peat, with the water-table less than a metre below the surface. More than 40,000 piles had to be driven just to prepare it for the first phase of development. The site was also administratively awkward, straddling the boroughs of (Labour-leaning) Greenwich and (Tory-leaning) Bexley, and therefore subject to different local policies and services. One of Bexley's building codes, imposed after the Thames had breached the river wall in 1953, was a

76 Cover of the GLC's 1970–71 Thamesmead report.

stipulation that any habitable rooms in buildings on its low-lying lands should stand at least 8 feet 6 inches (2.6 metres) above the high-water mark.

The GLC envisaged a self-contained mini-New Town of about 60,000 residents on the site, with a mixture of private and socially rented housing. It was conceived as a huge exercise in community building, based on the premise that a successful, diverse community could be produced from the drawing board with the right combination of layout and amenities – diversity at the time being construed only in terms of family size, age and social class. Understandably, the GLC needed a name for the development that was not associated with either borough, or with the marshland or the nearby landmarks of Belmarsh prison and Crossness sewage works. It was left to a local newspaper competition to decide on 'Thamesmead'. The GLC's planners, drawing on early proposals that had been developed by LCC staff for Hook, utilised the entire canon of Modernist architecture, urban design and planning, much of it derived from interwar ideas set out in the Athens Charter and the writings of Le Corbusier, Ebenezer Howard, Patrick Abercrombie and Clarence Perry.[7] Thamesmead would be organised around segregated land-use zones and feature tall apartment blocks at widely spaced intervals, deck-access 'streets in the sky', traffic-free neighbourhood units with local amenities and schools within walking distance, a central pedestrian precinct, and industrial estates to provide jobs. Six subterranean gas-fired boilers provided heat and hot water, which was included in every household's rent. Poor road and rail connectivity to the rest of the metropolis would be partially rectified by a new railway station and a tunnel beneath the Thames, while a 200-berth marina on the river and a shopping mall would help to ensure that Thamesmead would attract a population that was 'balanced' in terms of income and social class.

What made Thamesmead distinctive was the architects' and planners' solution to the marshy site. Seizing its limitations as an opportunity, housing and shops were elevated to a first-floor podium, connected by a network of bridges, cycle routes and footpaths, and with roads and garages beneath. It made for a futuristic-looking setting that decisively addressed one of the principal planning preoccupations of the time: the separation of pedestrian and motor traffic. The boggiest parts of the site were transformed into shallow holding lakes and canals to hold storm water, and the planners took advantage of this to add waterscapes as another distinctive element of their urban design. Penton House is one of four high-rise towers that overlook the central body of water, Southmere Lake. Edward Hollamby, the LCC architect who worked on early schematics for the project, allowed himself to get carried away with the imagery: 'We wanted to relate marsh and river and buildings. The idea was to raise everything on platforms, like ships, so that the town would float over the marshland – to relate the ships on the Thames to the ship-like platforms and towers of the town.'[8]

77 Tower blocks overlooking Southmere Lake.

Following planning orthodoxy, the site was divided into sectors, with Tavy Bridge – a raised public square and shopping area – and Lakeside Health Centre occupying Thamesmead Central; industry and commerce in Thamesmead East; and the main municipal housing zone in Thamesmead South (itself zoned into a regular area and the charmlessly named HRA, or Higher Rented Area, let to better-off tenants in the cause of a 'balanced' community). Thamesmead North (social housing) and Thamesmead West (private housing) were developed later, after embankments and walls had been installed along the riverside and the danger of flooding downgraded to the point where housing could follow more traditional design standards, with ground-floor homes. Terry Gooch and his family became Thamesmead's first residents when they moved from their cramped flat in Peckham, where they had an outside toilet and no bathroom, to Coralline Walk in 1968, arriving at their new address in a chauffeured car. Because of extensive ongoing construction, the Gooch family had no neighbours for six months.[9] When other council tenants did arrive, they were all families whose housing records had passed scrutiny and, following the coercive paternalism of housing management practice, they were matched to the different kinds of housing. No families with small children, for example, were assigned to Penton House or the other towers. Penton House itself, like the other towers, was thirteen storeys tall, with forty-eight flats. Like the maisonettes and deck-access terraces on the rest of the Southmere Estate, it was built using a pre-cast concrete panel system called Balency and Schuhl. A temporary factory was set up in West Thamesmead by the construction company, Cubitt, to produce wall panels that incorporated service elements, such as plumbing, wiring, gas pipework and ducting, thus allowing for fast and efficient construction.

The pre-cast system made for a Brutalist, sculptural appearance that sat well with Modernist sensibilities. Hubert Bennett, the GLC's chief architect, received the prestigious Patrick Abercrombie award from the Union Internationale des Architectes in 1969 in recognition of the design for Thamesmead. The judges praised the proposed development for its 'harmonious integration of human values, aesthetic expression and modern techniques'.[10] Richard MacCormac, writing in the *Architects' Journal* in 1972, observed that

> It represents a reaction by architects against the middle-class values of suburbia and the feeble aesthetics of the Mark I New Towns in favour of a bold act of communal architecture which conceives the town as a building and preserves the values of street life.[11]

The GLC touted Thamesmead as a 'City for the 21st Century', and in the early 1970s it attracted around 10,000 visitors a year – architects, students, sociologists and politicians. Across the Atlantic, the *Boston Globe* wrote that 'Every old American city needs a Thamesmead.'[12] The Gooch family, like many of their new neighbours, reported favourably on their new homes and on Thamesmead's amenities in comparison with those at their previous addresses, though Jean Gooch couldn't wait to put up wallpaper to soften the stark white modern décor. Pat Tompkins, the first resident of the new Area 3, recalled that 'We were all thrown together and immediately became friends with all our neighbours.' Salliann Heaton moved to Thamesmead in 1976, when she was twelve years old:

> We had great first impressions: we had the paddling pool and the park and the lake and we thought we were proper special because we'd been brought to Thamesmead. It was lovely ... When we moved to Thamesmead it felt like we could start a new chapter ... Thamesmead was like a giant playground. You never had to cross any roads, everywhere had flyovers.

Sheniz Bayraktar was just ten when she moved to Thamesmead: 'Everyone was excited because we all moved there at the same time. I had a bedroom of my own and I loved it from the start ... We were friendly with all our neighbours; we were like a big extended family.'[13] It was all consistent with a brief promotional film, *Living at Thamesmead*, produced in 1974 by the GLC.

The good feelings did not last long. In 1972, the Conservative government had introduced a 'Cost Yardstick' for municipal housing that forced the GLC to trim budgets at Thamesmead. It led in turn 'to the original richness and complexity of form being ironed out into grim and regimented housing blocks'.[14] The economic recession following the 1973 OPEC oil crisis and the three-day week and rolling power cuts of 1973–74 meant that construction work slowed considerably. The shopping mall, the marina and the new cross-river connection were dropped, and the new railway station never materialised. Thamesmead's isolation from the rest of the metropolis was cruelly underscored when the Docklands Light Railway, built in the 1980s, stopped short at Woolwich, 5 kilometres (3 miles) away. The planners' adherence to the dogma of zoning and land-use segregation resulted in the loss of serendipity and the vitality of the street life that residents had become used to in their former neighbourhoods. Areas for socialising and play were made available in Thamesmead, but they were segregated from the residential areas of the estate, precluding the spontaneity and creative disorder of older urban areas.

Meanwhile, Thamesmead's physical and social problems became glaringly apparent. Flats were prone to condensation and roofs tended to leak. A survey undertaken by the Thamesmead Community Association found that a third of households were affected to some extent. Frustrated with the response from the GLC and the building contractor, Cubitt, the Community Association printed a thousand posters that proclaimed 'We've Got Damp', posting them all over the estate:

> Soon it was quite impossible to route VIPs away from them. Their questions became embarrassing. Soon after this the GLC began taking much more determined action to cure the damp, bringing technologists in to occupy a flat and study the problem at first hand.[15]

Damp was not the only design problem. The canals and lakes proved difficult to clean and maintain, lending an impression of disorder and decay. Many of the vacant spaces beneath the buildings were 'an open invitation for vandals to gather, to break into and burn cars, sniff glue, or generally make mischief'.[16] And because there were more garages beneath the buildings than car owners upstairs, many of the garages themselves wound up as workshops, sheds or boat storage and changing rooms, confounding planners' assumptions about people's needs and behaviour.

The economic recession of the mid-1970s was directly reflected in the profile of Thamesmead residents. One account suggests that two thirds of the tenants were unable to pay their rent in 1975.[17] High levels of poverty and unemployment, in turn, made Thamesmead unattractive to retailing and private-sector service providers, further deepening the localised cycle of disadvantage. The place had already acquired a negative image nationally as a result of Stanley Kubrick's 1971 film *A Clockwork Orange*. Kubrick and his team had

> scouted dozens of locations in Greater London, searching for architecture that would be plausible both as a space produced by an authoritarian state and as one neglected enough to be overrun with the kind of wanton violence depicted in the film's first few scenes.[18]

Racial tension, meanwhile, had been an issue from the start. Robert Dyer, who moved from Lewisham to Thamesmead in 1976, when he was thirteen years old, recalled that

> At that time there were hardly any black families in Thamesmead, and I was the only black boy in my class ... There was a lot of racial tension. When the Vietnamese immigrants came to Thamesmead a few years later the far right seemed to focus their attention in their direction for a while.[19]

By the mid-1980s, racist violence on council estates had become a national issue, and Thamesmead was no exception. 'The walkways, corridors and courtyards that many architects believed would aid the production of communities instead left non-white residents visible and vulnerable.'[20]

As Simon Jenkins observed in his book *Outer London*, the mix of Brutalist medium-rise tower blocks and low-rise terraces that looked so terrific on paper had become a very visible failure:

> ... the architects have tried to recreate the harbour of Port Grimaud on the Cote d' Azur, with piazzas, lakes and sailing boats. Rubbish fills every corner; the concrete is stained and ugly and small boys wander about indolently smashing bottles and vandalizing cars. It is worth a visit to see how wrong-headed paternalist British architecture in the 1960s could be.[21]

By the mid-1980s, the idealistic dimension of the project had been entirely expunged. Thamesmead was just another struggling estate; Penton House was just another tower block. Before they knew it, planners' rationality and their predilection for efficient and tidy land-use patterns had led them to become social gatekeepers. Before they knew it, architects' evangelical belief in high-rise living led them to adopt system building, while their insistence on the primacy of architecture-as-art relegated both clients and users to passive beholders. Thamesmead North and Thamesmead West, built out in the 1980s and 1990s as mid-rise apartment buildings and winding drives of private housebuilders' standard brick houses, were unrecognisable from Southmere's towers and deck-access terraces. To the horror of the architectural commentariat, the Thatcher administration's right-to-buy legislation had meanwhile left its mark on the Southmere Estate, its Modernist aesthetic blemished by the symbols of home ownership: neo-Georgian doors, bottle-bottom glazing and fancy trimmings. But at least by now the only witnesses were the occasional videographers looking for a location to represent the social alienation associated with modern architecture and postwar planning (among those selecting Thamesmead: the makers of *The Misfits*, a teen TV series; and Aphex Twin's horror-themed music video for 'Come to Daddy').

The GLC was disbanded in 1986 and Thamesmead was taken over by a trust, run by residents,[22] that eventually devolved housing development and maintenance to the Gallions Housing Association, which in 2014 joined the larger Peabody Group.[23] Under Peabody's ten-year plan, Penton House and the other towers facing Southmere Lake have been refurbished, with new windows and improved communal areas and entrances. Elsewhere, the story is one of large-scale demolition and rebuilding. With ongoing redevelopment at the Royal Docks just across the river and the opening in 2022 of the Elizabeth Line as far as Abbey Wood station (little more than a kilometre – 0.6 miles – from Penton House), razing swathes of the estate in order to build for a more middle-class market was a plausible strategy. Peabody also plans a new £8 billion extension, Thamesmead Waterfront, with several thousand new homes and commercial and leisure space along more than a mile of undeveloped river frontage. Meanwhile, though, Peabody's first efforts at regeneration have been disappointing. In the Tavy Bridge area, redeveloped as Southmere Village with new homes, a new library, a new public square, community facilities and commercial space, 'the architects have created a placeless muddle', observes architecture critic Oliver Wainwright:

> This could have been an opportunity to make a spectacular waterside civic square, with proud public buildings of a calibre that finally fulfilled Thamesmead's dreams. But the result is a mess. The library, designed by Bisset Adams, looks like a temporary sales office, consisting of a white container covered in jazzy perforated patterns, perched at a jaunty angle on top of a glass box.[24]

Jane Jacobs would not have approved.

VI

GLOBAL LONDON

LONDON has long been a 'world city', one of a few in which a disproportionate amount of the world's business is conducted: organising trade and executing colonial, imperial and geopolitical strategies. It is now, in the lexicon of urban studies, a 'global city', concerned less with the orchestration of trade and the deployment of imperial power, and more with transnational corporate organisation, international banking and finance, fashion, design and the media. Along with New York, Tokyo and a few other cities, London is the site of extraordinary concentrations of activities associated with organising and managing the flows of capital, information and cultural products that collectively underpin the economic and cultural globalisation of the world. The shift in emphasis is a result of the evolution of the world economy. Beginning in the 1970s, North American and European manufacturers moved production facilities offshore to take advantage of cheap labour and to evade domestic trade unions. This created a need for specialised international financial services to facilitate the flow of components and goods. London already had a comparative advantage in the size and experience of its City financial sector and its long-standing familiarity with the international network of tax havens in former British territories (including Belize, the British Virgin Islands, the Cayman Islands, Hong Kong and Singapore). The introduction of desktop computers and the internet meant that geography became a decisive factor. Intermediate between New York and Tokyo,

78 The Docklands financial district on the Isle of Dogs.

London became pivotal in the emerging globe-spanning system of twenty-four-hour trading in currencies, stocks and specialised financial instruments.

Global London has meanwhile become distinctly multicultural. The 2021 census of population found that only 43 per cent of London's population identified as 'White British'. London is home to almost 350,000 Afro-Caribbeans, about 300,000 Indians and more than 100,000 each from Pakistan and Bangladesh, as well as to a large British-born ethnic minority population. The number of Asian-born residents increased significantly in the 1970s and 1980s, as family reunification followed the first wave of predominantly male immigrants drawn to the boom economy of the 1950s and 1960s. Meanwhile, hundreds of thousands moved to London during the UK's membership of the European Union, including more than 200,000 from France, 148,000 from Romania, 127,000 from Poland and 60,000 from Germany. In addition, the last several decades have seen the arrival of a mixture of refugees, asylum seekers and skilled migrants from around the world. An extraordinary number of different languages – more than 250 – are spoken across London's neighbourhoods.[1] The succession of different minority groups in particular districts is exemplified by the Jamme Masjid mosque in Brick Lane (Chapter 22): formerly a synagogue, before that a Methodist chapel, and before that a Huguenot chapel.

London's economy has been transformed, as dockland activities and warehousing have disappeared and the manufacturing base has been eroded, along with the deindustrialisation of the rest of the country. In its place has emerged a 'new economy' based on technology-intensive manufacturing, services (business, financial and personal), cultural-products industries (such as media, film and music), and design and fashion-oriented forms of production (such as clothing, furniture, product design and interior design). London has also fostered a tourist industry, beginning with the creation of the London Tourist Board in 1963 and continuing with the Greater London Authority's responsibility for the promotion and development of tourism. London is now the third most visited city in the world (after Hong Kong and Singapore), with more than 22 million inbound visitors each year, accounting for one in seven of the city's jobs and around 70 per cent of the aggregate turnover in London's pubs, bars, restaurants and hotels.[2] Overall, the growth of the highly paid financial and business services sector has been paralleled by the growth of a low-skilled, low-paid service sector and the decline of skilled middle-income employees in manufacturing industry, making London an engine of inequality, as well as of wealth.[3] Whereas in the rest of the UK the median income of the top 10 per cent of households is five times greater than the median income of the bottom 10 per cent, in London it is ten times greater.

London's social and economic disparities have been intensified by the transition to a political economy dominated by neoliberalism. Since the late 1970s, urban policy has become concerned more with providing a 'good business climate' than with the traditional concerns of civil society. Neoliberalism has meant a diminished role for the state, the privatisation of utilities, the sell-off of council housing to tenants and the handing-over of remaining social housing estates to housing associations that have effectively acted as agents of privatisation and gentrification. Particularly significant for London was the abolition of the GLC in 1986. Its municipal policies had consistently aggravated Conservative governments, and its abolition ensured that there was no overall strategic local government body for London until the creation of the Greater London Authority (GLA) in early 2000. 'Roll-back' neoliberalism soon contributed to social distress of the kind that interwar Keynesian economists and postwar welfare state planners had previously aspired to eradicate.[4]

Equally significant was the deregulation of financial markets in 1986. 'Light-touch' regulation of the financial sector was seen by the Thatcher government as essential to London's status as a world banking capital. Long-standing rules that barred foreign companies from operating in the City were scrapped, and face-to-face dealing on the floor of the Stock Exchange was replaced with screen-based trading. The result was the so-called Big Bang: a restructuring and realignment of firms in stock and bond markets and an overall recasting of the City's office employment profile. It also led, of course, to the shameful and irresponsible role of many City financial firms in the international financial meltdown of 2008 and the subsequent multi-year recession. Meanwhile, London's role as the pre-eminent financial hub of the global economy had been consolidated. The two districts whose physical fabric was most affected by the Big Bang were the City and Docklands. The boom in banking and financial services created a demand for high-tech, large-floor-plate offices that the existing building stock could not satisfy. This encouraged both the government and private investors in the development of a major new office district, Canary Wharf, 5 kilometres (3 miles) to the east of the City, on the site of the derelict quays of the Isle of Dogs. The signature building, One Canada Square (Chapter 23) is now surrounded by a forest of tall buildings. The Big Bang also created a great deal of wealth among a new, young class that, in turn, was promptly reflected in the built environment in various ways, including a spate of new-build gentrification projects in the form of loft apartments and riverside condominium towers.

The first elected mayor of London, Ken Livingstone, had committed the GLA to strengthening London's role as a major international financial centre in 2000. In a coup d'état against postwar planning orthodoxy, Livingstone actively supported the development of tall buildings (twenty storeys or more), believing the skyline to be an important means of asserting and consolidating London's status as a global city. It was also hoped that loosening height restrictions would help to secure 'planning gain' from developers: they would be allowed to build tall, so long as they contributed to public infrastructure and affordable housing. For someone branded 'Red Ken' by the Tory press, the role of developers' friend was unlikely and unexpected. With the appearance in 2004 of Norman Foster's forty-one-storey building at 30 St Mary Axe, Livingstone's strategy began to take form. The building was well received by the public, national media and the architectural press (making it instantly 'iconic') and was promptly nicknamed the 'Gherkin'. Since then, both the City and Canary Wharf have acquired distinctive clusters of towers and, with height restrictions no longer a concern, tall buildings have appeared as far away as Islington, and even across the river, where The Shard (Chapter 24) is the tallest of all.

London's amped-up role in the global economy, together with its infrastructure of high-end consumption, brought global investment, including 'flight capital' from the super-rich in less stable economies. When, following the financial crisis of 2008, Swiss banks were less willing to fulfil their traditional role of no-questions-asked banking, central London's property market filled the gap: somewhere for the global super-rich – the so-called ultra-high-net-worth individuals with more than £20 million in liquid assets – to park their money. The United Kingdom actively courted wealthy foreigners, offering 'golden visas' and a pathway to permanent residence, in return for an investment of at least £2 million. Between 2008 and 2022, when the scheme was closed, nearly 5,000 of these 'Tier I' visas were issued, a third of them to Chinese citizens and a further 18 per cent to Russians. Many of these new residents purchased real estate in London, as did many other overseas individuals. Some 40 per cent of all the new homes sold in London in 2020 were purchased by non-UK buyers (down from a staggering 75 per cent in 2013). By 2020, there were more than 85,000 properties in London belonging to overseas homeowners, while another 44,000 properties were owned by offshore companies.[5] Residential properties in high-end residential districts like Belgravia, Kensington and Mayfair became a form of reserve currency for the '1 per cent' as wealthy foreigners acquired 'super-prime' properties – homes costing more than £10 million – in which they may have no intention of living (except, perhaps, during one or two shopping binges each year). The consequent property bubble significantly overheated the housing market across the entire metropolis. There are signs, however, that London's super-prime real estate market, at least, is cooling off in the wake of the Russian invasion of Ukraine in 2022: sanctions on many ultra-high-net-worth Russians have denied them the opportunity to invest in the property market at any level. New laws on financial transparency were meanwhile introduced in 2022 to stem the flow of dodgy cash of any kind into the London property market.

The overheated real estate market has contributed to an acute shortage of affordable housing across the metropolis. By the late 1980s, the capacity of local authorities to deliver social housing had been significantly restricted, with housing associations (later renamed Registered Social Landlords) given the task of meeting the need for affordable housing, funding a significant part of their activity through private-sector borrowing. In the late 1990s, the New Labour government adopted the neoliberal policy of public–private partnerships as a means of kick-starting an 'urban renaissance'. The idea was for developers to be allowed to raze or renovate troublesome council estates, delivering a specified number of new affordable homes, cross-subsidising them by constructing more desirable apartments for private sale or rent. More than fifty London social housing estates have undergone 'regeneration' in this way, improving the quality of the housing stock across the metropolis, but also prompting accusations of state-led gentrification of low-income areas.

Public–private partnerships have also been crucial to the large-scale urban development projects that have been a signature feature of London's emergence as a global city. Located on extensive 'brownfield' sites (that had already gone through one or more cycles of industrial development), their scale and complexity have involved coalitions and partnerships among government agencies, international capital, international corporate interests, property developers and construction interests.[6] Docklands, London's first large-scale regeneration scheme, has been followed by Paddington Basin, King's Cross, Nine Elms, the South Bank and Olympic Park. All are characterised by a mix of residential, office, retail, leisure and public open spaces. At Nine Elms, for example, the landmark Battersea Power Station, renovated at a cost of £9 billion, is a mixed-use development that includes Apple's UK headquarters in 46,450 square metres (500,000 sq. ft) of office space in the old boiler room, as well as retailing and 'luxury' apartments. The developers contributed nearly £350 million to the construction of two new Tube stations on the Northern Line – Battersea Power Station and Nine Elms – allowing them a reduction in the number of statutorily required affordable housing units. Google's UK headquarters, meanwhile, occupies a new 'groundscraper' (Chapter 25) at King's Cross, the largest regeneration scheme in Europe. Together with the opening of the Elizabeth Line in 2022, large-scale brownfield regeneration schemes have effectively recast the geography of the metropolis.

FOURNIER STREET

22 Jamme Masjid, Spitalfields

COMMONLY known as Brick Lane Mosque, the Jamme Masjid in Spitalfields is heavily freighted with symbolism. As a house of worship for, successively, French Evangelical Protestants, Methodists, Jews and Muslims, it is emblematic of the East End's role as a transitional district: a place of arrival for wave after wave of immigrants and migrants. Just beyond the jurisdiction of the City of London's powerful guilds, less than a kilometre (half a mile) from the point of disembarkation at the Pool of London, and with a reputation for hosting nonconformity, Spitalfields and Bethnal Green were magnets for refugees and immigrants seeking economic opportunity and religious freedom. Rachel Lichtenstein's biography of Brick Lane provides a rich description of how successive waves of incomers to the area found work in London's docks and transport services and in local workshops, breweries and factories.[1] The Jamme Masjid was originally built as a chapel by the Huguenot community, religious refugees from Louis XIV's Revocation of the Edict of Nantes (1685), who brought with them their silk-weaving skills. The subsequent history of the building, on the corner of Brick Lane and Fournier Street, can be understood as a metaphor for London's changing demographics and, in particular, for both the successes and failures of London's multiculturalism.

79 Jamme Masjid, Brick Lane.

The chapel built by the Huguenots was completed in 1743 and named La Neuve Église (the 'New Church', to distinguish it from the French community's existing church in Threadneedle Street). The new chapel followed typical eighteenth-century English designs for meeting houses. Although now closely associated with Brick Lane, it is the Fournier Street frontage that is the principal elevation. Most of Fournier Street consists of handsome brick town houses built for the families of Huguenot master weavers. Sustained by a continuous supply of semi- and unskilled immigrant labour, Spitalfields had become an important centre for weaving and tailoring, famous especially for its fancy silks and brocades. Fournier Street was part of the prosperous quarter of 'Weaver Town', and the Huguenot community built its substantial chapel at the eastern end of the street. More humble weavers' dwellings were clustered around the tenter grounds a few blocks away – places where woven cloth was washed and then hooked to frames called tenters to dry. (This, incidentally, is the origin of the expression 'to be on tenterhooks'.)

The *Survey of London* notes that the Neuve Église is 'bold in scale and quietly dignified in expression'.[2] It was among the first buildings in London to be protected after the Town and Country Planning Act of 1947 provided for statutory listings (it was listed at Grade II* in 1950). The brick-built, two-storey Fournier Street elevation has a slightly projecting central element topped by a broad pediment. Two large doorcases at street level were given the full treatment of pilasters, keystones and architraves in stone and stucco, while the upper floor has six tall and evenly spaced arch-headed windows. A sundial in the centre of the pediment, dated 1743, carries the sombre Latin reminder *Umbra Sumus* ('We are all but shadow'). The narrower Brick Lane elevation has a fancy stone-dressed Venetian window on the upper floor and a large gable-end pediment but no street-level access. Next door on Brick Lane is a plain four-bay Georgian house, built at the same time as the chapel to serve as its vestry and school. The cellars under the house and the chapel were leased to Benjamin Truman, a local brewer, and continued to be occupied by brewers and wine merchants until the end of the nineteenth century.

It took only two or three generations for the Huguenot community to be assimilated into London's outer suburbs, mainly through intermarriage. The congregation at La Neuve Église dwindled. The social geography of the East End had been changing even as the chapel was under construction, with Irish weavers arriving in Spitalfields in the 1730s to take up work in the silk trade, following a decline in the Irish linen industry. By the mid-1700s, Jewish families were spreading into Spitalfields from Bethnal Green, where Sephardic Jews from Spain and Portugal had settled in the 1650s. In 1809, the trustees of the chapel leased it to the London Society for Propagating Christianity Among the Jews, but the society failed to have a noticeable impact on the religious adherence of the surrounding Jewish community, so

80 Jamme Masjid, Fournier Street elevation.

they moved elsewhere. In 1819 Methodists took over the lease, renamed the building 'Spitalfields Chapel', and kitted it out with a floor plan and furniture appropriate to their ceremonies.

The nineteenth century saw the steady impoverishment of Spitalfields: by mid-century, the East End had become the archetype of gloomy Victorian squalor, graphically described by Charles Dickens. Things got even worse after 1860, when a treaty between Britain and France allowed the import of cheaper French silks, plunging many weavers into ruin. After 1881, destitute Yiddish-speaking Ashkenazi Jews arrived in Spitalfields, after escaping from the pogroms that followed the assassination of the tsar of Russia. Brick Lane became the heart of the *shtetl*, with a local economy distinctive for its bagel bakeries and tailors' workshops. Charles Booth's careful statistical compilations and maps, published in *The Life and Labour of the People in London* (1889), showed Fournier Street (called Church Street at the time) and much of Brick Lane to be 'Fairly comfortable. Good ordinary earnings.' But many of the side streets and alleyways were categorised as 'Poor', 'Very poor, casual; chronic want' or 'Vicious, semi-criminal'. The district became especially notorious after the Jack the Ripper murders. Annie Chapman, the second victim, was found on Hanbury Street ('Mixed: some comfortable, others poor') off Brick Lane, just 125 metres (410ft) from the chapel; Mary Jane Kelly, the final victim, was found 250 metres (820ft) to the west of the chapel, in Dorset Street ('Vicious, semi-criminal').

With the surrounding population predominantly Jewish, the Methodists surrendered their lease to the trustees of the French Church. In 1898, a new lease was drawn up, this time with a group of orthodox Lithuanian Jews, the Machzike Hadath ('Strengtheners of the Faith'). They remodelled the attic space as a Torah school, added a new roof and furnished the interior for use as what was now to be called Spitalfields Great Synagogue, serving a congregation that had previously been attending makeshift synagogues in private homes. By the 1920s there were more than 200,000 Eastern European Jews in the East End. In the 1930s they became the focus of British anti-Semitism, which came to a head in 1936, when Oswald Mosley led 3,000 followers of the British Union of Fascists on a highly publicised march from Tower Hill towards the Jewish heartlands of Bethnal Green, Whitechapel and Spitalfields. They were turned back by anti-fascists, estimated to be well in excess of 100,000 in number. Jewish, Irish, socialist and communist groups set up barricades and halted the marchers in the 'Battle of Cable Street'. After the Second World War, the East End's Jewish community dwindled, as many families dispersed to North London suburbs such as Golders Green and Hendon (which became known as London's 'bagel belt'). By the 1970s, there were only about 15,000 Jews left in the East End, and today there are just a thousand or so. In Spitalfields, their place was taken by immigrants from south Asia and, in particular, from the Sylhet region of Bangladesh.

Unlike their predecessors, Bangladeshis came initially not as refugees, but as solitary workers in a post-colonial remittance economy. But before long, chain migration – with families from Sylhet moving into Spitalfields through word-of-mouth contact with friends and relatives already settled there – resulted in an established community. At first, the community relied on converted houses or shops to serve as mosques. The flexibility of Islamic rituals meant that a mosque could be created with the most basic alterations, demolishing walls to form small prayer halls. But after the Machzike Hadath moved to a new, purpose-built synagogue in Golders Green in 1970, an opportunity for a more prominent setting presented itself. The Machzike Hadath accepted a low bid, so that the synagogue could continue as a house of worship. The galleries were removed and the interior remodelled once more, with the old vestry and schoolhouse next door accommodating the administrative office and teaching facilities of the mosque complex and serving as its main entrance.

With space to accommodate more than 4,000 worshippers, the Brick Lane Mosque was one of the largest in the capital and the focal point of an increasingly well-established and growing Bangladeshi community. A new, purpose-built mosque – the East London Mosque – opened in the mid-1980s just half a kilometre away on Whitechapel Road, with a capacity of 7,000 congregants. But whereas the East London Mosque was affiliated with the Pakistani-based Islamic Congress Party and backed by financial support from the Gulf states, Brick Lane Mosque was associated with the Bangladeshi government, a range of political parties – including left-leaning groups – and local community activists with a secular, business-oriented outlook. Leveraging the lobbying power of community groups and their sheer weight of numbers in local elections, the Bangladeshi community was able to build alliances with white Labour Party activists and private organisations to secure public funding for community priorities. Brick Lane became the commercial artery of the community, a distinctive 'ethnoscape'[3] of curry houses, Asian video, music and book shops, barber shops, grocers selling Asian produce, butchers selling halal meat and clothing retailers selling brightly coloured sari fabrics; along with a couple of surviving bagel shops.

The consolidation of the Bangladeshi community in Spitalfields coincided with the neoliberal enterprise culture of the 1980s and a spirit of urban competitiveness. Spitalfields' proximity to the offices and tourist destinations of the City naturally made it the target of entrepreneurs and local government agencies seeking to exploit the district's distinctive character, simultaneously exoticising it and making it accessible, safe and visually appealing to visitors. For community leaders and local businesses, it was an opportunity to create a sense of place, to focus community pride and to draw visitors to Brick Lane's shops and restaurants; perhaps to create the Western world's first 'little Bangladesh'. For developers and policymakers, it was an opportunity to extend the booming City economy onto cheaper land and promote the diversification of the local economy through leisure and tourism, all with an attractive storyline of 'globalisation from below'.[4] A City Fringe Partnership involving the London Development Agency, the borough of Tower Hamlets and private businesses was established to promote 'Cityside', a strategic framework for regeneration designed to take advantage of central government grants. Through the City Fringe Partnership, Brick Lane was identified as a 'Developing Cultural Quarter' and the southern half of the street was branded as 'Banglatown'. Curry restaurants were the principal tourist draw, publicised by an annual, fortnight-long Curry Festival. Between 1989 and 2009, the number of outlets on Brick Lane selling Indian-, Bangladeshi- or Punjabi-style food grew from just eight to more than sixty. The City Fringe Partnership also promoted the Bengali New Year festival, Baishakhi Mela.

Together with these 'invented traditions', the Cityside strategy included grants for shop and restaurant owners to carry out frontage improvements and for the local authority to encode the streetscape as 'Banglatown': installing an ornamental Chinatown-style gateway arch at the southern end of Brick Lane near the mosque, adding street furniture with traditional motifs in red-and-green Bengali colours, and posting street signs in Bengali as well as English. Encouraged by all this, the Jamme Masjid erected a 25 metre (82ft) tall stainless-steel sculpture in 2009 at the corner of Fournier Street and Brick Lane. With its intricate surface pattern and the Islamic symbol of a crescent moon at the top of the tower, its resemblance to a minaret was controversial. For some, branding suddenly began to look like Islamisation.

> It was also regarded as being incongruous alongside a building that for more than two and a half centuries had served the religious needs of different faiths within the area. Local

> critics argued that it was at odds with the 'tradition of tolerance' and adaptability of this building to changing local needs and migration.[5]

Nevertheless, the area had been 'discovered'. Residential and industrial gentrification saw affluent households move into Spitalfields' Huguenot town homes and row houses, while design, media and fashion-related firms moved into its old industrial spaces. The Milanese fashion school, Istituto Marangoni, for example, took advantage not only of inexpensive real estate, but also of the opportunity to exploit a unique address, moving into old factory space on Fashion Street, a block away from the Jamme Masjid. Developers took over the huge Truman Brewery that marked the northern end of Banglatown, converting the complex to bars, nightclubs and studios for small independent businesses. Guidebook and media coverage, together with attention stemming from the popularity of Monica Ali's novel *Brick Lane* (2003) and its movie adaptation, brought international tourists into the heart of what had hitherto been a vibrant but relatively unknown area. Exoticised and edgy-but-safe, the transitional dynamism of Brick Lane was sustained by a lunch-time and night-time 'experience economy' catering to students and young white-collar workers. The proliferation of curry restaurants, however, meant there was intense competition, which led to aggressive kerbside touting by restaurant staff, while the sheer number of cheap restaurants gave the entire area a reputation for poor-quality food.[6] At the same time, the increasing multiculturalism of Brick Lane represented an intrusion upon the Bengali community's cohesiveness.[7] In a focus group held by Tower Hamlets Planning Department in 2002, older Bengali women

> stressed the point that they had to be escorted by their husbands and that they could not walk along Brick Lane at all because

> there are just too many men there, with all the visitors and [restaurant] staff. So, although it is their area, they are socially excluded from it.[8]

Gradually, gentrification, the rise of property values and the commodification of the Cityside 'cultural quarter' have all but eclipsed the distinctiveness of the Bangladeshi neighbourhood in the vicinity of the Jamme Masjid. The report of a detailed survey of Banglatown in 2020 by the Runnymede Trust concluded that 'The crisis facing Banglatown encapsulates a longer, broader and deeper set of concerns around migration and settlement; urban change and gentrification; global cities and [their] ordinary streets; changing consumer practices; and minority ethnic businesses and ethnic and intergenerational transformation.'[9] The cost of property – 20 per cent above the London average in 2020 – has led to the departure of many Bangladeshi families and businesses. In their place 'young urban creatives' and hipsters have arrived. Expensive shops, boutiques, cafés and Asian/European fusion restaurants have moved into the northern stretch of Brick Lane. Along the southern stretch – between the mosque and the old brewery complex – the number of curry restaurants fell to thirty-five in 2014 and to twenty in 2019. Many of them have been superseded by smarter restaurants serving alcohol, 'interspersed with Swedish delicatessens, French patisseries, pizza parlours and vegan cafes'.[10] The upper floors of many of the businesses, formerly used for offices and storage, have been converted to residential use under pressure of gentrification. Developers, meanwhile, have been given permission to replace the Truman Brewery buildings with a five-storey office, shopping mall and restaurant complex, displacing more than 300 small businesses, most of them independent 'microbusinesses'. The scale of change in the district begs the question of what next will become of the chapel/synagogue/mosque building.

23 One Canada Square, Isle of Dogs

STANDING on a site between the former Import and Export basins of the West India Docks, the fifty-storey, 263 metre (863ft) One Canada Square was the tallest structure in Europe when it was built in 1991. It remained London's tallest edifice for twenty-two years, until it was overtaken by the eighty-seven-storey Shard (310 metres; 1,017ft) in 2013. One Canada Square was the signature building in a regeneration project covering the entire 52 hectare (128 acre) West India Docks site, renamed Canary Wharf by developers and planners. By 2023, One Canada Square had become the progenitor of a cluster of thirty-six tall buildings – all more than twenty storeys – that constitute London's American-style 'edge city',[1] a major financial centre that has attracted its own residential towers, shops and restaurants – albeit with little of the diversity and none of the civic institutions that constitute a traditional city.

At one time the commercial heart of Britain's empire, employing more than 30,000 dockyard labourers and 20,000 more in dock-related industries, such as ship repairs, food processing, chemicals, engineering and transport, London's docks fell into a steep decline in the 1960s, first as a result of competition

81 Pelli's tower, One Canada Square.

from Rotterdam and other continental ports, and then as a result of the introduction of containerisation, which drew London's port facilities to Tilbury, 25 kilometres (15 miles) downstream. One by one, the docks closed: first the East India Docks in 1967, followed by the London Docks and the Surrey Docks in 1969, the West India Docks in 1980 and the Royal Docks in 1981. Dock employment registered with the Port of London Authority fell from 23,000 in 1967 to just over 4,000 in 1980, with predictably catastrophic effects for the surrounding working-class communities.[2] The district's population fell by almost 30 per cent between 1961 and 1981, by which time adult male unemployment stood at 21 per cent. Wharf-side equipment was left to rust, weeds began to sprout from cracks in the quaysides and warehouses fell into dereliction. It made for some terrific settings for East End gangster movies like *The Long Good Friday* and television series like *The Sweeney*, but the abandoned docks and their marooned neighbourhoods were widely regarded as emblematic of the decline of Britain's traditional economic base, a very visible source of embarrassment to the government. On the other hand, the docklands were *tabula rasa* for developers and planners. The 22 square kilometres (8.5 square miles) of redundant docklands space represented London's biggest redevelopment opportunity since the Great Fire of 1666.

In 1981, following a series of plans and reports, the central government, under Prime Minister Margaret Thatcher, took some 2,000 hectares (4,950 acres) of land out of the jurisdiction of the Port Authority and nearby local authorities and gave it to a specially created corporation – the London Docklands Development Corporation (LDDC) – with extensive powers and a mandate to regenerate the Docklands (now capitalised) by encouraging private investment. The model was based heavily upon the postwar Labour government's New Town Development Corporations, 'an extremely un-Thatcherite mechanism for achieving urban regeneration, involving a great deal of intervention in the market, and staffed primarily by public sector officials'.[3] The LDDC was equipped with property-acquisition rights and could grant planning consent to developers, circumventing the democratically elected local borough councils. In a more Thatcherite vein, the LDDC disdained the idea of any sort of master plan, preferring to rely on market-led redevelopment. The corporation's early work focused on marketing, and 'priming the pump': acquiring derelict land, making it serviceable and reconnecting the Isle of Dogs to the rest of London with roads, water, gas and electricity supplies and telephone lines. Within the Isle of Dogs, the LDDC constructed a series of canals to link the docks with the river and provide a framework for subsequent commercial development.[4]

The LDDC saw architecture and urban design as a means to establish a marketable sense of place for the Docklands, and had taken note of the trend for high-tech companies to be drawn to suburban business parks.

> As a result, the Island was paved in brick, and heavily landscaped around the refurbished dock basins. The details of the public realm – the seats, lighting, paving, etc. – were deliberately chosen to contrast, as far as possible, with the ex-industrial character of the area they inherited.[5]

The LDDC also designated the area around the West India and Millwall Docks as an Enterprise Zone – another Thatcherite innovation – absolving developers from local property taxes for a ten-year period, with no development land tax and a 100 per cent capital allowance for new commercial and industrial construction, to be offset against corporation and income taxes.[6] By 1987, several hundred companies had taken advantage of these breaks to move to the Docklands. Most of them occupied relatively small-scale light-industrial units arranged around parking courts, architecturally unremarkable, suburban in nature, and without any coherent public realm. Combined with the LDDC's bland landscaping, it lent a sense of generic placelessness to the early phase of Canary Wharf's development.

What rescued the project from relative anonymity was a combination of the City's inability to meet demand for high-tech, large-floor-plate offices for the booming international financial sector – supercharged by Britain's deregulation of financial markets in 1986 – and the vision and ambition of North American developers and investors. The 'Big Bang' of financial deregulation ended many of the City's insular and outdated practices and weakened the influence of its tight-knit old-boy networks. The booming financial services sector and the increasing necessity for office buildings to have up-to-date information technology capabilities, together with the City's adherence to its historic preservation policies, meant that rents for office space in the City were twice those of Paris and five times those in Frankfurt. As the *Financial Times* pointed out in 1985, 'the City of London, caught off balance by the speed of the revolution and determined to resist any development which threatens its architectural heritage, has so far been unwilling or unable to respond'.[7]

Meanwhile, the American real estate magnate G. Ware Travelstead, having identified the LDDC's vacant land and associated tax breaks, had begun to excite the interest of Reg Ward, the chief executive of the LDDC, with the prospect of replacing the LDDC's incremental development strategy with a single mega-project that would accommodate the 'overspill' of City financial service firms.[8] The scale of Travelstead's ambition implied a huge amount of public investment in infrastructure: on the face of it, a non-starter in the Thatcherite playbook. Upon learning of the proposed Canary Wharf project, however, the prime minister responded decisively in favour: it was an opportunity not only to market the Docklands to international investors, but also to sell the whole idea of 'global' London and of the United Kingdom as a rejuvenated, post-industrial economy. The Docklands were to become the flagship expression of neoliberal enterprise culture, fostering the growth of London's advanced business services and replacing a 'redundant' – both literally and figuratively – working-class population with a middle-class one. In spite of obstruction from City interests (and some internal Cabinet dissent), the government promptly committed to furnishing a new transportation infrastructure: a driverless light railway line – the Docklands Light Railway (DLR) – the Limehouse Link Road and Tunnel, and an extension to the Underground Jubilee Line, all connecting Canary Wharf to central London. Travelstead put together a consortium of US investment banks and began to court prospective tenants from the City with offers of reduced rents and other incentives. But his proposals quickly outgrew his ability to attract the required financial backing, and in 1987 his consortium was bought out by Toronto-based Olympia and York (O&Y). A private consortium, O&Y had risen to become the largest property development company in the world, with experience in developing large, prestige projects such as New York's World Financial Center at Battery Park City.

The momentum of the Canary Wharf project enabled O&Y to draw on £1.3 billion in public subsidies (equivalent to £4.7 billion in 2023) to develop 'Wall Street on Water'. The Chicago-based architectural firm Skidmore, Owings and Merrill (SOM) was engaged to create a master plan and several key buildings, with the Argentine-American architect César Pelli being given the commission for the flagship structure, One Canada Square. The master plan, devised by SOM partner Robert Turner, was based on a multi-level corridor beneath the principal buildings that carried a shopping centre, parking and a service spine for the whole development. A DLR station was integrated into the project, with a series of formal open spaces beyond, providing access to the water basins. The sheer height of Pelli's tower was its most remarkable feature; but it was innovative in using stainless steel cladding, which gave it a reflectivity that helped it to stand out in the landscape. It also has a distinctive louvred metal pyramid roof, 30 metres (98ft) wide and 40 metres (131ft) high, housing water tanks and maintenance and plant machinery.

With a mixture of hubris and superficial understanding of urbanisation typical of commercial architectural discourse, SOM claimed that their master plan incorporated the urban qualities of London's eighteenth- and nineteenth-century open spaces. Perhaps they were influenced by a need to subscribe to the historicism and revivalism that was characteristic of the current fad for postmodern architecture. Certainly the buildings that SOM designed for Phase One of Canary Wharf were infected with postmodern styling, with vestigial classical columns, pre-cast cutout pediments and overscaled entrances. The architectural press was not sympathetic. Tom Wilkinson, writing in *Architectural Record* in 1988, suggested that:

> The best that can be said for this piece of north American cultural colonisation is that it is not quite as bad as La Défense, the second business centre of Paris, where '60s Modernist planning made a central urban space that can only make sense if the whole of the French army is paraded upon it ... It is difficult to disagree with Royal Town Planning Institute President Francis Tibbald's [sic] remark that Canary Wharf 'as a piece of urban design is simply abysmal. A wonderful opportunity to create a new place in London with innovative urban forms has been missed ... The layout is simplistic and banal, the architecture lumpy and mediocre.'[9]

One Canada Square was completed in 1991, along with the rest of Phase One of Canary Wharf. A year later, only 40 per cent of the development was occupied, partly because the new transport infrastructure was incomplete, partly because of the attachment of financial services firms to City addresses, and partly because of planning and design accommodations made by the City in response to the competition represented by Canary Wharf; but mainly because of a collapse of the global property market. O&Y had been borrowing heavily against existing assets to continue with business expansion.[10] Unable to pay off their debts, O&Y filed for bankruptcy in 1992, and it took until 1997 for the development to regain momentum under a new consortium, the Canary Wharf Group.[11] Since then, rising demand for deep-floor-plate, grade-A office accommodation, along with the opening of the Jubilee Line extension in 1999, has seen the steady growth of Canary Wharf as a business centre.

Today Canary Wharf houses a daily working population of more than 120,000 – more than the docks and warehouses that preceded it – including more bankers than the City of London. One Canada Square has been joined by a collection of some of the most luxurious modern office and residential towers in the metropolis, most of them in the same glassy international style. They are set among plazas that 'cater for the new City workers' one-hour-and-no-more sandwich lunch which replaced the leisurely and alcoholic style of the 1960s and 1970s'.[12] The growth of the financial services sector has created a great deal of wealth among a new, young class fraction – including regular infusions of bonus-day millionaires – that has populated a spate of riverside loft apartments, converted warehouses and gated 'urban villages' on the Isle of Dogs, as well as the luxury residential towers of Canary Wharf. The result is a distinctive kind of suburbia that is dominated by affluent singles, child-free couples and empty nesters. With the opening of the Elizabeth Line in 2022, linking the area to Farringdon, in the City, in less than ten minutes, and to Heathrow in just 45 minutes, Canary Wharf is now even more attractive to both businesses and residents. Of wider significance is the effect of the growth of Canary Wharf not only on the regeneration of nearby parts of Poplar and the

Isle of Dogs, but also on the eastward shift of metropolitan development – the demonstrable success of Docklands regeneration providing momentum for mega-projects like the Olympic Park and the Westfield Shopping Centre at Stratford, and the O2 Arena at Greenwich.

82 Canary Wharf cityscape.

24 The Shard, London Bridge

THE Shard stands on what is an unlikely site for Europe's tallest building: on the 'wrong' side of the river from the City, amid the nineteenth- and early-twentieth-century workshops, warehouses and office buildings in the jumble of yards, lanes and streets around London Bridge Station. Its presence has sparked the regeneration of the district, now branded the London Bridge Quarter. The Shard itself was innovative in design and construction, and even before it had been completed it had become iconic, synonymous with London's new incarnation as a global city, its silhouette appearing on tourist knick-knacks and in civic and commercial branding. It was London's first twenty-four-hour mixed-use tower, described by its architect, Renzo Piano, as a 'vertical city', blending shops, offices, a hotel, apartments and observation decks.

In broader context, The Shard is part of the radical transformation of London's skyline. Until the 2000s, London had only a handful of tall buildings, scattered across the city: the Shell Centre (1961), Millbank Tower (1963), the BT Tower (1964), Centre Point (1967, Chapter 20) and Euston Tower (1970). Tower 42, the forty-seven-storey former National Westminster Tower, built in 1980 just to the north of Threadneedle Street, was the only true skyscraper in the City. A decade later, the

83 The Shard.

fifty-storey One Canada Square (Chapter 23) was built in the Docklands, seeding what eventually became a cluster of more than thirty tall buildings. In central London, meanwhile, building sites were in short supply and, until the early 2000s, building tall was discouraged by the City of London Corporation's historic preservation policies and its 'St Paul's Heights' guidelines, designed to protect views of the cathedral from the South Bank, from the Thames bridges and from certain points to the north, west and east. The first new skyscraper to appear in the City for almost a quarter-century was the forty-one-storey 30 St Mary Axe (the 'Gherkin'), opened in 2004. Since then, the City has acquired a distinctive cluster of novel and sculptural office towers, including Broadgate Tower, Heron Tower, 52 Lime Street (the 'Scalpel'), 122 Leadenhall (the 'Cheesegrater'), 8 Bishopsgate, 22 Bishopsgate, 100 Bishopsgate and 20 Fenchurch Street (the 'Walkie-Talkie'). Skyscrapers have also appeared across the river on the South Bank (One Blackfriars and the South Bank Tower, as well as The Shard), at Vauxhall and Nine Elms (One Nine Elms; St George Wharf Tower; DAMAC Tower; Gladwin Tower; Sky Garden), and at the Elephant and Castle (Highpoint; Strata; Two Fifty One; One The Elephant). Another seventeen buildings of twenty storeys or more were in the pipeline (with planning permission or under construction) in the City in early 2022, with an average height of thirty-eight storeys. In the rest of central London there were a further ninety-eight tall buildings in the pipeline, the majority of them residential towers in the 'build-to-rent' sector.[1]

The transformation of London's skyline has been the result of several converging factors. Developers, recognising the needs and opportunities presented by 'global' London's changing economy, see tall buildings as the best way to generate income and profit from the relatively small and incredibly expensive pockets of available land. International investors understand the same financial logic, and generally regard London as a predictably safe and stable environment for investment in property. This became especially significant in the 2000s, as investment in property became the solution to a moment when an accumulation of international capital could find few attractive alternatives for investment. London's property market has been especially attractive to the sovereign wealth funds of countries like Kuwait, Malaysia, Qatar and the United Arab Emirates, along with other quasi-sovereign investors, such as state-backed pension funds.[2] London's property market is also an 'advanced ecosystem for money laundering and financial crime'.[3] At the same time, the planning policies of both the Corporation of the City of London and the Greater London Assembly pivoted from restricting tall buildings to encouraging them. The City's resistance to the 'invasion' of foreign companies and modern architectural styles had led to open threats from the government for the abolition of the corporation. In response, the corporation reinvented itself with an institutional reform and rebranded its identity in the early 2000s as an outward-looking institution, open to London's new transnational elites.[4]

The corporation's 2002 Unitary Development Plan finally replaced the City's antiquated planning framework and signalled a willingness to permit high buildings where they would enhance the City's skyline. Beyond the City's jurisdiction, the GLA's first mayor, Ken Livingstone, saw tall office buildings as key to sustainable land-use strategies, densifying development around public transport nodes with office towers that might trigger the regeneration of entire districts. It was consistent with Livingstone's desire to boost London's global brand image through contemporary urban design and an enhanced skyline. 'For London to remain a competitive world city,' noted the 2004 *London Plan*, 'it must respond to the drivers of growth and continue to develop in a dynamic, organic manner, without inappropriate restraints.'[5] All of the key actors – developers, investors and policymakers – meanwhile came to recognise the value of

84 The Shard from Southwark Street.

not only building tall, but also of having tall buildings designed by 'starchitects', whose celebrity generally helps to lubricate the planning-approval process and to assist in promoting the building to prospective commercial tenants. Just as starchitects derive some of their professional standing through the visible presence of their built work in major cities, so the imagery of cities is derived in part from their association with starchitecture.[6] Celebrity and city branding become mutually reinforcing.

On the consumption side, London's new tall office buildings have been sought out by globalising businesses, for whom an iconic or prestige address serves to consolidate their status. New residential towers, on the other hand, have been targeted at the luxury and super-prime market. London has the highest number of super-rich individuals per capita of any city globally: more than 3,000 ultra-high-net-worth individuals domiciled in the metropolis and a further 6,000 ultra-high-net-worth individuals with second homes in the city. Not all of these are going to be wealthy Chinese visa holders, Russian oligarchs or Saudi princes.[7] A distinctive feature of this market is that, in many cases, units are sold 'off-plan' in advance of actual construction, through a global network of upmarket agencies and property investment fairs in cities such as Hong Kong, Singapore, Dubai and Cannes. Such is the demand for luxury apartments in London that it is not unusual for units to be bought off-plan and flipped at a profit to other buyers before projects are even completed. For some, a London property is a sort of safety deposit box; for others a private base for occasional shopping trips 'or, in the case of much illicit investment, the concealment and recycling of funds via offshore investment funds'. One way or another, observes Rowland Atkinson, 'much of London's new skyline is underused or lies entirely empty, so that one interpretation of this new landscape of super-prime residential development is that it is a kind of dead residential space or necrotecture'.[8] International middle-class investors also tend to buy off-plan, motivated more by a desire for reasonable gains in revenue and capital appreciation.[9]

The Shard's developer was Irvine Sellar, a character in the tradition of the ambitious and uncompromising property developers who had reshaped postwar London. Sellar had started his entrepreneurial career selling shirts in a chain of market stalls around the periphery of North London, before opening a shop on Carnaby Street at the height of 'Swinging London'.[10] The 'starchitect' that Sellar found to take on the design of the super-tall building he had in mind was Renzo Piano, a Pritzker Prize winner, whose portfolio included the Centre Pompidou in Paris, PricewaterhouseCoopers tower on Potsdamer Platz in Berlin, the Maison Hermès Tower in Tokyo, the Aurora Place towers in Sydney, and the New York Times Building in New York City. Finding a financier for the £1.85 billion project was more difficult. Credit Suisse had been lined up, but a slowdown in the global economy, combined with the US sub-prime credit crisis, put the deal in doubt, jeopardising the whole project. If work did not begin on time, consent to build The Shard would be voided, and the planning application, which had taken almost three years the first time around, would have to begin again. The situation was resolved just in time by Qatari investment, adding The Shard to a list of Qatari-owned or part-owned properties in London that includes whole or part ownership of prestige hotels (the Ritz, Claridge's, the Savoy, the Connaught, the Berkeley, the Churchill, Grosvenor House Suites and the InterContinental Park Lane), Harrods (Chapter 12), One Canada Square (Chapter 23), Chelsea Barracks, the former US embassy in Grosvenor Square, Heathrow airport, the exclusive Ivy restaurant and the private members' club Annabel's.[11] In Mayfair, a concentration of multi-million-pound Qatari-owned homes and offices has come to be known as 'Little Doha'. Thus a tiny emirate, a British protectorate from 1916 to 1971, whose citizen population is similar in size to that of Wigan or Wakefield, has deployed its vast surplus of oil and gas wealth to buy huge chunks of the capital that once ruled over it.

The Shard would be the Qataris' most prominent trophy. But its proposal – originally as 'London Bridge Tower' – met strong opposition. The eminent author and influential columnist Simon Jenkins, for example, described it as a 'monster': 'These gigantic buildings have no respect for the existing skyline ... If planning means anything, it must have some regard for the dominant Georgian and Victorian scale of London.'[12] The architectural press was ambivalent. Writer and design impresario Deyan Sudjic conceded that Piano was 'brilliant, innovative and sensitive', but complained that

> to judge by the sketches that have so far emerged, the Sellars [sic] tower is none of these things. The jagged pyramid with which Piano now proposes to skewer the London skyline would transform the look of the city permanently and not for the better.[13]

Simon Thurley of English Heritage (the organisation described by Ken Livingstone as 'the Taliban of British architecture')[14] claimed that the building would 'put a spike into the heart of historic London ... If built, it would be Europe's tallest building and London's greatest folly.'[15] The pejorative use of the term 'spike' was transmuted by the press into 'shard of glass', and impishly adopted by Sellar as 'The Shard'.

Thurley and English Heritage were not amused, insisting on a public inquiry. The case against The Shard was based on the long-standing assertion of the symbolism of historic landmarks in London's cityscape. Neil King QC wordily argued English Heritage's case. He conceded the 'striking architectural quality' of the tower, but added that such a building had to be 'in the right place'. He stressed the impact on views of St Paul's: 'From Parliament Hill ... the left-hand side of LBT [London Bridge Tower] would intersect the right-hand side of the dome, appearing therefore to grow out of it – a profoundly inappropriate effect.'[16] Counsel for Sellar sought to turn English Heritage's argument on its head, recalling the architectural eclecticism of the nineteenth century and advocating an aesthetic based on surprise and contrast in the cityscape. The GLA argued in favour of the project, asserting that it would be a truly world-class building, symbolic of London's role as a world city, and key to the regeneration of Southwark. It was the powerful business case for local regeneration that won the day.[17]

Construction began in 2009 on a site that had previously been occupied by Southwark Towers, a drab twenty-six-storey reinforced concrete office building constructed in the 1970s. The Shard was formally opened in 2012, topped out at 310 metres (1,017ft), with seventy-two habitable floors and a total floorspace of 11 hectares (27 acres). It was, as Piano conceded, decidedly *priapismo*. But it was also decidedly sensational, its crystalline quality making other glass skyscrapers look ordinary, unimaginative. Its jagged façades begin 20 metres (66ft) up, two facets on each side of the square base, all angled differently and covered with a total of more than 11,000 glass panels. The tapered shape of the tower was a product of Sellar's concept of a mixed-use skyscraper – which Piano stretched into the notion of a 'vertical city'. Retail units occupy the base, opening out onto the concourse of London Bridge Station, while the large floor plates above are for offices, allowing for the efficiencies of having people on the same floor. Each office floor is provided with three 'winter gardens'. Intermediate levels are allocated to restaurants (floors 31 to 33, centred on a triple-height atrium) and a luxury hotel and spa – the Shangri-La – with a corridor near the core and rooms around the perimeter, so that every guest room has a view. Luxury apartments occupy the narrowing top of the building, each occupying an entire floor or, in some cases, two floors. Above them, a viewing gallery and, finally, a 60 metre (197ft) spire. The mixed usage and the tapered shape are both reflected in the choices of material for the building structure:

> In the lower levels the floors are framed in steel because of the large spans, while in the upper levels the spans are smaller and post-tensioned concrete is more suitable. Spans are sufficiently low in the top few concrete floors to allow normal reinforced-concrete construction. The spire was framed in steel for ease of construction.[18]

The tower itself is integrated into the immediate surroundings with a 'sister' building – a seventeen-storey office tower, 'The Place', with the same floor-to-ceiling glazing and interior winter gardens as The Shard. The buildings share a new public space that leads to the redeveloped London Bridge transportation hub – one of the capital's busiest, used by about 54 million passengers a year. It has a large bus station, which was redeveloped as part of The Place, an Underground station served by the Northern and Jubilee lines, and a National Rail station with fifteen platforms.

85 The Shard and London's cityscape.

The whole ensemble is an exemplar of Livingstone's preferred strategy of densifying development around public transport nodes, saving land and minimising road traffic. On the other hand, the very success of The Shard has hastened the gentrification of much of Southwark, reducing the affordability of neighbourhood housing and displacing small businesses, as other developers seek to capitalise on the revitalising district. A symbol of Global London, The Shard is also emblematic of the acute social inequality associated with the growth of the super-prime property market, with developments conceived for investors and speculators leading to a glut of accommodation beyond the reach of ordinary people. The fact that the ten penthouse apartments at the top of The Shard (rumoured to have a price tag of £30–50 million each) remained unsold six years after the building's completion only adds insult to injury.[19]

25 Platform G, King's Cross

THE megastructure that emerged in 2023 between the approaches to St Pancras and King's Cross railway stations will be Google's UK headquarters. The newest landmark in the most recent recasting of London's restless urban landscape, it is the finishing touch to the transformation of the derelict lands surrounding the railway stations and the Regent's Canal basins that used to serve them. Platform G, as it is called, is part of an ensemble of brand new and restored 'heritage' buildings and landscaped public spaces that constitute the regenerated King's Cross Central district. Platform G is symbolic of a new dimension of London's economy, dominating a district that is itself emblematic of contemporary approaches to large-scale urban development. It is a manifestation of an entirely new type of building, incorporating 'smart' technologies and designed to accommodate the imperatives of information technology-based industries and the new 'workstyles' of their employees. It also reflects London's new economic geography, recast around a new economy based on technology-intensive services (business, financial and personal), cultural-products industries, and design- and fashion-oriented forms of production. Intimately tied in to complex flows and networks of information that are global in scope, London's

86 Platform G, artist's rendering.

new economy has now largely supplanted its manufacturing industries as the principal drivers of investment, growth and innovation.

Real estate consultant Rob Harris emphasises the catalytic role of digital technologies in reshaping London's economic geography. 'In the mid-1980s,' he notes, 'the fax machine and golf ball typewriter were leading-edge technologies. Personal computers were not widely available, and we had yet to experience the internet, email, mobile phones, social media, and digital media technology.' Until the latter part of the 1980s, central London's business geography was dominated by four tightly defined sub-markets: the 'Square Mile' of the City, with its financial services and associated businesses; Mayfair, with its advertising and media businesses, property firms and professional services; the 'Midtown' legal district around the Inns of Court and the Royal Courts of Justice; and Victoria, with its administrative and associated professional services businesses.[1]

But the launch of the first IBM personal computer in 1981, followed by the 'Big Bang' of financial reform in 1986, the introduction of Eudora (the first graphical user interface for email management) in 1988 and the release of the first world wide web software in 1991 not only supported the growing industries of the new economy, but also sharply increased their need for new premises. At first, London's technology firms sought out suburban settings in the corridor that stretches westwards from Hammersmith along the Thames Valley to Reading. Office parks provided new buildings equipped with the necessary wiring and designed to provide reconfigurable collaboration space, rather than banks of desks or warrens of cubicles. But by the late 1990s the new enabling technologies of smart phones and laptops and the blossoming of the internet prompted the emergence of innovative start-up companies that were able to find their niche in the relatively cheap vacant lofts and workshops of the East End. The most striking cluster of internet start-ups and specialised small to medium-sized high-tech businesses was in Shoreditch, where Old Street and City Road meet at 'Silicon Roundabout'. There soon developed a set of symbiotic relationships among a broad set of hybrid and crossover new-economy start-ups, allowing them to engage with each other in the same 'third places' (bars, coffee bars and pubs), to collaborate with one another, review each other's products and create jobs that cross-fertilise and share skill sets. It resulted in a distinctive hipster ecology characterised by an affinity with edgy and neo-bohemian elements.

But as the available workspaces were taken up, pushing up rents, small high-tech and creative businesses were forced to begin to push further into the East End. Large corporations – Cisco, Facebook, Google, McKinsey and Microsoft – began to move in, attracted by the creative buzz and cachet of the district and easily able to afford higher rents. Nevertheless, space was limited, and the big firms increasingly needed technologically advanced buildings with large floor plates that could accommodate new building management systems and the distribution of desktop technology for large workforces. Central London was the preferred location, to take advantage of the external economies of being situated among cultural, educational and research institutions, accessible to both clients and a large, specialised workforce. One option for developers was to build tall on one of the few available large-scale building sites in one of the city's principal office districts – now five of them: Canary Wharf, as well as the City, Mayfair, Midtown and Victoria. Another was to partner with local government in developing 'brownfield' land on derelict industrial sites, assembling unified parcels of land to accommodate the large footprint buildings required by the global office economy. 'The result was a series of "mega schemes" forming a necklace of integrated and master-planned office campuses around the fringe of central London, focused primarily, but not exclusively, on major rail and Underground hubs and including a large element of public realm, and a high retail and leisure content.'[2] The foundation for this strategy lay in a Private Finance Initiative established by the Conservative government in 1992 to leverage private-sector capacity to deliver public-sector infrastructure and services in areas affected by deindustrialisation and urban decay. It was expanded and rebranded by the Labour government in 1997 as a public–private partnership, with award-winning architect Richard Rogers appointed as head of an Urban Task Force charged with charting 'urban renaissance'.[3] In London, Ken Livingstone's GLA administration included a small but influential Architecture and Urbanism Unit, with Rogers as its chief advisor. Between 2005 and 2015, public–private partnerships regenerated more than fifty social housing estates across London, directly affecting over 164,000 residents.[4] Meanwhile, the Architecture and Urbanism Unit also encouraged the idea of public–private partnerships as the mechanism for large-scale property-led regeneration schemes on brownfield sites.

The derelict railway lands immediately around King's Cross and the nearby canal basins provided a massive site, ripe for regeneration. By the 1970s, the adjacent streets were run-down, and the seedy area around the station had acquired a reputation for drug use, prostitution and drunkenness. The vast, empty railway lands, for a long time a void in the fabric of central London, were an attractive target for both government and developers. After some stuttering attempts in the 1980s, an ambitious public–private partnership was established in 2000, boosted by the selection of St Pancras as the terminal for high-speed trains to Europe, the ongoing renovation of the St Pancras Renaissance Hotel (Chapter 11) and the construction of the British Library – the largest public building constructed in Britain in the previous hundred years – on the site of the old Midland Railway goods depot just to the west of St Pancras Station. The complex financial, legal and political growth machine behind King's Cross Central involved Camden and Islington borough councils, the

Channel Tunnel Rail Link and London and Continental Railways (the landowner), as well as the developer, Argent, and its bankers and venture capitalists. The Department of Transport provided cash grants, underwrote a bond issue and provided property development rights around King's Cross Station.

The 27 hectare (67 acre) site has fifty new and renovated buildings, twenty new streets, ten new public parks and squares and three new bridges across the Regent's Canal. Almost half of the net square footage is office space, a quarter is residential space (almost 2,000 apartments), and the rest a mix of educational, hotel and retail space. Character and place identity is provided by several legacy structures from the railway era. The Great Northern Hotel (1854), one of the earliest purpose-built railway hotels in the country, has been restored as a luxury boutique hotel, and King's Cross Station has been given a makeover. The brick arches of the restored Coal Drops Yard buildings provide a framework for a new retail quarter. The old goods yard and Granary Building have been redeveloped for Central Saint Martins College of Art and Design, and Granary Square, originally wharfage for the canal basins built by the Great Northern Railway to load the rail cars from the barges, has become a public space, embellished with more than a thousand fountains. The old Fish and Coal Offices now house the headquarters, flagship store and showroom for product designer Tom Dixon; and three landmark gasometer frames have been refurbished, re-erected next to Regent's Canal, and used to frame circular luxury condominium buildings of differing heights (to mirror the movement of the original gasholders).

Altogether, King's Cross Central has become the kernel of a newly branded 'knowledge quarter', KQ, that extends to the neighbouring Francis Crick Institute (a biomedical research centre), the British Library and the Alan Turing Institute for data science and artificial intelligence, initially hosted in the British Library. King's Cross Central itself has meanwhile emerged as

87 Platform G 'landscraper', artist's rendering.

88 Battle Bridge Place and the Platform G building, artist's rendering.

London's newest tech quarter, with a range of international businesses, including AstraZeneca, the Global Music Data Alliance, YouTube and Meta, as well as Google. After leasing the slice of land immediately to the west of the King's Cross approaches, Google hired starchitect Bjarke Ingels and designer Thomas Heatherwick for Platform G. Their design reflects the amenity-rich corporate campuses favoured by big tech companies, adapted for a metropolitan setting. It is 'smart', with thousands of interconnected devices to improve comfort and energy efficiency, and 'green', with a wooden façade system and a huge rooftop garden. The long, tapering site – 330 metres (1,083ft) – allows for the large floor plates required by Google to accommodate flexible, collaborative work spaces. It is not a beautiful thing, but it is monumental in size and scope, stepping up from eight floors in the south to twelve in the north: a massive 'groundscraper'. Its narrow southern façade faces one of the new squares, Battle Bridge Place, which leads to new entrances to the railway station and to King's Cross St Pancras Tube station. The building stands on a plinth of retailing and dining, with street frontage facing one of the new streets, King's Boulevard. Google also promises a 'market hall' for small businesses and a community, education and event space at street level. The floors above will have 76,000 square metres (818,000 sq. ft) of office space. There are no internal weight-bearing pillars or columns inside to hamper the open-plan office floors, though the wide-open spaces are broken up by staff amenities that include an auditorium and events space, cafés and a 'wellness centre', with a gym, an indoor basketball court and a 25 metre (82ft) multi-lane swimming pool. The campus-like theme is continued on the roof, with a 200 metre running track and a series of different garden settings and habitats, planted in 40,000 tonnes of soil.[5]

Still under construction at the time of writing, Platform G has been treated respectfully, but not warmly by the architectural press. Like the rest of King's Cross Central, it will be regarded as evidence of London's perpetual ability to remake itself and to take advantage of shifting economic circumstances: a platform for the newest dimension of Global London. It will doubtless be taken as evidence of the effectiveness of brownfield regeneration via public–private partnerships as an engine of 'urban renaissance'. In that vein, King's Cross Central has already won recognition as the 'Most Innovative Development of the Past 20 Years' at the Property Awards 2015, the 'Best Project Five Years On' at the 2017–18 London Planning Awards, and the Mayor's Planning Award for Excellence at the 2017–18 London Planning Awards.[6] It is worth noting, however, that while regeneration and public–private partnerships were originally conceived as strategies aimed at addressing the renaissance of low- and middle-income communities affected by deindustrialisation and urban decay, regeneration in practice has been geared more towards attracting upper-income households and international business. Writing at an early stage of the King's Cross regeneration programme, planning professor Michael Edwards conceded that

> There is perhaps one element in all this that can be chalked up as a victory for local community demands: Camden has insisted that the new streets being created as part of the Argent development will be adopted as public highways and thus subject to normal police powers, rather than private security patrols.[7]

As it turns out, facial recognition technology is being used to surveil the tens of thousands of visitors that frequent the site each day, 'to ensure everyone who visits King's Cross has the best possible experience', as the property developer, Argent, puts it. Google executives, for their part, were in the process in mid-2023 of evaluating the possibility of digitally tracking their own staff through company badges. Having invested so much in an enormous state-of-the art office building designed to facilitate in-person teams, the company has had to confront a significant cultural shift in the aftermath of the covid pandemic, which has seen central London's workers coming into the office, on average, only 2.3 days per week.[8]

Epilogue

COLLECTIVELY, the twenty-five buildings described in this book tell the story of the development of London as a sprawling and cosmopolitan metropolis and world city, mercantile, industrial and imperial in character. They also reflect its evolution as a municipality that developed a broad scope of progressive management and planning, before it eventually reinvented itself as a post-industrial arena for global capital. The biographies of individual buildings have provided a series of lenses through which we can discern the history of the metropolis as a whole. London's built environment consists of a layered legacy, the product of a sequence of demographic, economic and technological changes, the rise and fall of imperial power, changing ideals in architecture, urban design and planning, and changing preferences and aspirations among different socio-economic and ethnic groups.

Over more than three centuries, successive rounds of investment, disinvestment and reinvestment have taken place on a resilient framework based on Greater London's natural physiography, its transport systems and its socio-economic geography. The ancient cores of the metropolis – Westminster and the City – are surrounded by the distinctive social ecologies of the West End, the East End and North London. On the other side of the river is the jumble of South London's inner suburbs. Around outer London, the combination of physical features and transport corridors has produced seven sectors with distinctive social and economic profiles. Clockwise: North London, the Lea Valley, Northeast London, the Thames Estuary, South London, the Thames Valley and Northwest London.[1]

We can recognise the legacy of a pre-modern layer of building that extended across the commercial and administrative cores of the City and Westminster, respectively, and across the patrician heartland of the West End estates. Outliers of the pre-modern layer also survive in the successors of ancient settlements that have anchored the structure of the metropolis as a 'city of villages'. This oldest layer was overwritten by the institutional framework and pre-automobile suburbs of the Victorian and Edwardian era, as industrialisation and new transport networks fostered the development of finely differentiated inner-tier districts. A third layer was added as the Underground system and the rise of car ownership led to the rapid growth of distinctive owner-occupier suburbs, while 'footloose' industries attracted blue-collar suburbs around industrial corridors, and the blossoming of municipal socialism found expression in large LCC and local-authority housing estates. A fourth distinctive layer emerged after the Second World War, as economic recovery and the reassertion of consumer markets added high-rise commercial buildings, while the social revolution embodied in the welfare state led to slum clearance and the appearance of everyday Modernism in the form of social housing, schools and clinics across the entire metropolis. The most recent layer is the product of a counter-revolution, as the political climate shifted decisively away from a sense of patrician obligation and stewardship and towards a market-driven regime. Several decades of a neoliberal political economy have resulted in an emasculated planning system and a significant shift in the role of the state, from being a regulator of markets and provider of welfare services to becoming a facilitator of markets and agent of business. In practice, this has involved the dismantling of welfare-state landscapes to make room – both physically and economically – for a new layer of commercial and residential building supercharged by global investment.

Each of these layers – including elements of the most recent layer – has been subject to the cyclical 'creative destruction' of property redevelopment in search of greater returns. During the Second World War, it was a matter of plain destruction, wrought by the Blitz and, later, V1 and V2 rockets. After the war, the cumulative loss of important buildings, as well as much of the more basic fabric of the city, became the focus of an emergent conservation movement. A long-running public debate surrounding the tensions between modernisation and conservation centred around the loss of London landmarks, such as the London Coal Exchange, St James's Theatre in King Street, the Doric arch and Great Hall at Euston Station, and the Army and Navy Club; and the prospective loss of entire districts – Piccadilly Circus, Whitehall, Covent Garden, Oxford Street and Regent Street – targeted for redevelopment by planners and property companies. Gradually, the historic preservation and conservation of London's built environment became an accepted goal, bolstered by the listing of buildings of special architectural or historical interest under the 1947 Town and Country Planning Act and by the Civic Amenities Act of 1967 that gave local authorities the power to establish conservation areas.

Simon Jenkins notes that 'Respecting a city's history and character was enough to make its fabric desirable and prosperous.'[2] As we have seen, London's buildings and streets, protected from demolition, have proven particularly versatile. Changing occupancy and adaptive re-use have added new chapters to the living history of many individual buildings. Georgian town homes have become office buildings; warehouses, factories and office buildings have become luxury apartment buildings; government buildings have become mixed-use developments; churches have become residences, cafés and warehouses. Meanwhile, the desirability of older districts has been made clear in the extent of gentrification across London, a phenomenon that was accelerated by the Rent Act of 1957 (which made it much easier for landlords to evict long-term tenants and render older properties available for sale) and by the expanded availability of mortgage credit in the 1960s. Recently, the wealthy and super-wealthy have populated a 'third wave' of gentrification, based on new-build projects on brownfield sites along the riverside and around transport hubs,[3] and have colonised established 'alpha' districts like Kensington and Mayfair.[4]

The desirability of London real estate has driven the inflation of property values and intensified the inequality that has always been a hallmark of the city. The average price of a detached house in Greater London in 2022 was just over £1 million; semis averaged £660,000; while terraced houses went for an average of £553,000.[5] (The median salary in Greater London in 2022 was £41,900.) But these averages mask the way in which wealth and poverty have condensed in particular localities. Detached houses, for example, ranged in average sale price from £636,737 in Barking and Dagenham to £4,016,000 in Kensington and Chelsea. At finer levels of resolution, the disparities are even more glaring. The townscapes of the West End, the riverlands along the Thames between Nine Elms and Vauxhall and around the Isle of Dogs, and the sequestered cocktail-belt suburbs of outer London stand in stark contrast to aging inner-city neighbourhoods, local-authority 'sink' estates and the fading suburbs of semi-detached homes that were put up cheaply and in a hurry in the boom years of the 1930s.

These disparities underscore what has become of London. Poverty and inequality have certainly been a constant throughout London's development. But the metropolis that had at one time developed a progressive administrative framework that was committed to strategic governance and functionality and to the mitigation of poverty no longer has the same sense of progress, improvement and social mission as the Victorians or the Edwardians, let alone the New Elizabethans of the welfare state. New-build gentrification, corporate office towers and the tourist ecology of west-central London have together numbed broad tracts of the urban fabric, rendering much of central London available only to visitors or the very wealthy. With much of the rest of London already gentrified, the neoliberal political economy of the past several decades has targeted scores of local-authority estates for demolition, to make way for profitable private-sector developments.[6] While developers of regeneration projects larger than ten units are typically required to deliver a specified number of statutorily 'affordable' homes, there has been a significant net loss of social housing.

The Heygate Estate, just southeast of the Elephant and Castle shopping centre in Southwark, provided an early example of what can go wrong. The estate was built in 1974, but in the late 1990s the council stopped all but minimal maintenance of its 1,212 homes and began preparations for 'decanting' more than 3,000 residents prior to the estate's regeneration.[7] The council had to spend several million pounds on demolition and clearance, before transferring ownership of the land to its private-sector partner. The initial agreement was for 35 per cent of the 2,535 new units on the estate – now called Elephant Park – to be affordable housing. This was renegotiated to 25 per cent after submission of a financial viability assessment. The final tally of social rented units in Elephant Park was under a hundred, meaning that few former leaseholders were able to exercise their right to return; meanwhile, some households had to accept below-market compensation for the flat they had been encouraged to purchase under the Thatcher administration's right-to-buy legislation.[8] London's affordable housing problem is set to continue, driven by the arithmetic of a fixed supply of land and buildings as the denominator and a growing population as the numerator. Having overtaken its prewar peak of 8.5 million in 2015, London's population is now set to hit at least 11 million by 2050. On top of the existing shortage of affordable housing, London will need between 50,000 and 60,000 new homes each year for the next twenty years to keep pace with its rising population: 30,000 to 40,000 units a year in excess of current housebuilding rates.

Meanwhile, the biographies of the twenty-five buildings described in this book point to the overall resilience of the city and its built environment. Some of them, such as Spencer House, Rochelle Street School and the Hoover factory, are among the more than 26,000 buildings in Greater London that are statutorily protected through listing (more than 9,000 of them with Grade I status). Others feature as part of one or other of the statutory conservation areas that together account for about 17 per cent of the built fabric of the metropolis. Yet others will be protected through the hidden hand of the marketplace, refurbished through gentrification or renovated by wealthy purchasers. That still leaves half or more of the existing fabric of the city as an underappreciated assemblage of living histories. One of the lessons of the buildings described in this book is that every building – protected or not – carries a story, a biography that reflects not only the circumstances of its creation, but also key aspects of the unfolding history of one of the world's most interesting cities.

Notes

INTRODUCTION

1 See, for example, N. Pevsner et al., *The Buildings of England: London* (6 vols), Yale University Press, London, 1994–97; J. Summerson, *Georgian London*, Yale University Press, London, 1988; K. Allinson, *Architects and Architecture of London*, Routledge, London, 2008.
2 J.N. Entrikin, *The Betweenness of Place*, Palgrave, London, 1991; P. Claval and J.N. Entrikin, 'Cultural geography: Place and landscape between continuity and change', in G. Benko and U. Strohmayer (eds), *Human Geography: A history for the twenty-first century*, Taylor and Francis, London, 2004, pp. 39–60.
3 T. Gieryn, 'What buildings do', *Theory and Society*, 31 (2002), p. 35.
4 P. Hall, *Cities in Civilization*, Weidenfeld and Nicolson, London, 1998.
5 P.L. Knox, *London: Architecture, building and social change*, Merrell, London, 2015.
6 P.L. Knox, *Metroburbia: The anatomy of Greater London*, Merrell, London, 2017.
7 J. Davis, *Waterloo Sunrise: London from the Sixties to Thatcher*, Princeton University Press, London, 2022.
8 O.S. Smith, *Boom Cities: Architect planners and the politics of radical urban renewal in 1960s Britain*, Oxford University Press, London, 2019.
9 C. Hay, 'The winter of discontent thirty years on', *Political Quarterly*, 80/4 (2009), pp. 545–52.
10 Knox, *Metroburbia*, p. 162.

PART I – GEORGIAN LONDON

1 G. Hodgson, '1688 and all that: Property rights, the Glorious Revolution and the rise of British capitalism', *Journal of Institutional Economics*, 13/1 (2017), pp. 79–107.

2 J. Summerson, *Georgian London*, Yale University Press, London, 1988, p. 135.
3 H. Greig, *The Beau Monde: Fashionable society in Georgian London*, Oxford University Press, London, 2013.
4 M. Girouard, *The English Town: A history of urban life*, Yale University Press, New Haven, CT, 1990, p. 153.
5 J. White, *A Great and Monstrous Thing: London in the eighteenth century*, Harvard University Press, Cambridge, MA, 2013.
6 D. Keene, 'Growth, modernization and control: The transformation of London's landscape c.1500–c.1760', *Proceedings of the British Academy*, 107/7 (2001), p. 36.
7 ibid., p. 25.
8 Summerson, *Georgian London*, p. 7.

CHAPTER 1 – SPENCER HOUSE, ST JAMES'S

1 J. Friedman, *Spencer House: Chronicle of a great London mansion*, Zwemmer, London, 1993, p. 18.
2 H. Walpole, *Horace Walpole's Correspondence*, Yale Online edition, vol. 18, p. 211.
3 R. Stewart, *The Town House in Georgian London*, Yale University Press, London, 2009, p. 191.
4 H. Greig, *The Beau Monde: Fashionable society in Georgian London*, Oxford University Press, London, 2013.
5 M.H. Port, 'West End palaces: The aristocratic town house in London, 1730–1830', *London Journal*, 20/1 (1995), pp. 17–46; also Stewart, *The Town House in Georgian London*.
6 P. Guillery, 'Cavendish Square and Spencer House: Neo-classicism, opportunity and nostalgia', *Georgian Group Journal*, 23 (2015), pp. 75–96.
7 G.A. Stelter, 'The classical ideal: Cultural and urban form in eighteenth century Britain and America', *Journal of Urban History*, 10/4 (1984), p. 352.
8 Friedman, *Spencer House*, p. 19.
9 S. Jones, 'Roman taste and Greek gusto: The Society of Dilettanti and the building of Spencer House, London', *Antiques Magazine*, 141/6 (1992), pp. 968–77.
10 F.H.W. Sheppard (ed.), 'St James's Place', in *Survey of London*, Vols 29 and 30: *St James Westminster, Part 1* (1960), at British History Online, www.british-history.ac.uk/survey-london/vols29-30/pt1/pp511-541 (accessed 3 July 2023); also G. Jackson-Stops, 'Spencer House, London', *Country Life*, 29 November 1990, pp. 42–47.
11 Sheppard, 'St James's Place'.

12 T. Malton, *A Picturesque Tour through the Cities of London and Westminster, 1792*, vol. ii, Gale ECCO, Print Editions, London, 2018, p. 108.
13 Friedman, *Spencer House*, p. 190.
14 Greig, *The Beau Monde*, p. 7.
15 J. Rendell, *The Pursuit of Pleasure: Gender, space and architecture in Regency London*, Rutgers University Press, New Brunswick, NJ, 2002.

CHAPTER 2 – BEDFORD SQUARE, BLOOMSBURY

1 A. Byrne, *Bedford Square: An architectural study*, Athlone Press, London, 1990, p. 9.
2 S. Jenkins, *Landlords to London: The story of a capital and its growth*, Book Club Associates, London, 1975, p. 55.
3 J. Summerson, *Georgian London*, Yale University Press, London, 1988, p. 23.
4 D.J. Olsen, *Town Planning in London: The eighteenth and nineteenth centuries*, Yale University Press, London, 1982, p. 18.
5 Jenkins, *Landlords to London*.
6 P. Booth, 'From property rights to public control: The quest for public interest in the control of urban development', *Town Planning Review*, 73/2 (2002), pp. 153–70.
7 C.W. Chalkin, 'Urban housing estates in the eighteenth century', *Urban Studies*, 5/1 (1968), pp. 67–84.
8 Camden History Society, *Streets of Bloomsbury and Fitzrovia*, London, 1997.
9 ibid.
10 J. Ayres, *Building the Georgian City*, Yale University Press for the Paul Mellon Centre for Studies in British Art, London, 1998.
11 H.W. Lawrence, 'The greening of the squares of London: Transformation of urban landscapes and ideals', *Annals of the Association of American Geographers*, 83/1 (1993), pp. 90–118.
12 Olsen, *Town Planning in London*, p. 44.
13 ibid., pp. 147–49.
14 Jenkins, *Landlords to London*, p. 57.
15 E. Walford, 'Russell Square and Bedford Square', in *Old and New London*, vol. 4, London, 1878, pp. 564–572, at British History Online, www.british-history.ac.uk/old-new-london/vol4/pp564-572 (accessed 3 July 2023).
16 *Morning Chronicle*, 8 March 1815; cited in T. Longstaffe-Gowan, *The London Square: Gardens in the midst of town*, Paul Mellon Centre for Studies in British Art, London, 2012, p. 78.

17 Byrne, *Bedford Square*, p. 46.
18 ibid., p. 48.
19 B. Cherry and N. Pevsner, *The Buildings of England, London 4: North*, Yale University Press, London, 1998, pp. 323–24.

CHAPTER 3 – NO. 2 WAREHOUSE, IMPORT DOCK, WEST INDIA QUAY

1 H. Hobhouse (ed.), 'The West India Docks: The buildings, introduction', in *Survey of London*, Vols 43 and 44: *Poplar, Blackwall and Isle of Dogs* (1994), at British History Online, www.british-history.ac.uk/survey-london/vols43-4/pp281-284 (accessed 3 July 2023).
2 N. Draper, 'The City of London and slavery: Evidence from the first dock companies, 1795–1800', *Economic History Review*, 61/2 (2008), pp. 432–66.
3 See, for example, E. Williams, *Capitalism and Slavery* (third edition), University of North Carolina Press, Chapel Hill, NC, 2021; C. Hall, N. Draper, K. McClelland, K. Donington and R. Lang, *Legacies of British Slave-ownership: Colonial slavery and the formation of Victorian Britain*, Cambridge University Press, Cambridge, 2014.
4 W.M. Stern, 'The first London Dock boom and the growth of the West India Docks', *Economica*, 19/73 (1952), p. 61.
5 J. Schneer, 'London's docks in 1900: Nexus of empire', *Labour History Review*, 59/3 (1994), pp. 20–33.
6 M. Taylor, 'The British West India interest and its allies, 1823–1833', *English Historical Review*, 133/565 (2018), pp. 1478–511.
7 Stern, 'The first London dock boom', pp. 59–77.
8 Hobhouse, 'The West India Docks'.
9 J. Conrad, *The Children of the Sea*, Dodd, Mead and Company, New York, 1896, p. 132.
10 Hobhouse, 'The West India Docks'.
11 J. Schneer, *London 1900: The imperial metropolis*, Yale University Press, London, 1999, p. 42.
12 F. Driver and D. Gilbert, ''Heart of empire? Landscape, space and performance in imperial London', *Environment and Planning D: Society and Space*, 16 (1998), p. 21.
13 *Baedeker* (1879), p. 118, cited in ibid., p. 21.
14 Schneer, *London 1900*.
15 Based on the Bank of England's inflation calculator: www.bankofengland.co.uk/monetary-policy/inflation/inflation-calculator
16 Schneer, *London 1900*, p. 51.

PART II – VICTORIAN LONDON I: WORKSHOP METROPOLIS

1 K. Polanyi, *The Great Transformation*, Beacon Press, Boston, MA, 1957.
2 J. White, *London in* the *Nineteenth Century*, Jonathan Cape, London, 2007.
3 D.E.B. Weiner, *Architecture and Social Reform in Late Victorian London*, Manchester University Press, Manchester, 1994.
4 A. Black, S. Pepper and K. Bagshaw, *Books, Buildings and Social Engineering: Early public libraries in Britain*, Ashgate, London, 2009.
5 M. Kaika and E. Swyngedouw, 'Fetishizing the modern city: The phantasmagoria of urban technological networks', *International Journal of Urban and Regional Research*, 24/1 (2000), p. 122.
6 C. Otter, *The Victorian Eye: A political history of light and vision in Britain, 1800–1910*, University of Chicago Press, Chicago, IL, 2008; also P.D. Joyce, *The Rule of Freedom: Liberalism and the modern city*, Verso, London, 2003; T. Crook, *Governing Systems: Modernity and the making of public health in England, 1830–1910*, University of California Press, Berkeley, CA, 2016.
7 H. McLeod, *Class and Religion in the Late Victorian City*, Routledge, London, 2017.
8 S. Thurley, *The Building of England: How the history of England has shaped our buildings*, William Collins, London, 2013, p. 365.
9 N. Mansfield and M. Trustram, 'Remembering the buildings of the British labour movement: An act of mourning?' *International Journal of Heritage Studies*, 19/5 (2013), pp. 442–43.
10 C. Brooks and A. Saint (eds), *The Victorian Church: Architecture and society*, Manchester University Press, Manchester and New York, 1995.
11 A. Briggs, *The Age of Improvement: 1783–1877*, Longman, London, 1959.
12 S.D. Koven, 'Borderlands: Women, voluntary action and child welfare in Britain, 1840 to 1914', in S.D. Koven and S. Michel (eds), *Mothers of a New World: Maternalist politics and the origins of welfare states*, Routledge, London, 2013, pp. 94–135.
13 P.L. Knox, *Better by Design? Architecture, urban planning, and the good city*, Virginia Tech Publishing, Blacksburg, VA, 2020. Open source: https://publishing.vt.edu/site/books/m/10.21061/better-by-design/ (accessed 4 July 2023).
14 J. White, *Rothschild Buildings: Life in an East End tenement block*, Routledge and Kegan Paul, London, 1980, pp. 159, 162.
15 M.P. Collins, 'The London County Council's approach to town planning, 1909–1945', *London Journal*, 42/2 (2017), pp. 172–91.

CHAPTER 4 – FAIRFIELD WORKS, BOW

1 C. O'Brien, B. Cherry and N. Pevsner, *The Buildings of England, London 5: East*, Yale University Press, London, 2005, p. 622.
2 L. Raw, *Striking a Light: The Bryant and May matchwomen and their place in labour history*, Bloomsbury, London, 2011, p. 28.
3 Charles Booth Archive, London School of Economics, B346/75–77.
4 A.F. Weber, *The Growth of Cities in the Nineteenth Century: A study in statistics*, Cornell University Press, Ithaca, NY, 1963, p. 369 (originally published by Macmillan, 1899).
5 A. Mearns, *The Bitter Cry of Outcast London: An inquiry into the condition of the abject poor*, James Clarke & Co., London, 1883, pp. 2, 3.
6 Raw, *Striking a Light*.
7 *London Evening Standard*, 17 July 1888, p. 3.
8 P. Thompson, *Socialists, Liberals and Labour: The struggle for London, 1885–1914*, Routledge and Kegan Paul, London, 1967, p. 53.
9 *East London Observer*, Saturday 29 June 1912, p. 7.
10 *East London Observer*, Saturday 6 December 1913, p. 7.
11 *London Evening Standard*, 14 July 1898, p. 3.
12 L.J. Satre, 'After the match girls' strike: Bryant and May in the 1890s', *Victorian Studies*, 26/1 (1982), pp. 7–31.
13 P. Wright, *A Journey Through Ruins: The last days of London*, Oxford University Press, Oxford, 2009, p. 239.
14 S. Zukin, *Loft Living: Culture and capital in urban change*, Radius, New York, 1988.
15 Wright, *A Journey Through Ruins*, p. 243.

CHAPTER 5 – LAMBETH WORKHOUSE, LAMBETH

1 D.R. Green, 'Icons of the new system: Workhouse construction and relief practices in London under the old and new poor law', *London Journal*, 34/3 (2009), pp. 264–84.
2 K. Morrison, *The Workhouse: A study of poor-law buildings in England*, English Heritage, Swindon, 1999.
3 M.A. Crowther, *The Workhouse System 1834–1929*, Routledge, London, 2016, p. 121.
4 D.R. Green, 'Pauper protests: Power and resistance in early nineteenth-century London workhouses', *Social History*, 31/2 (2006), pp. 137–59.
5 S. Donovan and M. Rubery, 'Doing the amateur casual: Victorian investigative journalism and the legacy of James Greenwood's "A Night in a Workhouse"', *Victorian Studies*, 63/3 (2021), pp. 401–30.

6 ibid.
7 Morrison, *The Workhouse*, p. 121.
8 www.workhouses.org.uk/Lambeth/ (accessed 3 July 2023).
9 *Daily Telegraph*, 11 September 1888. Cited in J. White, *Rothschild Buildings: Life in an East End tenement block 1887–1920*, Routledge and Kegan Paul, London, 1980, p. 123.
10 M. Doolittle, 'The duty to provide: Fathers, families and the workhouse in England, 1880–1914', in B. Althammer, A. Gestrich and J. Gründler (eds), *The Welfare State and the 'Deviant Poor' in Europe, 1870–1933*, Palgrave Macmillan, London, 2014, pp. 58–77.
11 ibid.
12 Crowther, *The Workhouse System*, p. 36.

CHAPTER 6 – SHAFTESBURY PARK ESTATE, BATTERSEA

1 S. Morris, 'Market solutions for social problems: Working-class housing in nineteenth-century London', *Economic History Review*, 54/3 (2001), pp. 525–45; J. Maltby and J. Rutterford, 'Investing in charities in the nineteenth century: The financialization of philanthropy', *Accounting History*, 21/2–3 (2016), pp. 263–80; M. MacDonald and C. Howorth, 'Roots of social enterprise: Entrepreneurial philanthropy', *Social Enterprise Journal*, 14/1 (2018), pp. 4–21.
2 R. Haywood, 'Railways, urban form and town planning in London, 1900–1947', *Planning Perspectives*, 12 (1997), pp. 37–69; H.J. Dyos, 'Workmen's fares in South London, 1860–1914', *Journal of Transport History*, 1/1 (1953), pp. 3–19.
3 C. Thom, *Survey of London: Volume 50, Battersea: Part 2: Houses and Housing*. Yale University Press for English Heritage, London, 2013, p. 251.
4 *Morning Post*, 24 July 1848, p. 8.
5 J. Burnett, *A Social History of Housing, 1815–1985* (second edition), Routledge, London, 1986.
6 The Artizans' and General Properties Company Ltd., *Artizans' Centenary, 1867–1967*, London, 1967.
7 K. Bailey, 'Developing Victorian Battersea: The story of James Lord and George Todd, Junior', *London Journal*, 40/1 (2015), pp. 56–79.
8 Thom, *Survey of London*, p. 53.
9 ibid., p. 264.
10 *London Evening Standard*, Monday 20 July 1874, p. 2.
11 Thom, *Survey of London*, p. 265.
12 J. McCalman, 'Respectability and working-class politics in late-Victorian London', *Historical Studies*, 19/74 (1980), p. 111.

13 Thom, *Survey of London*, p. 251.
14 Dyos, 'Workmen's fares', p. 8.
15 S.T. Abernethy, 'Opening up the suburbs: Workmen's trains in London, 1860–1914', *Urban History*, 42/1 (2015), p. 76.
16 A.A. Jackson, *Semi-detached London: Suburban development, life and transport*, Allen and Unwin, London, 1973, p. 24.
17 N. Kelvin (ed.), *The Collected Letters of William Morris*, vol. 2: *1893–96*, Princeton University Press, Princeton, NJ, 1987, p. 227.
18 McCalman, 'Respectability and working-class politics', pp. 108, 112, 114.
19 www.house-historian.co.uk/london/morrison-street/ (accessed 3 July 2023).
20 ibid.

CHAPTER 7 – ROCHELLE STREET SCHOOL, BETHNAL GREEN

1 T.F.T. Baker (ed.), 'Bethnal Green: The West, Shoreditch Side, Spitalfields, and the Nichol', in *A History of the County of Middlesex*, vol. 11: *Stepney, Bethnal Green*, Victoria County History, London, 1998, at British History Online, www.british-history.ac.uk/vch/middx/vol11/pp103-109 (accessed 3 July 2023).
2 T.F.T. Baker (ed.), 'Bethnal Green: Building and social conditions from 1876 to 1914', in *A History of the County of Middlesex*, vol. 11: *Stepney, Bethnal Green*, Victoria County History, London, 1998, at British History Online, www.british-history.ac.uk/vch/middx/vol11/pp126-132 (accessed 3 July 2023).
3 ibid.
4 ibid.
5 R. Dennis, 'The geography of Victorian values: Philanthropic housing in London, 1840–1900', *Journal of Historical Geography*, 15/1 (1989), p. 41.
6 P. Gardner, *The Lost Elementary Schools of Victorian England: The people's education*, Routledge, London, 2018.
7 J.D. Hirst, 'Public health and the public elementary schools, 1870–1907', *History of Education*, 20/2 (1991), pp. 107–18.
8 H.W. Schupf, 'Education for the neglected: Ragged schools in nineteenth-century England', *History of Education Quarterly*, 12/2 (1972), pp. 162–83.
9 T.F.T. Baker (ed.), 'Bethnal Green: Education', in *A History of the County of Middlesex*, vol. 11: *Stepney, Bethnal Green*, Victoria County History,

London, 1998, at British History Online, www.british-history.ac.uk/vch/middx/vol11/pp242-260 (accessed 3 July 2023).

10 J. Martin, '"Hard-headed and large-hearted": Women and the industrial schools, 1870–1885', *History of Education*, 20/3 (1991), p. 188.

11 D.E.B. Weiner, *Architecture and Social Reform in Late Victorian London*, Manchester University Press, Manchester, 1994, p. 3.

12 B.W. Richardson, *The Health of Nations: A review of the works of Edwin Chadwick*, London,1887, vol. 1, p. 306. Cited in Hirst, 'Public health and the public elementary schools', p. 110.

13 E.R. Robson, 'School planning', *The Builder*, 30 (1872), p. 525.

14 E.R. Robson, *School Architecture: Being practical remarks on the planning, designing, building, and furnishing of school-houses. With 300 Illustrations*, J. Murray, London, 1877.

15 A.C. Doyle, 'The naval treaty', *The Strand*, October/November 1893.

16 Cited in Weiner, *Architecture and Social Reform*, p. 54.

17 M. Girouard, *Sweetness and Light: The Queen Anne movement, 1860–1900*, Yale University Press, New Haven, CT, 1977.

18 Anon., *The Extravagant Expenditure of the London School Board*, Effingham Wilson, London, 1876, at https://en.wikisource.org/wiki/The_Extravagent_Expenditure_of_the_London_School_Board (accessed 3 July 2023).

19 Historic England, 'Former Nichol Street Infant School', https://historicengland.org.uk/listing/the-list/list-entry/1065260 (accessed 3 July 2023).

20 Final Report of the School Board for London, p. 39. Cited in F. Kelsall, 'The board schools: School building 1870–1914', in R. Ringshall, M. Miles and F. Kelsall, *The Urban School: Buildings for education in London, 1870–1980*, Greater London Council/Architectural Press, London, 1983, p. 24.

21 Named after the street that marked the boundary between the metropolitan boroughs of Shoreditch and Bethnal Green.

22 R.V. Steffel, 'The Boundary Street Estate: An example of urban redevelopment by the London County Council, 1889–1914', *Town Planning Review*, 47/2 (1976), pp. 161–73.

23 Cited in L. Chester, *All my Shows are Great: The life of Lew Grade*, Aurum, London, 2010, p. 16.

24 M. Young and P. Willmott, *Family and Kinship in East London*, Routledge, London, 1957.

25 J. Boughton, *Municipal Dreams: The rise and fall of council housing*, Verso, London, 2018.

CHAPTER 8 – CHRIST CHURCH, TURNHAM GREEN

1 C. Brooks, 'Introduction', in C. Brooks and A. Saint (eds), *The Victorian Church: Architecture and society*, Manchester University Press, Manchester and New York, 1995, p. 4.
2 C. Wakeling, 'The nonconformist traditions: Chapels, change and continuity', in Brooks and Saint, *The Victorian Church*, pp. 82–97.
3 S. Thurley, *The Building of England: How the history of England has shaped our buildings*, William Collins, London, 2013, p. 365.
4 A. Saint, 'Anglican church-building in London, 1790–1890', in Brooks and Saint, *The Victorian Church*, pp. 30–50.
5 K. Inglis, *Churches and the Working Classes in Victorian England*, Routledge, London, 2013, p. 7.
6 M.H. Port, *Six hundred New Churches: The Church Building Commission, 1818–1856*, Spire Books, Reading, 1961.
7 J. Wolffe, 'The chicken or the egg? Building Anglican churches and building congregations in a Victorian London suburb', *Material Religion*, 9/1 (2013), p. 39.
8 B. Cherry and N. Pevsner, *The Buildings of England, London 3: North West*, Yale University Press, London, 2002, p. 392.
9 https://gilbertscott.org/christ-church-turnham-green/ (accessed 3 July 2023).
10 A. Gowans, 'Review', *Journal of the Society of Architectural Historians*, 24/2 (1965), p. 178.
11 A.W.N. Pugin, *Contrasts: A parallel between the noble edifices of the fourteenth and fifteenth centuries and similar buildings of the present day shewing the present decay of taste*, London, 1836. See also J. Lubbock, *The Tyranny of Taste: The politics of architecture and design in Britain, 1550–1960*, Yale University Press, London, 1995.
12 G.G. Scott, *Personal and Professional Recollections*, edited by his son, G.G. Scott, Sampson Low, Marston, Searle and Rivington, London, 1879, pp. 87–88. Cited in J. Banerjee, 'The Cambridge Camden Society and the Ecclesiological Society', Victorian Web, https://victorianweb.org/religion/eccles.html (accessed 3 July 2023).
13 *The Ecclesiologist*, 1 (1842), pp. 56–59.
14 P. Jones, 'Architecturing modern nations: Architecture and the state', in G. Delanty and E. Isin (eds), *Handbook of Historical Sociology*, Sage, London, 2002, pp. 301–11.
15 G. Braithwaite, *Struggling, Closed and Closing Churches Research Project*, Church Building Council, London, 2020.

PART III – VICTORIAN LONDON 2: HEART OF EMPIRE

1 P.L. Knox and P. Taylor (eds), *World Cities in a World-System*, Cambridge University Press, Cambridge, 1995.
2 P. Hugill, *World Trade Since 1431: Geography, technology, and capitalism*, Johns Hopkins University Press, Baltimore, MD, 1993.
3 E.J. Hobsbawm, *Industry and Empire: An economic history of Britain since 1750*, Weidenfeld and Nicolson, London, 1968.
4 J. Schneer, *London 1900: The imperial metropolis*, Yale University Press, London, 1999, p. 19.
5 F. Harrison, 'London improvements', *New Review*, 7 (1892), p. 414; cited in D. Gilbert and F. Driver, 'Capital and empire: Geographies of imperial London', *GeoJournal*, 51 (2000), pp. 23–32.
6 M. Kaika, 'Architecture and crisis: Re-inventing the icon, re-imag(in)ing London and re-branding the City', *Transactions of the Institute of British Geographers*, 35 (2010), pp. 453–74.
7 D.J. Olsen, *The Growth of Victorian London*, Batsford, London, 1976, p. 329.
8 Gilbert and Driver, 'Capital and empire', p. 26.
9 I.S. Black, 'Rebuilding "The Heart of the Empire": Bank headquarters in the City of London, 1919–1939', *Art History*, 22/4 (1999), pp. 593–618.
10 Schneer, *London 1900*.
11 J. Auerbach, *The Great Exhibition of 1851: A nation on display*, Yale University Press, London, 1999.
12 C. Ross and J. Clark, *London: The illustrated history*, Penguin Books for the Museum of London, London, 2011, p. 234.
13 Gilbert and Driver, 'Capital and empire', p. 28.

CHAPTER 9 – FOREIGN AND COMMONWEALTH OFFICE, WHITEHALL

1 S. Bradley and N. Pevsner, *The Buildings of England, London 6: Westminster*, Yale University Press, London, 2003, pp. 266–67.
2 Cited in B. Porter, *The Battle of the Styles: Society, culture and the design of a new Foreign Office, 1855–1861*, Bloomsbury Publishing, London, 2011, p. 1.
3 A. Sutcliffe, *London: An architectural history*, Yale University Press, London, 2006, p. 105.
4 I. Toplis, *The Foreign Office: An architectural history*, Mansell, London, 1987; B. Porter, 'Architecture and empire: The case of the "Battle of

the Styles", 1855–61', *British Scholar*, II/2 (2010), pp. 181–96; Porter, *The Battle of the Styles*; G.A. Bremner, 'Nation and empire in the government architecture of mid-Victorian London: The Foreign and India Office reconsidered', *Historical Journal*, 48/3 (2005), pp. 703–42; K. Mays, 'How the Victorians un-invented themselves: Architecture, the Battle of the Styles, and the history of the term *Victorian*', *Journal of Victorian Culture*, 19/1 (2014), pp. 1–23.

5 Porter, *The Battle of the Styles*, p. 183.

6 M. Herford, 'Architecture in Victorian London and the question of style', *Literature and Aesthetics*, 31/1 (2021), pp. 1–23.

7 Porter, 'Architecture and empire', p. 190.

8 Bremner, 'Nation and empire'.

9 Herford, 'Architecture in Victorian London', p. 15.

10 E.K. Morris, 'Symbols of empire: Architectural style and the government offices competition', *Journal of Architectural Education*, 32/2 (1978), p. 10.

11 J. Dittmer, 'Theorizing a more-than-human diplomacy: Assembling the British Foreign Office, 1839–1874', *Hague Journal of Diplomacy*, 11 (2016), p. 101.

12 K. Hamilton, 'Accommodating diplomacy: The Foreign and Commonwealth Office and the debate over Whitehall redevelopment', *Contemporary British History*, 18/3 (2004), p. 201.

13 O.S. Smith, *Boom Cities: Architect planners and the politics of radical urban renewal in 1960s Britain*, Oxford University Press, London, 2019.

14 A. Sharr and S. Thornton, *Demolishing Whitehall: Leslie Martin, Harold Wilson and the architecture of white heat*, Routledge, London, 2016.

15 Hamilton, 'Accommodating diplomacy', pp. 207, 209.

16 A. Seldon, *The Foreign Office: An illustrated history of the place and its people*, HarperCollins, London, 2000.

CHAPTER 10 – VICTORIA AND ALBERT MUSEUM, SOUTH KENSINGTON

1 J. Physick, *The Victoria and Albert Museum: The history of its building*, Phaidon/Christie's, Oxford, 1982.

2 B. Black, *On Exhibit: Victorians and their museums*, University Press of Virginia, Charlottesville, VA, 2000, p. 4.

3 A. Arieff, 'Reading the Victoria and Albert Museum', *Victorian Poetry*, 33/3–4 (1995), pp. 406, 409.

4 A. Burton, *Vision and Accident: The story of the Victoria and Albert Museum*, V&A Publications, London, 1999, p. 43.

5 L. Purbrick, 'The South Kensington Museum: The building of the house of Henry Cole', in M. Pointon (ed.), *Art Apart: Art institutions and ideology across England and North America*, Manchester University Press, Manchester, 1994, p. 74.
6 S. Forgan and G. Gooday, 'Constructing South Kensington: The buildings and politics of T.H. Huxley's working environments', *British Journal for the History of Science*, 29/4 (1996), pp. 435–68; B. Robertson, 'The South Kensington Museum in context: An alternative history', *Museum and Society*, 2/1 (2004), pp. 1–14.
7 T. Barringer, 'The South Kensington Museum and the colonial project', in T. Barringer and T. Flynn (eds), *Colonialism and the Object: Empire, material culture and the museum*, Routledge, London, 1998, pp. 11–27; see also E. Said, *Orientalism*, Vintage Books, New York, 1978.
8 A. Segall and B. Trofanenko, 'The Victoria and Albert Museum: A subversive, playful pedagogy in action', in D.E. Clover, K. Sanford, L. Bell and K. Johnson (eds), *Adult Education, Museums and Art Galleries*, Sense Publishers, Rotterdam, 2016, pp. 53–63.
9 Barringer, 'The South Kensington Museum and the colonial project', p. 23.
10 ibid., p. 11.
11 Burton, *Vision and Accident*, pp. 179–80.
12 ibid., p. 199.
13 E. Wilson, 'The rhetoric of urban space', *New Left Review*, 1/209 (1995), p. 156.
14 Segall and Trofanenko, 'The Victoria and Albert Museum', p. 60.
15 L. Sandino, 'Politics and the narrative agency in the history of the Victoria and Albert Museum', in I. Goodson, A. Antikainen, P. Sikes and M. Andrews (eds), *The Routledge International Handbook on Narrative and Life History*, Routledge, London, 2016, pp. 392–402; see also Burton, *Vision and Accident*.
16 G. Debord, *La société du spectacle*, Les Éditions Gallimard, Paris, 1967.
17 Segall and Trofanenko, 'The Victoria and Albert Museum'.

CHAPTER 11 – ST PANCRAS STATION AND HOTEL, CAMDEN

1 F. Fisher, 'Inside London's railway termini, c.1870–1939', *London Journal*, 45/2 (2020), p. 219.
2 B. Black, *Hotel London: How Victorian commercial hospitality shaped a nation and its stories*, Ohio State University Press, Columbus, OH, 2019, p. 79.
3 Cited in ibid., p. 34.

4 D. Taylor, *Ritzy: British hotels, 1837–1987*, Millman, London, 2003.
5 G. Biddle, *Victorian Stations: Railway stations in England and Wales 1830–1923*, David and Charles, Newton Abbot, 1973, p. 74.
6 H.J. Dyos, 'Railways and housing in Victorian London', *Journal of Transport History*, 2/1 (1955), pp. 90–100.
7 E. Walford, 'Agar Town and the Midland Railway', in *Old and New London*, vol. 5, London, 1878, pp. 368–373, at British History Online, www.british-history.ac.uk/old-new-london/vol5/pp368-373 (accessed 4 July 2023).
8 *The Builder*, 8 October 1853, p. 1.
9 W.H. Barlow, 'Description of the St Pancras Station and Roof, Midland Railway', *Minutes of the Proceedings of the Institution of Civil Engineers*, 29 (1870), p. 81.
10 S. Bradley, *St Pancras Station*, Profile Books, London, 2007, p. 69.
11 Walford, 'Agar Town and the Midland Railway'.
12 S. Thurley, *The Building of England: How the history of England has shaped our buildings*, William Collins, London, 2013, p. 419.
13 J. Simmons, *The Victorian Railway* (second edition), Historical Publications, London, 2003, p. 156.
14 Fisher, 'Inside London's railway termini', p. 229.
15 Thurley, *The Building of England*, p. 419.
16 M. Herford, 'Architecture in Victorian London and the question of style', *Literature and Aesthetics*, 31/1 (2021), pp. 1–23.
17 K. Clark, *The Gothic Revival: An essay in the history of taste*, John Murray, London, 1996 (first published in 1928), p. 188.
18 G.G. Scott, *Personal and Professional Recollections*, edited by his son, G.G. Scott, Sampson Low, Marston, Searle and Rivington, London, 1879, p. 98.
19 Black, *Hotel London*, p. 85.
20 Bradley, *St Pancras Station*, p. 113.
21 L. Skipper, 'The evolution of wallpaper interior design schemes in a commercial setting: The interiors of the St Pancras Renaissance Hotel (Midland Grand Hotel), London 1870s–1980s', *Journal of Design History*, 30/3 (2016), p. 318.
22 *The Engineer*, 2 August 1901; cited in L. Allington-Jones, 'The phoenix: The role of conservation ethics in the development of St Pancras railway station', *Journal of Conservation and Museum Studies*, 11/1 (2013), p. 4.
23 G.A. Bremner, *Building Greater Britain: Architecture, imperialism and the Edwardian Baroque revival, 1885–1920*, Yale University Press for the Paul Mellon Centre for Studies in British Art, London, 2023.
24 Black, *Hotel London*, p. 86.
25 R. Bloomfield, 'St Pancras Chambers: Models, bigwigs, rockers: All aboard. A Victorian-era landmark draws professionals seeking to ride

the transformation of a grimy London district', *Wall Street Journal*, 26 October 2012, p. M.3.

26 A. Lansley, S. Durant, A. Dyke, B. Gambrill and R Shelton, *The Transformation of St Pancras Station*, Laurence King, London, 2008.

27 E. Riot, 'A European perspective on the planning of major railway stations: Considering the cases of St Pancras Station and Paris Gare du Nord', *Town Planning Review*, 85/2 (2014), pp. 191–202.

28 G. Roberts, 'St Pancras Station: Victorian "cathedral of the railways"', *Engineering History and Heritage*, 162/3 (2009), pp. 157–66.

CHAPTER 12 – HARRODS, KNIGHTSBRIDGE

1 F. Trentmann, 'Beyond consumerism: New historical perspectives on consumption', *Journal of Contemporary History*, 39/3 (2004), pp. 373–401.

2 K. Morrison, *English Shops and Shopping: An architectural history*, Paul Mellon Centre for Studies in British Art, London, 2003.

3 ibid., p. 125.

4 W. Lancaster, *The Department Store: A social history*, Leicester University Press, London, 1995; S. Elvins, 'History of the department store', in J. Stobart and V. Howard (eds), *The Routledge Companion to the History of Retailing*, Routledge, London, 2019, pp. 136–53.

5 F.H.W. Sheppard (ed.), 'Brompton Road: South side', in *Survey of London*, vol. 41: *Brompton* (1983), at British History Online, www.british-history.ac.uk/survey-london/vol41/pp9-32 (accessed 4 July 2023).

6 B. Cherry and N. Pevsner, *The Buildings of England, London 3: North West*, Yale University Press, London, 2002, p. 539.

7 G. Crossick and S. Jaumain, 'The world of the department store: Distribution, culture and social change', in G. Crossick and S. Jaumain (eds), *Cathedrals of Consumption: The European department store, 1850–1939*, Ashgate, Aldershot, 1999, p. 22.

8 D. Chaney, 'The department store as a cultural form', *Theory, Culture and Society*, 1/3 (1983), p. 25.

9 A. Trachtenberg, *The Incorporation of America: Culture and society in the gilded age*, Hill and Wang, New York, 1982, p. 131.

10 R. Sennet, *The Fall of Public Man*, Knopf, New York, 1976, p. 144.

11 P. Lara-Betancourt, 'Displaying dreams: Model interiors in British department stores, 1890–1914', in A.I. Lasc, P. Lara-Betancourt and M.M. Petty (eds), *Architectures of Display: Department stores and modern retail*, Taylor and Francis, London, 2017, p. 33.

12 https://archive.org/details/harrods-for-everything-images/page/xvi/mode/2up (accessed 4 July 2023).

13 S. Callery, *Harrods, Knightsbridge: The story of society's favourite store*, Ebury Press, London, 1991.
14 J. Giles, *The Parlour and the Suburb: Domestic identities, class, femininity and modernity*, Berg, Oxford, 2004.
15 E.D. Rappaport, *Shopping for Pleasure: Women in the making of London's West End*, Princeton University Press, Princeton, NJ, 1999.
16 Elvins, 'History of the department store', p. 141.
17 R. Laermans, 'Learning to consume: Early department stores and the shaping of modern consumer culture', *Theory, Culture and Society*, 10/1 (1993), p. 95.
18 Elvins, 'History of the department store', p. 143.
19 L.S. Sanders, *Consuming Fantasies: Labor, leisure, and the London shopgirl*, Ohio State University Press, Columbus, OH, 2006.
20 E. Carlson, 'The girl behind the counter: Elizabeth Sparhawk-Jones and the modern shop girl', *Panorama: Journal of the Association of Historians of American Art*, 5/1 (2019), p. 10.
21 T. Sutherst, *Death and Disease Behind the Counter*, Kegan Paul, Trench & Co., London, 1884, p. 42. Quoted in K.K. Bradshaw, 'Reality, expectations and fears: Women shop assistants in London, 1890–1914', doctoral dissertation, George Mason University, 2019.
22 Laermans, 'Learning to consume', p. 86.
23 S. Ashmore, 'Extinction and evolution: Department stores in London's West End, 1945–1982', *London Journal*, 31/1 (2006), pp. 41–63.

CHAPTER 13 – ADMIRALTY ARCH, WHITEHALL

1 G. A. Bremner, *Building Greater Britain: Architecture, imperialism and the Edwardian Baroque revival, 1885–1920*, Yale University Press for the Paul Mellon Centre for Studies in British Art, London, 2023, p. 185.
2 D. Cannadine, 'The context, performance and meaning of ritual: The British monarchy and the "invention of tradition" c. 1820–1977', in E. Hobsbawm and T. Ranger (eds), *The Invention of Tradition*, Cambridge University Press, Cambridge, 2012, pp. 101–64.
3 M.H. Port, *Imperial London: Civil government building in London 1851–1915*, Yale University Press for the Paul Mellon Centre for Studies in British Art, London, 1995.
4 T. Smith, '"A grand work of noble conception": the Victoria Memorial and imperial London', in F. Driver and D. Gilbert (eds), *Imperial Cities: Landscape, display and identity*, Manchester University Press, Manchester, 1999, p. 21.

5 G.A. Bremner, '"Imperial Peace Memorial": The Second Anglo-Boer War and the origins of the Admiralty Arch, 1900–05', *British Art Journal*, 5/3 (2004), p. 64.
6 S. Bradley and N. Pevsner, *The Buildings of England, London 6: Westminster*, Yale University Press, London, 2003, p. 656.
7 Bremner, *Building Greater Britain*, pp. 182–83.
8 H.M. Cundall, 'The memorial to the Great Queen: The story of its making told by its maker, Thomas Brock, R.A.', *Pall Mall Magazine*, June 1911, p. 848; cited in J. Plunkett, 'A tale of two statues: Memorializing Queen Victoria in London and Calcutta', *Interdisciplinary Studies in the Long Nineteenth Century*, 33 (2022).
9 ibid.
10 Smith, '"A grand work of noble conception"', p. 30.
11 Bradley and Pevsner, *The Buildings of England,* p. 645.

PART IV – METRO LONDON

1 P. Thane, 'Women in the British Labour Party and the construction of state welfare, 1906–1939', in S.D. Koven, and S. Michel (eds), *Mothers of a New World: Maternalist politics and the origins of welfare states*, Routledge, London, 2013, pp. 343–77.
2 P.L. Knox, *Metroburbia: The anatomy of Greater London*, Merrell, London, 2017.
3 R. Bowdler, 'Between the wars: 1914–1940', in J. Honer (ed.), *London Suburbs*, Merrell Holberton/English Heritage, London, 1999, pp. 103–30.

CHAPTER 14 – COUNTY HALL, LAMBETH

1 P.L. Knox, *London: Architecture, building and social change*, Merrell, London, 2015.
2 K. Young and P.L. Garside, *Metropolitan London: Politics and urban change 1837–1981*, Edward Arnold, London, 1982, p. 21.
3 P. Hall, *Cities in Civilization*, Weidenfeld and Nicolson, London, 1998.
4 ibid., p. 702.
5 J. Davis, *Reforming London: The London government problem 1855–1900*, Clarendon Press, Oxford, 1988.
6 H. Hobhouse (ed.), *Survey of London: County Hall* (Monograph 17), Guild & School of Handicraft, London, 1991.
7 *Westminster Gazette*, Monday 17 July 1922, p. 6.

8 S. Pankhurst, *Workers' Dreadnought*, 22 July 1922, p. 2.
9 Hobhouse, *Survey of London*, p. 75.
10 B. Cherry and N. Pevsner, *The Buildings of England, London 2: South*, Yale University Press, London, 2002, p. 355.
11 S.D. Pennybacker, *A Vision for London 1889–1914: Labour, everyday life and the LCC experiment*, Routledge, London, 1995.
12 Hobhouse, *Survey of London*, pp. 70–91.
13 ibid., p. 70.
14 ibid., p. 118.
15 ibid., p. 70.
16 Pennybacker, *A Vision for London*.
17 E. Harwood, 'Review: *A Vision for London, 1889–1914*', *Victorian Studies*, 39/4 (1996), pp. 572–74.
18 A. Saint (ed.), *Politics and the People of London: The London County Council, 1889–1965*, Bloomsbury Academic, London, 1989.
19 D. Thomas, 'London's green belt: The evolution of an idea', *Geographical Journal*, 129/1 (1963), p. 17.
20 P.L. Knox, *Metroburbia: The anatomy of Greater London*, Merrell, London, 2017.
21 P.L. Knox, *Better by Design? Architecture, urban planning, and the good city*, Virginia Tech Publishing, Blacksburg, VA, 2020. Open source: https://publishing.vt.edu/site/books/m/10.21061/better-by-design/ (accessed 4 July 2023).
22 O. Hatherley, *Red Metropolis: Socialism and the government of London*, Repeater Books, London, 2020.
23 Knox, *Metroburbia*.
24 I. Sinclair, *London Orbital*, Penguin Books, London, 2003, p. 13.
25 Hobhouse, *Survey of London*, p. 118.
26 Hatherley, *Red Metropolis*, p. 21.

CHAPTER 15 – DUNROAMIN, AMERSHAM

1 P. Oliver, I. Davis and I. Bentley, *Dunroamin: The suburban semi and its enemies*, Barrie & Jenkins, London, 1981.
2 A.A. Jackson, *Semi-detached London: Suburban development, life and transport*, Allen and Unwin, London, 1973.
3 P.L. Knox, *Better by Design? Architecture, urban planning, and the good city*, Virginia Tech Publishing, Blacksburg, VA, 2020. Open source: https://publishing.vt.edu/site/books/m/10.21061/better-by-design/ (accessed 4 July 2023).
4 N. Barratt, *Greater London: The story of the suburbs*, Random House, London, 2012.

5 F.M.L. Thompson, *The Rise of Suburbia*, Leicester University Press, Leicester, 1982.
6 S. Gunn and R. Bell, *Middle Classes: Their rise and sprawl*, Cassell, London, 2002.
7 A.A. Jackson, *London's Metro-Land*, Capital History, London, 2006.
8 *Sunday Dispatch*, 18 October 1931.
9 J.W.R. Whitehand and C.M.H. Carr, 'England's interwar suburban landscapes: Myth and reality', *Journal of Historical Geography*, 25/4 (1999), pp. 483–501.
10 Oliver et al., *Dunroamin.*
11 J.B. Priestley, 'Introduction' in *The Beauty of Britain*, Batsford, London, 1935, p. 3.
12 J.B. Priestley, *English Journey*, Folio Society, London, 1997 (first published in 1934), p. 325.
13 J.M. Richards, *The Castles on the Ground: The anatomy of suburbia*, Architectural Press, London, 1946, p. 35.
14 P. Abercrombie, 'Introduction', in P. Abercrombie (ed.), *The Book of the Modern House: A panoramic survey of contemporary domestic design*, Hodder and Stoughton, London, 1939, p. xix.
15 G. Orwell, 'A clergyman's daughter', in *The Complete Novels*, Penguin Modern Classics, London, 1976 (first published in 1935), p. 368.
16 C. Williams-Ellis, *England and the Octopus*, Council for the Protection of Rural England, London, 1928, p. 24.
17 J. Giles, *The Parlour and the Suburb: Domestic identities, class, femininity and modernity*, Berg, Oxford, 2004.
18 R. Madigan and M. Munro, 'Gender, house and "home": Social meanings and domestic architecture in Britain', *Journal of Architectural and Planning Research*, 8/2 (1991), pp. 116–32.
19 Giles, *The Parlour and the Suburb.*
20 P.L. Knox, *Metroburbia: The anatomy of Greater London*, Merrell, London, 2017.

CHAPTER 16 – DOLPHIN SQUARE, PIMLICO

1 T. Gourvish, *Dolphin Square: The history of a unique building*, A&C Black, London, 2014, p. 92.
2 P.L. Knox, *London: Architecture, building and social change*, Merrell, London, 2015.
3 J. Giles, *The Parlour and the Suburb: Domestic identities, class, femininity and modernity*, Berg, Oxford, 2004.

4 W. Carey, *William Carey's Pimlico: History, analysis, gazetteer*, Maypole Press, London, 1986, p. 102.
5 K.F. Morris, *A History of Dolphin Square*, Dolphin Square Trust, London, 1995.
6 ibid.
7 City of Westminster, *Conservation Area Audit, Dolphin Square*, City of Westminster Planning and City Development, London, 2008.
8 Gourvish, *Dolphin Square*.
9 ibid.
10 S. Danczuk and D. Smith, *Scandal at Dolphin Square: A notorious history*, History Press, Cheltenham, 2022, p. 47.
11 ibid.
12 Morris, *A History of Dolphin Square*, p. 105.
13 Gourvish, *Dolphin Square*, p. 292.
14 Morris, *A History of Dolphin Square*, pp. 37–38.
15 H. Porter and A. Davidson, 'Another dark chapter for London's most scandalous address', *Vanity Fair*, December 2014, at www.vanityfair.com/style/scandal/2014/12/scandal-dolphin-square-london (accessed 4 July 2023).
16 E. Malnick, 'Disgraced Lord Sewel who was "filmed snorting cocaine with prostitutes" allowed continued access to parliament', *Daily Telegraph*, 4 October 2017, at www.telegraph.co.uk/news/2017/10/14/disgraced-lord-sewel-filmed-snorting-cocaine-prostitutes-allowed/ (accessed 4 July 2023).

CHAPTER 17 – HOOVER FACTORY, PERIVALE

1 P. Hall, 'The new industrial areas', in J.T. Coppock and H.C. Prince (eds), *Greater London*, Faber and Faber, London, 1964, pp. 121–39.
2 S. Alexander, 'A new civilization? London surveyed 1928–1940s', *History Workshop Journal*, 64 (2007), pp. 297–320.
3 W. Hitchmough, *Hoover Factory: Wallis, Gilbert and Partners*, Phaidon, London, 1992, p. 8.
4 R. Loader and J. Skinner, 'Management, construction and architecture: The development of the model factory', *Construction History*, 7 (1991), pp. 83–103.
5 T. Wallis, 'Factories', *Journal of the Royal Institute of British Architects*, 25 February 1933, pp. 301–02.
6 J.S. Skinner, *Form and Fancy: Factories and factory buildings by Wallis, Gilbert and Partners, 1916–1939*, Liverpool University Press, Liverpool, 1997.

7 A. Schwartzman, *London Art Deco*, Hudson Hills Press, Manchester, 2006.
8 Hitchmough, *Hoover Factory*.
9 D. Thompson, 'Inside the Hoover building', *Spirit of Progress*, 2/4 (2001), p. 13.
10 B. Elliott, 'Modern, moderne, and modernistic: Le Corbusier, Thomas Wallis and the problem of Art Deco', in P. Caughie (ed.), *Disciplining Modernism*, Palgrave Macmillan, London, 2009, pp. 128–46.
11 Hitchmough, *Hoover Factory*.
12 N. Pevsner, *The Buildings of England*, vol. 3, part 4: *Middlesex*, Penguin, London, 1951.
13 B. Cherry and N. Pevsner, *The Buildings of England, London 3: North West*, Yale University Press, London, 2002, pp. 76 and 191.
14 D.K. Bolton, H.P.F. King, G. Wyld and D.C. Yaxley, 'Perivale: Economic and social history', in T.F.T. Baker, J.S. Cockburn and R.B. Pugh (eds), *A History of the County of Middlesex*, vol. 4: *Harmondsworth, Hayes, Norwood with Southall, Hillingdon with Uxbridge, Ickenham, Northolt, Perivale, Ruislip, Edgware, Harrow with Pinner*, Victoria County History, London, 1971, at British History Online, www.british-history.ac.uk/vch/middx/vol4 (accessed 6 September 2023).
15 P.L. Knox, *Metroburbia: The anatomy of Greater London*, Merrell, London, 2017.
16 E. Platt, *Leadville: A biography of the A40*, Picador, London, 2000.
17 G. Stamp, 'Guinness isn't good for you: Britain's best twentieth-century buildings may be listed, but cynical, greedy corporations are still finding ways to demolish them – and more than architecture is at stake', *Apollo*, 162/522 (2005), p. 81.
18 M. Airs, 'Protecting the historic environment: The legacy of W.G. Hoskins', *Journal of Architectural Conservation*, 12/3 (2006), pp. 19–33.
19 J. Davis, *Waterloo Sunrise: London from the Sixties to Thatcher*, Princeton University Press, London, 2022, p. 14.

PART V – POSTWAR LONDON

1 D. Johnson, *The London Blitz: The City ablaze, December 29, 1940*, Stein and Day, New York, 1980, pp. 196–97.
2 L. Glasheen, 'Bombsites, adventure playgrounds and the reconstruction of London', *London Journal*, 44/1 (2019), pp. 54–74.
3 T. Atkinson and B. Atkinson (eds), *Missing Buildings*, Hwæt Books, London, 2015.
4 E. Harwood, *Space, Hope and Brutalism: English architecture, 1945–1975*, Yale University Press for the Paul Mellon Centre for Studies in British

Art, London, 2015; R. Wakeman, *Practicing Utopia*, University of Chicago Press, Chicago, IL, 2016.

5 P.L. Knox, *Better by Design? Architecture, urban planning, and the good city*, Virginia Tech Publishing, Blacksburg, VA, 2020. Open source: https://publishing.vt.edu/site/books/m/10.21061/better-by-design/ (accessed 4 July 2023).

6 H. Wardle and L. Obermuller, 'The Windrush generation', *Anthropology Today*, 34/4 (2018), pp. 3–4.

7 K.H. Perry, *London is the Place for Me: Black Britons, citizenship and the politics of race*, Oxford University Press, Oxford, 2015; C. Schofield and B. Jones, '"Whatever community is, this is not it": Notting Hill and the reconstruction of "race" in Britain after 1958', *Journal of British Studies*, 58/ 1 (2019), pp. 142–73.

8 See D. Sandbrook, *White Heat: A history of Britain in the Swinging Sixties*, Little, Brown, London, 2006.

9 O.S. Smith, *Boom Cities: Architect planners and the politics of radical urban renewal in 1960s Britain*, Oxford University Press, London, 2019.

10 A. Marwick, 'The cultural revolution of the long sixties: Voices of reaction, protest, and permeation', *International History Review*, 27/4 (2005), pp. 780–806; L. Tickner, *London's New Scene: Art and culture in the 1960s*, Yale University Press, London, 2020.

11 J. Davis, *Waterloo Sunrise: London from the Sixties to Thatcher*, Princeton University Press, London, 2022.

12 R. Porter, *London: A social history*, Hamish Hamilton, London, 1994, p. 363.

13 Davis, *Waterloo Sunrise*, p. 5.

14 O.S. Smith, 'The inner city crisis and the end of urban modernism in 1970s Britain', *Twentieth Century British History*, 27/4 (2016), pp. 578–98.

CHAPTER 18 – NATIONAL THEATRE, WATERLOO

1 L. Kruger, '"Our National House": The ideology of the National Theatre of Great Britain', *Theatre Journal*, 39/1 (1987), pp. 35–50.

2 https://artsandculture.google.com/story/JQVxhoZl2REA8A (accessed 4 July 2023).

3 P. Dillon, 'National Theatre, 1976. Architect, Denys Lasdun', in D. Staples and D. Hamer (eds), *Modern Theatres 1950–2020*, Routledge, London, 2021, pp. 259–69.

4 D. Lasdun, 'Architectural aspects of the National Theatre', *Journal of the Royal Society of Arts*, 125/5256 (1977), pp. 780–92.

5 ibid., p. 789.
6 Dillon, 'National Theatre, 1976', p. 262.
7 Lasdun, 'Architectural aspects of the National Theatre', p. 785.
8 E. Harwood, *Space, Hope and Brutalism: English architecture, 1945–1975*, Yale University Press for the Paul Mellon Centre for Studies in British Art, London, 2015.
9 M. Billington, *Guardian*, 12 March 1976.
10 M. Hills, 'The National Theatre, London, as a theatrical/architectural object of fan imagination', in N. van Es, S. Reijnders, L. Bolderman and A. Waysdorf (eds), *Locating Imagination in Popular Culture: Place, tourism and belonging*, Routledge, London, 2021, p. 297.
11 D. Rosenthal, *The National Theatre Story*, Oberon Books, London, 2013, p. 238.
12 G. Baeten, 'From community planning to partnership planning: Urban regeneration and shifting power geometries on the South Bank, London', *GeoJournal*, 51 (2000), pp. 293–300.
13 S. Murray, 'The evolution and transformation of Bankside, London, 1947–2019', *Journal of Urban History*, 47/1 (2021), pp. 68–84.
14 P. Newman and I. Smith, 'Cultural production, place and politics on the south bank of the Thames', *International Journal of Urban and Regional Research*, 24/1 (1999), pp. 9–24.
15 A. Fair, 'The limits of 1960s radicalism: The Fun Palace versus the National Theatre', in B. Calder (ed.), *Setting the Scene: Perspectives on twentieth-century theatre architecture*, Routledge, London, 2015, p. 175.

CHAPTER 19 – ABBEY ROAD STUDIOS, ST JOHN'S WOOD

1 D.J. Olsen, 'Victorian London: Specialization, segregation, and privacy', *Victorian Studies*, 17/3 (1974), pp. 272–73.
2 A.P. Vadillo, *Women Poets and Urban Aestheticism*, Palgrave Macmillan, London, 2005, p. 134.
3 ibid., p. 118.
4 A.M. Eyre, *Saint John's Wood: Its history, its houses, its haunts, and its celebrities*, Chapman and Hall, London, 1913, p. 296.
5 R. Tames, *St John's Wood and Maida Vale Past*, Historical Publications, London, 1998, p. 58.
6 Vadillo, *Women Poets and Urban Aestheticism*, p. 128.
7 Tames, *St John's Wood and Maida Vale Past*, p. 129.
8 H. Massey, *The Great British Recording Studios*, Hal Leonard, Lanham, MD, 2015, p. 2.

9 A. Leve and R. Morgan, *1963: The year of the revolution: How youth changed the world with music, art, and fashion*, Harper Collins, London, 2013; J. Walford, *Sixties Fashion from 'Less is More' to Youthquake*, Thames & Hudson, London, 2013.
10 L. Tickner, *London's New Scene: Art and culture in the 1960s*, Yale University Press, London, 2020.
11 A. Marwick, 'The cultural revolution of the long sixties: Voices of reaction, protest, and permeation', *International History Review*, 27/4 (2005), pp. 780–806.
12 P. Atkinson, 'Abbey Road studios, the tourist, and Beatles heritage', in E. Mazierska and G. Gregory (eds), *Relocating Popular Music*, Palgrave Macmillan, London, 2015, pp. 129–47.
13 Massey, *The Great British Recording Studios*.
14 D. Bacon and N. Maslov, *The Beatles' England: There are places I'll remember*, 910 Press, San Francisco, CA, 1982.
15 C. Gibson, 'Recording studios: Relational spaces of creativity in the city', *Built Environment*, 31/3 (2005), p. 203.
16 S. Bennett, 'Behind the magical mystery door: History, mythology and the aura of Abbey Road Studios', *Popular Music*, 35/3 (2016), pp. 396–417.
17 T. Brabazon, 'We're one short for the crossing: Abbey Road and popular memory', *Transformation*, 3 (2002), pp. 1–16.

CHAPTER 20 – CENTRE POINT, ST GILES

1 'Centre Point symbol of the sixties', *Building*, 24 May 1968, pp. 99–106.
2 B. Cherry and N. Pevsner, *The Buildings of England, London 4: North*, Yale University Press, London, 1998, p. 316.
3 *Hansard*, vol. 508. Second Reading of Town and Country Planning Bill, 1 December 1952, p. 1115.
4 O. Marriott, *The Property Boom*, Hamish Hamilton, London, 1967, p. 8.
5 P.J. Ambrose and R.J. Colenutt, *The Property Machine*, Penguin, Harmondsworth, 1975; P. Scott, *The Property Masters*, E. and F.N. Spon, London, 1996.
6 S. Jenkins, *Landlords to London: The story of a capital and its growth*, Book Club Associates, London, 1975, p. 216.
7 A. Kefford, 'Actually existing managerialism: Planning, politics and property development in post-1945 Britain', *Urban Studies*, 58/12 (2021), p. 2446.
8 F. Mort, 'Fantasies of metropolitan life: Planning London in the 1940s', *Journal of British Studies*, 43/1 (2004), p. 124.

9 Marriott, *The Property Boom*, p. 105.
10 ibid., pp. 112–16; Jenkins, *Landlords to London*, p. 221.
11 'Seifert on our skyline', *Sunday Times*, 13 February 1972, supplement; quoted in E. Harwood, *Space, Hope and Brutalism: English architecture, 1945–1975*, Yale University Press for the Paul Mellon Centre for Studies in British Art, London, 2015, p. 401.
12 Scott, *The Property Masters*, p. 195.
13 P.L Knox, *Better by Design? Architecture, urban planning, and the good city*, Virginia Tech Publishing, Blacksburg, VA, 2020. Open source: https://publishing.vt.edu/site/books/m/10.21061/better-by-design/ (accessed 4 July 2023).
14 E. Harwood, 'Keeping the past in England: The history of post-war listing', *Journal of Architecture*, 15/5 (2010), pp. 671–82.
15 M. Raco, D. Durrant and N. Livingstone, 'Slow cities, urban politics and the temporalities of planning: Lessons from London', *Environment and Planning C: Politics and Space*, 36/ 7 (2018), p. 1184.

CHAPTER 21 – PENTON HOUSE, THAMESMEAD

1 P. Chadwick and B. Weaver (eds), *The Town of Tomorrow: 50 years of Thamesmead*, Here Press, London, 2019.
2 P.L. Knox, *Better by Design? Architecture, urban planning, and the good city*, Virginia Tech Publishing, Blacksburg, VA, 2020. Open source: https://publishing.vt.edu/site/books/m/10.21061/better-by-design/ (accessed 4 July 2023).
3 J. Boughton, *Municipal Dreams: The rise and fall of council housing*, Verso, London, 2018.
4 P. Scott, 'Friends in high places: Government–industry relations in public sector house-building during Britain's tower block era', *Business History*, 62/4 (2020), pp. 545–64.
5 J. Jacobs, 'Downtown is for people', in W. Whyte Jr. (ed.), *The Exploding Metropolis*, Doubleday, Garden City, NY, 1958, p. 157.
6 O.S. Smith, *Boom Cities: Architect planners and the politics of radical urban renewal in 1960s Britain*, Oxford University Press, London, 2019, pp. 95–101.
7 Knox, *Better by Design?*
8 D. Cruickshank, 'Thamesmead, London 1964–1998', *RIBA Journal*, 105/1 (1998), p. 62.
9 A. Markowitz, *The Making, Unmaking, and Remaking of Thamesmead: A story of urban design, decline, and renewal in postwar London*, Bartlett Development Planning Unit, Working Paper 193, 2017.

10 D. Danaher and J.D. Williamson, '"New Town Blues": Planning versus mutual', *International Journal of Social Psychiatry*, 29/2 (1983), p. 147.
11 R. MacCormac, 'Thamesmead New Town. Part 1, A riverside development', *Architects' Journal*, 156/41 (1972), p. 830.
12 I. Menzies, 'Needed: A Thamesmead', *Boston Globe*, 23 November 1970, p. 10.
13 Quoted in Chadwick and Weaver, *The Town of Tomorrow*, pp. 165 and 169.
14 Cruickshank, 'Thamesmead, London 1964–1998', p. 62.
15 T. Aldous, 'London's New Town', *Illustrated London News*, 1 July 1974, p. 33.
16 V.G. Wigfall, *Thamesmead: Back to the future – a social history of Thamesmead*, Greenwich Community College Press, London, 1997, p. 96.
17 ibid.
18 S. Babish, '"A place in London's future": A Clockwork Orange, Thamesmead and the urban dystopia of the modernist large-scale plan', *Screen*, 59/2 (2018), p. 201.
19 Chadwick and Weaver, *The Town of Tomorrow*, p. 162.
20 S. Wetherell, *Foundations: How the built environment made twentieth-century Britain*, Princeton University Press, Princeton, NJ, 2000, p. 100.
21 S. Jenkins, *Outer London*, HarperCollins, London, 1981, p. 42.
22 V. Symes, 'Under new management: The case of Thamesmead', *Journal of Architectural and Planning Research*, 8/4 (1991), pp. 276–86.
23 P. Ford and K. Baikie, 'Thamesmead: Kickstarting the transformation of a stalled New Town', *Geography*, 103/2 (2018), pp. 102–04.
24 O. Wainwright, 'What happened to the Cockney Rivieras? The botched regeneration of brutalist utopia Thamesmead', *Guardian*, 30 November 2022.

PART VI – GLOBAL LONDON

1 P. Baker and J. Eversley, *Multilingual Capital: The languages of London's schoolchildren and their relevance to economic, social, and educational policies*, Battlebridge Publications, London, 2000.
2 A. Smith, 'Destination London: An expanding visitor economy', in A. Smith and A. Graham (eds), *Destination London: The expansion of the visitor economy*, University of Westminster Press, London, 2019, pp. 1–13.
3 C. Hamnett, *Unequal City: London in the global arena*, Taylor and Francis, London, 2003.
4 N. Brenner and N. Theodore, 'Neoliberalism and the urban condition', *City*, 9 (2005), pp. 101–07.

5 R. Atkinson, *Alpha City: How London was captured by the super-rich*, Verso, London, 2021, p. 86.
6 P.L. Knox, 'Reflexive neoliberalism, urban design, and regeneration machines', in H. Westlund and T. Haas (eds), *In the Post-Urban World*, Routledge, London, 2017, pp. 82–96; E. Swyngedouw, F. Moulaert and A. Rodriguez, 'Neoliberal urbanization in Europe: Large-scale urban development projects and the New Urban Policy', in N. Brenner and N. Theodore (eds), *Spaces of Neoliberalism: Urban restructuring in North America and Europe*, Blackwell, Oxford, 2002, pp. 195–229.

CHAPTER 22 – JAMME MASJID, SPITALFIELDS

1 R. Lichtenstein, *On Brick Lane*, Hamish Hamilton, London, 2007.
2 F.H.W. Sheppard (ed.), 'The Wood-Michell estate: Fournier Street', in *Survey of London*, vol. 27: *Spitalfields and Mile End New Town* (1957), at British History Online, www.british-history.ac.uk/survey-london/vol27/pp199-225 (accessed 4 July 2023).
3 S. Shaw, S. Bagwell and J. Karmowska, 'Ethnoscapes as spectacle: Reimaging multicultural districts as new destinations for leisure and tourism consumption', *Urban Studies*, 41/10 (2004), pp. 1983–2000.
4 S.J. Shaw and N.E. Macleod, 'Creativity and conflict: Cultural tourism in London's city fringe', *Tourism, Culture and Communication*, 2/3 (2000), pp. 165–75.
5 A. Spicer, 'Jamme Masjid mosque and layered landscapes', in E. Nelson and J. Wright (eds), *Layered Landscapes: Early modern religious space across faiths and cultures*, Routledge, London, 2017, p. 223.
6 N. Frost, 'Green curry: Politics and place-making on Brick Lane', *Food, Culture & Society*, 14/2 (2011), pp. 225–42.
7 G. Mavrommatis, 'The new "creative" Brick Lane: A narrative study of local multicultural encounters', *Ethnicities*, 6/4 (2007), pp. 498–517.
8 Shaw, et al., 'Ethnoscapes as spectacle', p. 1993.
9 Runnymede Trust, *Beyond Banglatown: Continuity, change, and new urban economies in Brick Lane*, Runnymede Trust, London, 2020, p. 3.
10 ibid., p. 11.

CHAPTER 23 – ONE CANADA SQUARE, ISLE OF DOGS

1 J. Garreau, *Edge City: Life on the new frontier*, Random House, New York, 1992.

2 S. Brownill, *Developing London's Docklands: Another great planning disaster?* Paul Chapman, London, 1990.
3 J. Brown, '"Rolling back the frontiers of the state, only to see them re-imposed in Docklands?": Margaret Thatcher, Michael Heseltine and the contested parenthood of Canary Wharf', in A. Mullen, S. Farrall and D. Jeffery (eds), *Thatcherism in the 21st Century*, Palgrave Macmillan, Cham, Switzerland, 2020, p. 93.
4 H. Hobhouse (ed.), 'Modern Docklands: The background to redevelopment', in *Survey of London*, Vols 43 and 44: *Poplar, Blackwall and Isle of Dogs* (1994), at British History Online, www.british-history.ac.uk/survey-london/vols43-4/pp686-691 (accessed 6 September 2023).
5 M. Carmona, 'The Isle of Dogs: Four development waves, five planning models, twelve plans, thirty-five years, and a renaissance ... of sorts', *Progress in Planning*, 71 (2009), p. 98.
6 T. Oc and S. Tiesdell, 'The London Docklands Development Corporation (LDDC), 1981–1991: A perspective on the management of urban regeneration', *Town Planning Review*, 62/3 (1991), pp. 311–30.
7 *Financial Times*, 5 September 1985, p.27.
8 Brown, '"Rolling back the frontiers of the state ..."'.
9 T. Wilkinson, 'The architecture of the Big Bang', *Architectural Review*, May 1988, p. 4.
10 A. Hallsworth and J.M. Bobe, 'How the interest rate cat ate the Docklands Canary', *Area*, 25/1 (1993), pp. 64–69.
11 D.L.A. Gordon, 'The resurrection of Canary Wharf', *Planning Theory and Practice*, 2/2 (2001), pp. 149–68.
12 A. Sutcliffe, *London: An architectural history*, Yale University Press, London, 2006, p. 204.

CHAPTER 24 – THE SHARD, LONDON BRIDGE

1 New London Architecture, *London Tall Buildings Survey 2022*, New London Architecture, London, 2022.
2 D. Craggs, 'Skyscraper development and the dynamics of crisis: The new London skyline and spatial recapitalization', *Built Environment*, 43/4 (2015), pp. 500–19.
3 R. Atkinson, *Alpha City: How London was captured by the super-rich*, Verso, London, 2021, p. 83. See also A. Minton, *Big Capital: Who is London for?* Penguin UK, London, 2017.
4 M. Kaika, 'Architecture and crisis: Re-inventing the icon, re-imag(in)ing London and re-branding the City', *Transactions of the Institute of British Geographers*, 35 (2010), pp. 453–74.

5 Greater London Authority, *The London Plan*, Greater London Authority, London, 2004, p. 5.

6 P.L. Knox and K. Pain, 'Globalization, neoliberalism and international homogeneity in architecture and urban development', *Informationen zur Raumentwicklung*, 5/6 (2010), pp. 417–28.

7 Wealth-X, *UHNW Cities: Residential footprint*, Wealth-X Institute, London, 2017; R. Atkinson, R. Burrows, L. Glucksberg, H.K. Ho, C. Knowles and D. Rhodes, 'Minimum city? The deeper impacts of the "super-rich" on urban life', in R. Forrest, S.Y. Koh and B. Wissink (eds), *Cities and the Superrich: Real estate, elite practices and urban political economies*, Palgrave, London, 2016; Minton, *Big Capital*.

8 R. Atkinson, 'Necrotecture: Lifeless dwellings and London's super-rich', *International Journal of Urban and Regional Research*, 43/1 (2019), pp. 2–3.

9 H.K. Ho and R. Atkinson, 'Looking for big "fry": the motives and methods of middle-class international property investors', *Urban Studies*, 55/9 (2017), pp. 2040–56.

10 H. Watson, *The Shard: The vision of Irvine Sellar*, Constable, London, 2017.

11 R. Davies, 'How Qatar bought up Britain', Observer, 5 November 2022, at www.theguardian.com/business/ng-interactive/2022/nov/05/how-qatar-bought-up-britain (accessed 4 July 2023).

12 S. Jenkins, 'Ken falls victim to Big Apple envy', *Evening Standard*, 18 January 2001.

13 D. Sudjic, 'Don't come to me with your storeys', *Observer*, 19 November 2000.

14 Quoted by Robert Gibson, '"Taliban" slur upsets EH', *Estates Gazette*, 17 November 2001.

15 Quoted in Watson, *The Shard*, p. 124.

16 H. Wright, 'The Shard', *Blueprint*, 315 (2012), p. 52.

17 M. Appert and C. Montes, 'Skyscrapers and the redrawing of the London skyline: A case of territorialisation through landscape control', *Articulo: Journal of Urban Research*, Special issue 7 (2015); M. Appert (trans. O. Waine), 'Skyline policy: The Shard and London's high-rise debate', *Metropolitics*, 14 December 2011, at https://metropolitics.org/Skyline-policy-the-Shard-and.html (accessed 4 July 2023).

18 J. Parker, 'Engineering The Shard, London: Tallest building in western Europe', *Proceedings of the Institution of Civil Engineers*, 166/CE2 (2013), p. 68.

19 R. Neate, 'Ghost towers: Half of new-build luxury London flats fail to sell', *Guardian*, 26 January 2018.

CHAPTER 25 – PLATFORM G, KING'S CROSS

1 R. Harris, *London's Global Office Economy: From clerical factory to digital hub*, Routledge, London, 2021.
2 ibid., p. 202.
3 J. Punter (ed.), *Urban Design and the British Urban Renaissance*, Routledge, London, 2010.
4 Greater London Assembly, *Knock It Down or Do It Up? The challenge of estate regeneration*, GLA, London, 2015.
5 T. Schröpfer, 'Google King's Cross', in *Dense + Green Cities: Architecture as urban ecosystem*, Birkhäuser, Basel, 2020, pp. 250–57.
6 M. Adelfio, I. Hamiduddin and E. Miedema, 'London's King's Cross redevelopment: A compact, resource efficient and "liveable" global city model for an era of climate emergency?', *Urban Research & Practice*, 14/2 (2021), pp. 180–200.
7 M. Edwards, 'King's Cross: Renaissance for whom?', in Punter, *Urban Design and the British Urban Renaissance*, p. 203.
8 Centre for Cities: www.centreforcities.org/press/office-politics-press-release/ (accessed 4 July 2023).

EPILOGUE

1 P.L. Knox, *Metroburbia: The anatomy of Greater London*, Merrell, London, 2017.
2 S. Jenkins, 'The battle for the soul of London', *New Statesman*, 2–8 June 2023, p. 53.
3 P.L. Knox, 'Reflexive neoliberalism, urban design, and regeneration machines', in H. Westlund and T. Haas (eds), *In the Post-Urban World*, Routledge, London, 2017, pp. 82–96.
4 R. Atkinson, *Alpha City: How London was captured by the super-rich*, Verso, London, 2021; C. Knowles, *Serious Money*, Allen Lane, London, 2022.
5 www.statista.com/statistics/1029318/average-price-of-detached-dwellings-in-london-by-borough/ (accessed 4 July 2023).
6 A. Minton, *Big Capital: Who is London for?* Penguin UK, London, 2017.
7 E. Wall, *Contesting Public Spaces: Social lives of urban redevelopment in London*, Routledge, London, 2022.
8 Knox, 'Reflexive neoliberalism'.

Select Bibliography

Atkinson, P., 'Abbey Road studios, the tourist, and Beatles heritage', in E. Mazierska and G. Gregory (eds), *Relocating Popular Music*, Palgrave Macmillan, Basingstoke, 2015, pp. 129–147.

Atkinson, R., *Alpha City: How London was captured by the super-rich*, Verso, London, 2021.

Ayres, J., *Building the Georgian City*, Yale University Press for the Paul Mellon Centre for Studies in British Art, London, 1998.

Barratt, N., *Greater London: The story of the suburbs*, Random House, London, 2012.

Black, B., *Hotel London: How Victorian commercial hospitality shaped a nation and its stories*, Ohio State University Press, Columbus, OH, 2019.

Boughton, J., *Municipal Dreams: The rise and fall of council housing*, Verso, London, 2018.

Bremner, G.A., 'Nation and empire in the government architecture of mid-Victorian London: The Foreign and India Office reconsidered', *Historical Journal*, 48/3 (2005), pp. 703–42.

Bremner, G.A., *Building Greater Britain: Architecture, imperialism and the Edwardian Baroque revival, 1885–1920*, Yale University Press for the Paul Mellon Centre for Studies in British Art, London, 2023.

Brooks, C. and A. Saint (eds) *The Victorian Church: Architecture and society*, Manchester University Press, Manchester and New York, 1995.

Burton, A., *Vision and Accident: The story of the Victoria and Albert Museum*, V&A Publications, London, 1999.

Byrne, A., *Bedford Square: An architectural study*, Athlone Press, London, 1990.

Callery, S., *Harrods, Knightsbridge: The story of society's favourite store*, Ebury Press, London, 1991.

Carmona, M., 'The Isle of Dogs: Four development waves, five planning models, twelve plans, thirty-five years, and a renaissance … of sorts', *Progress in Planning*, 71 (2009), pp. 87–151.

Carmona, M. and F. Wunderlich, *Capital Spaces: The multiple complex spaces of a global city*, Routledge, London, 2012.

Chadwick, P. and B. Weaver (eds), *The Town of Tomorrow: 50 years of Thamesmead*, Here Press, London, 2019.

Crowther, M.A., *The Workhouse System 1834–1929*, Routledge, London, 2016.

Davis, J., *Reforming London: The London government problem 1855–1900*, Clarendon Press, Oxford, 1988.

Davis, J., *Waterloo Sunrise: London from the Sixties to Thatcher*, Princeton University Press, Princeton, NJ, 2022.

Dennis, R., 'The geography of Victorian values: Philanthropic housing in London, 1840–1900', *Journal of Historical Geography*, 15/1 (1989), p. 41.

Donovan, S. and M. Rubery, 'Doing the amateur casual: Victorian investigative journalism and the legacy of James Greenwood's "A Night in a Workhouse"', *Victorian Studies*, 63/3 (2021), pp. 401–30.

Draper, N., 'The City of London and slavery: Evidence from the first dock companies, 1795–1800', *Economic History Review*, 61/2 (2008), pp. 432–66.

Driver, F. and D. Gilbert, 'Heart of empire? Landscape, space and performance in imperial London', *Environment and Planning D: Society and Space*, 16 (1998), pp. 11–28.

Friedman, J., *Spencer House: Chronicle of a great London mansion*, Zwemmer, London, 1993.

Gardner, P., *The Lost Elementary Schools of Victorian England: The people's education*, Routledge, London, 2018.

Giles, J., *The Parlour and the Suburb: Domestic identities, class, femininity and modernity*, Berg, Oxford, 2004.

Gourvish, T., *Dolphin Square: The history of a unique building*, A&C Black, London, 2014.

Greig, H., *The Beau Monde: Fashionable society in Georgian London*, Oxford University Press, Oxford, 2013.

Hall, C., N. Draper, K. McClelland, K. Donington and R. Lang, *Legacies of British Slave-ownership: Colonial slavery and the formation of Victorian Britain*, Cambridge University Press, Cambridge, 2014.

Hamnett, C., *Unequal City: London in the global arena*, Taylor and Francis, London, 2003.

Harwood, E., *Space, Hope and Brutalism: English architecture, 1945–1975*, Yale University Press for the Paul Mellon Centre for Studies in British Art, London, 2015.

Hatherley, O., *Red Metropolis: Socialism and the government of London*, Repeater Books, London, 2020.

Haywood, R., 'Railways, urban form and town planning in London, 1900–1947', *Planning Perspectives*, 12 (1997), pp. 37–69.

Hitchmough, W., *Hoover Factory: Wallis, Gilbert and Partners*, Phaidon, London, 1992.

Hobhouse, H. (ed.), *Survey of London: County Hall* (Monograph 17), Guild & School of Handicraft, London, 1991.

Jackson, A.A., *Semi-detached London: Suburban development, life and transport*, Allen and Unwin, London, 1973.
Jackson, A.A., *London's Metro-Land*, Capital History, London, 2006.
Jenkins, S., *Landlords to London: The story of a capital and its growth*, Book Club Associates, London, 1975.
Jenkins, S., *Outer London*, HarperCollins, London, 1981.
Joyce, P.D., *The Rule of Freedom: Liberalism and the modern city*, Verso, London, 2003.
Knox, P.L., *London: Architecture, building and social change*, Merrell, London, 2015.
Knox, P.L., *Metroburbia: The anatomy of Greater London*, Merrell, London, 2017.
Koven, S. and S. Michel (eds), *Mothers of a New World: Maternalist politics and the origins of welfare states*, Routledge, London, 2013.
Lansley, A., S. Durant, A. Dyke, B. Gambrill and R. Shelton, *The Transformation of St Pancras Station*, Laurence King, London, 2008.
Longstaffe-Gowan, T., *The London Square: Gardens in the midst of town*, Paul Mellon Centre for Studies in British Art, London, 2012.
Matera, M., *Black London: The imperial metropolis and decolonization in the twentieth century*, University of California Press, Los Angeles, CA, 2015.
McLeod, H., *Class and Religion in the Late Victorian City*, Routledge, London, 2017.
Minton, A., *Big Capital: Who is London for?* Penguin, London, 2017.
Morris, K.F., *A History of Dolphin Square*, Dolphin Square Trust, London, 1995.
Morris, S., 'Market solutions for social problems: Working-class housing in nineteenth-century London', *Economic History Review*, 54/3 (2001), pp. 525–45.
Morrison, K., *The Workhouse: A study of poor-law buildings in England*, English Heritage, Swindon, 1999.
Morrison, K., *English Shops and Shopping: An architectural history*, Paul Mellon Centre for Studies in British Art, London, 2003.
Oliver, P., I. Davis and I. Bentley, *Dunroamin: The suburban semi and its enemies*, Barrie & Jenkins, London, 1981.
Olsen, D.J., *The Growth of Victorian London*, Batsford, London, 1976.
Olsen, D.J., *Town Planning in London: The eighteenth and nineteenth centuries*, Yale University Press, London, 1982.
Ortolano, G., 'Planning the urban future in 1960s Britain', *Historical Journal*, 54/2 (2011), pp. 477–507.
Otter, C., *The Victorian Eye: A political history of light and vision in Britain, 1800–1910*, University of Chicago Press, Chicago, IL, 2008.
Pennybacker, S.D., *A Vision for London 1889–1914: Labour, everyday life and the LCC experiment*, Routledge, London, 1995.

Perry, K.H., *London Is the Place for Me: Black Britons, citizenship and the politics of race*, Oxford University Press, Oxford, 2015.
Pevsner, N. et al., *The Buildings of England: London* (6 vols), Yale University Press, London, 1994–97.
Physick, J., *The Victoria and Albert Museum: The history of its building*, Phaidon/Christie's, Oxford, 1982.
Port, M.H., *Imperial London: Civil government building in London 1851–1915*, Yale University Press for the Paul Mellon Centre for Studies in British Art, London, 1995.
Porter, B., *The Battle of the Styles: Society, culture and the design of a new Foreign Office, 1855–1861*, Bloomsbury Publishing, London, 2011.
Punter, J. (ed.), *Urban Design and the British Urban Renaissance*, Routledge, London, 2010.
Rappaport, E.D., *Shopping for Pleasure: Women in the making of London's West End*, Princeton University Press, Princeton, NJ, 1999.
Raw, L., *Striking a Light: The Bryant and May matchwomen and their place in labour history*, Bloomsbury, London, 2011.
Rawley, J.A., *London, Metropolis of the Slave Trade*, University of Missouri Press, Columbia, MO, 2003.
Rendell, J., *The Pursuit of Pleasure: Gender, space and architecture in Regency London*, Rutgers University Press, New Brunswick, NJ, 2002.
Rosenthal, D., *The National Theatre Story*, Oberon Books, London, 2013.
Runnymede Trust, *Beyond Banglatown: Continuity, change, and new urban economies in Brick Lane*, Runnymede Trust, London, 2020.
Rycroft, S., *Swinging City: A cultural geography of London 1950–1974*, Taylor and Francis, London, 2010.
Sanders, L.S., *Consuming Fantasies: Labor, leisure, and the London shopgirl*, Ohio State University Press, Columbus, OH, 2006.
Schneer, J., *London 1900: The imperial metropolis*, Yale University Press, London, 1999.
Schröpfer, T., 'Google King's Cross', in *Dense + Green Cities: Architecture as urban ecosystem*, Birkhäuser, Basel, 2020, pp. 250–57.
Seldon, A., *The Foreign Office: An illustrated history of the place and its people*, HarperCollins, London, 2000.
Smith, O.S., *Boom Cities: Architect planners and the politics of radical urban renewal in 1960s Britain*, Oxford University Press, Oxford, 2019.
Stewart, R., *The Town House in Georgian London*, Yale University Press, London, 2009.
Summerson, J., *Georgian London*, Yale University Press, London, 1988.
Sutcliffe, A., *London: An architectural history*, Yale University Press, London, 2006.
Thurley, S., *The Building of England: How the history of England has shaped our buildings*, William Collins, London, 2013.

Tickner, L., *London's New Scene: Art and culture in the 1960s*, Yale University Press, London, 2020.
Toplis, I., *The Foreign Office: An architectural history*, Mansell, London, 1987.
Trentmann, F., 'Beyond consumerism: New historical perspectives on consumption', *Journal of Contemporary History*, 39/3 (2004), pp. 373–401.
Wakeman, R., *Practicing Utopia*, University of Chicago Press, Chicago, IL, 2016.
Wall, E., *Contesting Public Spaces: Social lives of urban redevelopment in London*, Routledge, London, 2022.
Watson, H., *The Shard: The vision of Irvine Sellar*, Constable, London, 2017.
Weiner, D.E.B., *Architecture and Social Reform in Late Victorian London*, Manchester University Press, Manchester, 1994.
Wetherell, S., *Foundations: How the built environment made twentieth-century Britain*, Princeton University Press, Princeton, NJ, 2000.
White, J., *London in the Twentieth Century: A city and its people*, Viking, London, 2001.
White, J., *London in the Nineteenth Century*, Jonathan Cape, London, 2007.
White, J., *London in the Eighteenth Century: A great and monstrous thing*, Bodley Head, London, 2017.
Wigfall, V.G., *Thamesmead: Back to the future – a social history of Thamesmead*, Greenwich Community College Press, London, 1997.
Young, K. and P.L. Garside, *Metropolitan London: Politics and urban change 1837–1981*, Edward Arnold, London, 1982.

Index

INDEX